A POET'S NOTEBOOK

A Poet's Notebook

by
EDITH SITWELL

An Atlantic Monthly Press Book

Little, Brown and Company · Boston

1950

Published October 1950
Reprinted November 1950

ATLANTIC—LITTLE, BROWN BOOKS
ARE PUBLISHED BY
LITTLE, BROWN AND COMPANY
IN ASSOCIATION WITH
THE ATLANTIC MONTHLY PRESS

PRINTED IN THE UNITED STATES OF AMERICA

Acknowledgments for
A Notebook on William Shakespeare

My most grateful thanks are due to the following authors, translators, editors, and publishers, all of whom have treated me with the greatest kindness.

The executors of the late Mr. Harley Granville Barker and Messrs. Sidgwick & Jackson for permission to include an extract from *Prefaces to Shakespeare*. To Mr. A. M. Bayfield and the Cambridge University Press for the extract from *A Study of Shakespeare's Versification*. To Mr. Edmund Blunden and Messrs. Jonathan Cape for the passages from *The Mind's Eye*. To the executors of the late Dr. A. C. Bradley and Messrs. Macmillan for the passages from *Shakespearean Tragedy*. To Sir Edmund Chambers and the Clarendon Press for the quotations from *William Shakespeare*. To Mrs. F. M. Cornford and Messrs. Edwin Arnold for the quotations from the late Dr. F. M. Cornford's *The Origin of Attic Comedy*. To Mrs. Laurence Binyon and Messrs. Macmillan for permission to include lines from the late Mr. Binyon's translation of Dante's *The Inferno*. To Mr. Mark Van Doren and Messrs. Allen & Unwin for the quotations from *The Plays of Shakespeare*. To the executors of the late Professor Edward Dowden and the Oxford University Press for a quotation from the Prefaces to the Oxford Edition of *Shakespeare*. To Mr. Lewis Richard Farnell and the Clarendon Press for permission to quote from *Cults of the Greek States*. To Mrs. James Joyce and Messrs. John Lane, The Bodley Head, for permission to include an

Acknowledgments

extract from the late Mr. James Joyce's *Ulysses*. To Dr. Gilbert Murray, O.M., Sir Idris Bell, C.B., O.B.E., and the Oxford University Press for permission to quote from Dr. Murray's *Hamlet and Orestes* (annual Shakespeare Lecture for the British Academy, 1914); and to Dr. Murray and Messrs. Allen & Unwin for the lines from Dr. Murray's translation of Euripides's *Hippolytus*. To Mr. Francis Maitland and Messrs. Thomas Nelson & Sons for the excerpts from Henri Poincaré's *Science and Method* (translated by Mr. Maitland). To the executors of the late Sir James Frazer, O.M., and Messrs. Macmillan for the passages from Pausanius's *Description of Greece;* and to the executors of the late Sir Arthur Quiller-Couch and the Cambridge University Press for passages from *Shakespeare's Workmanship* and the Preface to *All's Well that Ends Well* (the Cambridge Edition of *Shakespeare*). To Mr. Harold Rosenberg and the Editor of *View* for the passages from *Notes on Identity*, with special reference to the Mixed Philosopher, Soren Kierkegaard: *View*, May 1946. To Mr. Stephen Spender and the Editor of *New Writing*, for permission to quote the passages on *Macbeth* from Penguin *New Writing, No. 6*. To Dr. Caroline Spurgeon and the Clarendon Press for permission to quote from *Shakespeare's Imagery and What It Tells Us*. To Dr. E. M. W. Tillyard, Master of Jesus College, Cambridge, and to Messrs. Chatto & Windus for the passages from *The Elizabethan World Picture* and *Shakespeare's History Plays*. To Mr. Edward MacCurdy and Messrs. Duckworth for the passage from Mr. MacCurdy's translation of Leonardo da Vinci's *Notebook*. And to Harcourt, Brace & Co. for the material in the Preface from *Towards a New Architecture* by Le Corbusier.

For all the great kindness shown me by these authors, translators, editors, and publishers, I am deeply grateful.

If by any inadvertence I have used any copyright material for which permission was not asked, or have failed to return thanks where thanks are due, I offer my very sincere apologies, which I hope will be accepted by those concerned.

I must also thank the Editor of *New Writing* and *Daylight* for his kind permission to include the essay on *King Lear*, and the

Acknowledgments

Notes on Iago, which appeared, first, in *New Writing;* the Editor of the *Nineteenth Century and After* for permission to include the essay on *Measure for Measure* and the Editor of *View* for permission to quote a large part of the essay on *Macbeth*, many of the General Notes, and the Notes on "Clowns and Fools," which appeared, first, in *View.*

My most grateful thanks are due, also, to Miss F. E. Woolford, who has kindly undertaken the secretarial work connected with this book, and whose invaluable help has been beyond praise.

E. S.

Acknowledgments for A Poet's Notebook

My most grateful thanks are due to the following authors, translators, editors, and publishers, all of whom have treated me with the greatest kindness: To Messrs. Burns, Oates, and Washbourne for permission to include extracts from St. Thomas Aquinas's *Summa Theologica.* To Monsieur Gaston Bachelard and the Editor of *Minotaure.* To Mr. Edward Hoskyns and the Oxford University Press for the extract from Barth: *The Epistle to the Romans.* To Mr. A. M. Bayfield and The Cambridge University Press for the passage from *A Study of Shakespeare's Versification.* To Mr. Gordon Bottomley and Messrs. Constable for the lovely verse from *Poems of Thirty Years.* To Professor Bradley and Messrs. Macmillan for the passage from *Shakespearean Tragedy.* To Monsieur Nicholas Calas and the Editor of *View* for an extract from an essay on Yves Tanguy. To Mr. Martin Armstrong and Messrs. Victor Gollancz for the two sentences by Cézanne, quoted in *Major Pleasures of Life.* To Monsieur Georges Chirico and the Editor of *Minotaure.* To Monsieur Jean Cocteau, Mr. Ernest Boyd, and Messrs. Allen and Unwin for the quotations from *Opium.* To Monsieur Jean Cocteau and Messieurs Gallimard

Acknowledgments

for the quotations from *Le Rappel à l'Ordre* and *Orphée*. To Mr. Tickner Edwards and Messrs. Methuen for the passage from *The Lore of the Honey Bee*. To the executors of the late Mr. Roger Fry and to Mr. A. E. Zwemmer for the extract from *Matisse*. To Miss Ruth Pielkova and Messrs. Heinemann for the quotation from Paul Gauguin's *Letters*. To Captain Anthony M. Ludovici and Messrs. Constable for the quotation from van Gogh: *Letters of a Post-Impressionist*. To Miss Ruth Pielkova and Messrs. Heinemann for the quotation from *Letters to an Artist*. To the executors of Gerard Manley Hopkins and the Oxford University Press for extracts from *Poems;* to Messrs. Sheed and Ward for a quotation from St. John of the Cross: *The Ascent of Mount Carmel*. To the executors of the late Mr. James Joyce and to Messrs. John Lane, The Bodley Head, for a quotation from *Ulysses*. To the Oxford University Press for the quotation from Kierkegaard: *Christian Discourses*. To Mr. Lincoln Kirstein and the Editor of *View* for the extract from an essay on Pavel Tchelitchew. To Mr. Kenneth Sisam and the Clarendon Press for that lovely discovery made by Mr. Sisam, "The Maid of the Mor," also for the fragment from "Sir Orfeo" (p. 247), from *Fourteenth Century Verse and Prose*. To Dr. D. S. MacColl and Messrs. Jackson, Son and Co., Ltd., 73 West George Street, Glasgow, C.2, for the quotations from Mr. D. S. MacColl's *19th Century Art*. To Mr. Walter de la Mare and Messrs. Constable for the lovely passage about Isabell Pennell, for the phrase of Thomas Nashe about Poetry, and the quotation from Mrs. Elizabeth Mary Wright's *Rustic Speech and Folklore* — all these from *Come Hither*. To Sir Arthur Quiller-Couch and the Cambridge University Press for the passage from *Shakespeare's Workmanship*. To Mr. Edgell Rickword and Messrs. Lawrence and Wishart for the passage from *Rimbaud: The Boy and the Poet*. To Messrs. Faber and Faber for passages from Miss Helen Rootham's translation of Arthur Rimbaud's *Les Illuminations*. To Messrs. R. B. Haldane and J. Kemp, and to Messrs. Kegan Paul, Trench, Trubner and Co. Ltd. for the passages from Schopenhauer's *The World as Will and Idea*. To Mr. W. Force Stead and Messrs. Jonathan Cape for the quotations from Christopher

Acknowledgments

Smart's *Rejoice with the Lamb*. To Messrs. Heinemann for the quotations from A. C. Swinburne's *Essays and Studies, Miscellanies*, and *Contemporaries of Shakespeare*. To Mr. Arthur Symons and Messrs. Jonathan Cape for the quotation from Mr. Symons's *Blake;* to Mr. Arthur Symons and Messrs. Elkin Mathews for quotations from *Baudelaire: a Study*. To Mr. Arthur Symons and Messrs. Constable for the quotations from *The Symbolist Movement in French Literature* and *The Romantic Movement in English Poetry*. To Mr. Arthur Symons and Messrs. Martin Secker and Warburg for the quotations from *Studies in Seven Arts*. To Messrs. Methuen for the quotation from Tauler's *Sermons*. To Messrs. P. J. and A. E. Dobell for the quotations from Thomas Traherne's *Centuries of Meditation*. To Messrs. E. Dannreuther and Messrs. William Reeves for the quotations from Richard Wagner's *Beethoven*. To Mr. W. A. Ellis and Messrs. Kegan Paul, Trench, Trubner and Co. Ltd. for the quotation from *Wagner's Prose Works*. To Mr. Charles Williams and the Oxford University Press for the many quotations from *A New Christian Year*, in which I first read the passages here given from St. Thomas Aquinas's *Summa Theologica*, St. Bernard, St. Clement, Barth, St. John of the Cross, St. Ignatius, Kierkegaard, Benjamin Whichcote, and Tauler. To Professor J. Dover Wilson and the Cambridge University Press for passages from *What Really Happened in Hamlet*. To Mrs. Elizabeth Mary Wright and the Oxford University Press for a quotation from *Rustic Speech and Folklore*.

In my essay on Shakespeare, I should have said that, of two of the phrases applied by me to Falstaff, the first, "alive from the roots, a part of universal nature," is by Mr. Arthur Symons, and occurs in *Studies in Seven Arts* (not applied to Shakespeare), and the second, "a gross . . . enormity of sensation," is by Dr. D. S. MacColl, and occurs in *19th Century Art*, where it is applied to works by Courbet. Dr. MacColl, however, used the word "Zolaesque," not "physical."

Finally, I owe a debt of gratitude to the following publishers and editors who have kindly allowed me to make certain quotations from my own works: To Messrs. Gerald Duckworth for

Acknowledgments

permission to make quotations from *Pleasures of Poetry* and *Aspects of Modern Poetry*. To Messrs. Faber and Faber for quotations from *Alexander Pope*. To Messrs. Victor Gollancz for quotations from *Edith Sitwell's Anthology*.

For all the great kindness shown me by these authors, translators, editors, and publishers I am deeply grateful.

If by any inadvertence I have used any copyright material for which permission was not asked, or have failed to return thanks where thanks are due, I offer my very sincere apologies, which I hope will be accepted by those concerned.

E. S.

Preface

For many years I have read with the fury of a cannibal hunting heads, with the reverence of a pilgrim approaching Mecca upon his knees. As a result of these — perhaps contrasted — passions, I have been in the habit of keeping notebooks, filled, not only with my own reactions towards poems, but also with passages from other writers — some artists in the other arts, some mystics, and with passages from the writings of the Saints that seemed to me to throw light on the various problems of poetry.

The Saints and Mystics, for instance, in their records of their experiences, cast a great light on the processes of inspiration.

That exquisite passage in the *Aurora,* in which Jacob Boehme speaks of a wonderful religious experience in which he watched the growth of a flower, might be the record also, of the growth of a poem. Since a poem is formed, grows gradually, in the same way, and with the same processes, from the same manner of seed. "In the divine power there is, hidden in secret . . . the astringent quality, which is a quality of the kernel, pith or hidden being, a sharp compaction or penetration . . . very sharp and harsh or astringent, which generates hardness and also coldness."

.   .   .   .   .   .

The second quality, or second spirit of God . . . is the sweet quality, which worketh in the astringent, so that it is altogether lovely, pleasant and mild or meek.

.   .   .   .   .   .

[xi]

For when men speak of the mercy of God the Father, they speak of his *power*, of the fountain spirits.

.   .   .   .   .   .

The astringent or harsh quality is the heart, pith, or kernel in the divine power, the contraction, compaction or imaging, forming or impression; for it is the sharpness and cold, as it is seen that the harsh astringent cold *drieth* the water, and maketh it sharp ice.

The sweet quality is the allaying or warming, whereby the harsh or astringent and cold quality becometh thin and *soft*, whence the water taketh the original.

Thus the astringent quality is, and is called, the heart, and the sweet is called barm, or warm, or softening, or mitigating: they are the two qualities out of which the heart or Son of God is generated.

For the astringent or harsh quality, in its stock or kernel, when it qualifieth or operateth in its own power, is a darkness: the sweet quality, in its own power, is a moving, boiling, warming and rising light, a source or fountain of meekness and well-doing.

.   .   .   .   .

The third quality, or the third spirit of God, in the Father's power, is the bitter quality: which is a penetrating or forcing of the sweet and the astringent or harsh qualities, and which is trembling, penetrating and rising up.

The astringent or harsh quality is the kernel or stock, and is sour or *attractive*; and the sweet is the light, *mollifying* and softening; and the bitter is *penetrating* or triumphing, which riseth up and triumpheth in the astringent or harsh quality, and in the sweet.

Preface

This is the source of joy, or the cause of the laughing, elevating joy, whereby a thing trembleth and jubilateth for joy: whence the heavenly joy existeth.

That wonderful passage, only the beginning of which I have quoted, would have been included in the main body of my present *Poet's Notebook*, but it is so long that it would have distorted the shape of the book. Were it not for this, it would form part of the section called "On the Poet, the Natural World, and Inspiration."

.   .   .   .   .   .

In my notebooks there are many passages about the importance of fire in poetry . . . "la flamme est de nature animale" (that important statement made by Novalis, and so often forgotten in this age of damp, spiritless, misty verse), and on the importance that poetry should be *essential* — in the original meaning of that word, that is, that it should have a central core; on the importance, too, that all words should be re-created, come fresh, as it were, from the spirit. . . . "Each word," said John Livingston Lowes, on Coleridge, in *The Road to Zanadu*, "has been transmuted, through the imaginative intensity of one compelling act.

"Give Coleridge one word from an old narrative, let him mix it with two in his thought; and then (translating terms of music into terms of words) 'out of three sounds he [will] frame, not a fourth sound, but a star.' "

It is with the processes that go to form that star, that many of these notes are occupied.

There are copious notes on color, and on light, as well as what Eisenstein, in *The Film Sense*, called synesthesia. (Speaking of one person known to him, Eisenstein said, "The scale of vowels was seen by him not as *colours*, but as a scale of varying *light values*.")

[xiii]

Preface

Apropos of synesthesia, many years ago one of my earliest poems aroused great wrath, because of the line:

The morning light creaks down again.

Yet in the record of Samuel Hearne's Journey from Prince of Wales Fort in Hudson Bay to the Northern Ocean, 1795, we find this passage:

"I do not remember to have met with any travellers into high Northern latitudes, who remarked their having heard the Northern Lights make any noise in the air as they vary their colours or position; which may probably be owing to the want of perfect silence at the time they made their observations on these meteors. I can positively affirm, that on still nights I have heard them make a rustling and crackling noise like the waving of a large flag in a fresh gale of wind."

A sound due to some electrical process? Possibly.

In any case, I had not read that passage when I wrote the poem.

Among the notes by artists in the other arts which seem to me to throw a light on the problems of poetry, there are many by the great architect Monsieur Le Corbusier. For instance:

"The plan bears within itself a primary and pre-determined rhythm . . . with results which can range from the simplest to the most complex, all coming within the same law. Unity of law is the law of a good plan: a simple law capable of infinite modulation."

And this, about Unity:

"The Greeks on the Acropolis set up temples which are animated by a single thought. It is on this account that there are no other architectural works on this scale of grandeur. We shall be able to talk 'Doric' when man, in nobility of aim and

[xiv]

complete sacrifice of all that is accidental in art, has reached the higher levels of the mind: austerity."

I do not believe in austerity in poetry, which should be full of sensuous beauty; but I do believe in the sacrifice of all that is accidental in art. The sensuousness must be essential.

Then, too, there is this passage about cubic volume, which seems to me to apply to consonantal values: "Then there comes in the sensation of density. . . . Marble is denser, both to the eye and to the mind, than is wood, and so forth. Always you have gradation."

(These quotations from Monsieur Le Corbusier are from his book *Towards a New Architecture*, translated by Frederick Etchells.)

There are notes, too, on human beings. These beings range from the little boys who, dressed in Shakespeare's clothes, climbed an apple tree outside his house (when he, who had been sweet "as the honey of Hybla, my old lad of the castle," had long been in the grave) — and from among the branches, peered through the windows — to Shakespeare's Wife . . . "in New Place a slack dishonoured body, that once was comely, once as sweet, as fresh as cinnamon, now her leaves falling, all bare, frighted of the narrow grave and unforgiven."

So said James Joyce, in *Ulysses*. But we know nothing of her, and can only guess at why he left her and why, after many years, he returned.

Speculations, beliefs, theories, the beginnings of inspirations — all these go to the making of a notebook.

There are, too, such words of comfort as these, taken from a letter written by Goethe to Schiller (November 19, 1796) and dealing with the utterances of some ninny:

"Would not these utterances turn the Hippocrene into ice, and make Pegasus cast his skin? But things were the same five-and-twenty years ago, when I began, and will be so long after

I am gone. However, it cannot be denied that it does seem as if certain views and principles, without which no one ought to approach a great work of art, must by degrees become more general."

"As it was in the beginning, is now and ever shall be. World without end" is the only answer to *that*.

E. S.

Contents

A NOTEBOOK ON WILLIAM SHAKESPEARE

Preface   xi

I   The Hymn to Life   3

II   Of the Clowns and Fools   10

III   Comedy and Tragedy   19

IV   Some General Notes on the Tragedies   21

V   *Macbeth*   30

VI   *King Lear*   55

VII   *Hamlet*   89

VIII   *Othello, the Moor of Venice*   94

IX   *Timon of Athens*   117

X   *Measure for Measure*   121

XI   *Antony and Cleopatra*   131

XII   *Julius Caesar*   139

XIII   The Historical Tragedies   145

XIV   The Comedies   146

XV   *All's Well that Ends Well*   148

A POET'S NOTEBOOK

I   On the Poet's Nature   153

II   On the Nature of Poetry   158

[xvii]

Contents

III   On Technical Matters   177

IV   Some Necessities of Poetry   194

V   On Morality in Poetry   197

VI   On Simplicity   198

VII   On the Senses   201

VIII   On Over-Civilization   204

IX   On the Need for the Refreshing of the Language   206

X   On the Poet's Labor   207

XI   On Imagery in Poetry   208

XII   On the Poet, the Natural World, and Inspiration   209

XIII   On the Power of Words   211

XIV   On Ben Jonson   217

XV   On the Augustans   218

XVI   On Alexander Pope   219

XVII   On Blake   222

XVIII   On Baudelaire   225

XIX   On Verlaine   227

XX   On Chaucer   229

XXI   On Certain Poems by Dunbar, Skelton, Gower, and a Poem by an Anonymous Poet   236

XXII   On Herrick   254

XXIII   On Smart, with a Note on Gerard Manley Hopkins   261

XXIV   On Wordsworth   269

A Notebook on William Shakespeare

I. The Hymn to Life

In these gigantic works, there are the differences in nature, in matter, in light, in darkness, in movement, that we find in the universe.

Sometimes the identities of which the world is composed belong, as it were, to the different grades in the series of existence, — to the mineral kingdom, the vegetable kingdom, the brute creation. Or they are one of the elements: Water: Hamlet. Air: Romeo and Juliet. Fire: Lear. (Goethe said that "Time is an element." Time may be said to be the other element in Lear, of whom Coleridge said "old age is a character." But in King Lear, the character is more than old age: it is Time itself. Time is the essence of Lear's being, the space in which that being exists.) The fourth element, Earth, is always present. Shakespeare knew that there is no fragment of clay, however little worth, that is not entirely composed of inexplicable qualities.

Characters such as Falstaffe are "lumps of the world," "are still alive from the roots, a part not yet cut off from universal nature," and they have a gross physical enormity of sensation which approaches a kind of physical godhead.

Shakespeare is like the sun, that common-kissing Titan, having a passion for matter, pure and impure, an energy beyond good and evil, an immense benevolence creating without choice or preference, out of the need of giving birth to

[3]

life. "Never was there such a homage to light, to light and the principle of life." [1]

Antony swears

> By the fire
> That quickens Nilus' slime.

Antony and Cleopatra, I, 3

Poor Pompey, the bawd's tapster in *Measure for Measure*, excuses himself to his judge by saying:

> Truly, sir, I am a poor fellow that would live.

And Shakespeare, if no one else, forgives him, for to Shakespeare life is holy, and Pompey, Mrs. Quickly, and other earthy characters, of this, as of every other kind, hold in them the principle, and the love, of life. These, and Nilus' slime, are worthy in his eyes of the light and heat of the sun.

> None does offend, none, I say, none;

King Lear, IV, 6

said the old mad King upon the dark moor. And so said his loving creator. The terrible storms of the most gigantic tragedies ever born from the heart of Man, though they are vast as the upheavals of Nature, are not blind as these. It is no fault of the sun if we wreck our world. . . . In *King Lear*, in *Timon of Athens*, the diatribes are only the reverse side of love.

"We are really for brief moments Primordial Being itself, and feel its indomitable desire for being, and joy in existence. The struggle, the pain, the destruction of phenomena appear

---

[1] This was said by Arthur Symons of a still great, though infinitely lesser artist than Shakespeare, and an artist in a different medium — Edouard Manet. But it seems still more applicable to Shakespeare.

to us something necessary . . . considering the fertility of the universal will." [2]

"There's sap in it yet," says Antony to his Queen before darkness falls. Sap in the event, sap in the heart of Man.

Old Falstaffe, with his heat and intemperance, his love of life, is to Shakespeare, as to Prince Hal, ". . . thou latter spring . . . all hallow'en summer."

Only that which is too cold for Hell (as was, perhaps, Iago, once a native) is condemned. Only the hard heart offends. But this, too, though it is more inflexible than marble or than the cold of death, must be investigated.

"Then let them anatomise Regan," said the old outcast King, "see what breeds about her heart. Is there any cause in Nature that makes these hard hearts?"

To Shakespeare, generation and the processes of generation, Death and the processes of Death, are holy.

In these hymns to life, the very blood of the beings, the animate heat, is spirit. . . . "Not fire, it does not take its origin from fire, but derives from the solar ray. . . . The blood acquires remarkable and most excellent powers, and is analogous to the stars. . . ."

"The heat of the sun and of animals,[3] not only that which is stored up in semen, but even that of any excrementitious matter, although divers in nature, still contains a vital principle." "Now," continues Harvey, "I maintain the same thing of the innate heat of the blood. I say that they are not fire and they do not derive their origin from fire. They rather share the nature of some other, and that a more divine body or substance. They act by no faculty or property of the elements; but as there is something inherent in the semen which makes it prolific, and as in producing an animal, it surpasses

[2] Nietzsche, *The Birth of Tragedy*.
[3] Aristotle, quoted by William Harvey *On Generation*.

the power of the elements — as it is a spirit, namely, and the inherent nature of that spirit corresponds to the element of the stars, so there is a spirit, a certain force, inherent in the blood, acting superiorly to the powers of the elements . . . and the nature, yea, the soul in this spirit and blood is identical with the nature of the stars."

In beings like Othello, the blood, "by reason of its admirable properties and powers, is spirit. It is celestial, something analogous to heaven, vicarious of heaven . . . the innate heat, the sun of the microcosm, the fire of Plato. . . ." In such beings as Juliet's nurse, "in so far as it is spirit, it is the hearth, the Vesta, the household divinity." [4]

That splendor of the blood ran through all grand animal nature, — in that "globe of sinful continents," poor old Sir John Falstaffe, the "honeysuckle villain," the "honey seed rogue," whose heart was killed because a King, in whose word he had trusted, seemed to break faith with him.

It runs in the veins of the Dauphin's horse, that being of air and fire.

DAUPHIN: What a long Night is this! I will not change my Horse with any that treades but on foure pasternes: Ça ha! he bounds from the Earth, as if his entrayles were hayres: *le Cheval volant*, the Pegasus, *chez les narines de feu!* When I bestryde him, I soare, I am a Hawke: he trots the ayre; the Earth sings when he touches it; the basest horne of his hoofe is more Musicall than the Pipe of Hermes.

ORLEANS: Hee's of the colour of the Nutmeg.

DAUPHIN: And of the heat of the Ginger. It is a Beast for Perseus: hee is pure Ayre and Fire; and the dull elements of Earth and Water never appeare in him, but only in patient stillnesse while his Rider mounts him: hee is indeed a Horse; and all other Jades you may call Beasts.

[4] William Harvey, *op. cit.*

The Hymn to Life

CONSTABLE: Indeed, my Lord, it is a most absolute and excellent Horse.

DAUPHIN: It is the Prince of Palfrayes, his Neigh is like the bidding of a Monarch, and his countenance enforces Homage.

The Life of King Henry the Fifth, III, 7

Such plays as *King Henry the Fourth* (Parts I and II) and *King Henry the Fifth* are giant hymns to the physical glory of Life, and the characters seem "the animalisation of God."

. . . banish plumpe Jacke, and banish all the World.

First Part of *King Henry the Fourth*, II, 4

(That round berry the world, with its sweetness . . . the world with its earthiness and juice; the old happy laughing world that forgets it must die.)

"Thou knowest," said the "honeysuckle villain," "in the state of Innocency Adam fell: and what should poore Jacke Falstaffe do in the dayes of Villainy? Thou seest, I have more flesh than another man, and therefore more frailty." [Part I, III, 3] ". . . If Sacke and Sugar be a fault, Heaven helpe the wicked: if to be old and merry be a sinne, then many an olde Hoste that I know is damned."

He was sinful, yes, but not diabolic.

Throughout the days of that "latter spring . . . all hallow'en summer" (as the Prince called the old man) the sun danced, although "the fortune of us that are the Moone's men doeth ebbe and flow like the Sea, being governed as the Sea is by . . . the Moone." [First Part of *King Henry the Fourth*, I, 2]

The hours go by, but nobody cares. The shades of night seem companions of these "Dianae's Forresters, gentlemen of the Shade, minions of the Moone."

Certain characters that we do not see, but that are known to the beings of this world — Robin Nightwork, for instance,

[7]

and old Jane Nightwork ("old, old, Master Shallow") and Cousin Silence whom we do see – are like sweet shadows, remembered from youth, and still haunting the brain of that earthy old man, Sir John Falstaffe, whose redness is from Adam!

Stupidity and lean Virtue are only shadows, too, but these will soon pass away under the great dancing sun, or they are a cool resting-place for laughter:

SHALLOW: For the other, Sir John: Let me see: Simon Shadow!
FALSTAFFE: Yea, marry, let me have him to sit under: he's like to be a cold souldier.
SHALLOW: Where's Shadow?
SHADOW: Heere, sir.

.   .   .   .   .   .

SHALLOW: Do you like him, Sir John?
FALSTAFFE: Shadow will serve for Summer: pricke him: For we have a number of shadowes to fill up the Muster-Booke.
Second Part of King Henry the Fourth, III, 2

But the shade of Sir John Falstaffe "partook" as da Vinci said Shadow must do, "of the nature of universal matter."

It is better to be a fat old man who "sweates to death, And Lards the leane earth as he walkes along" [First Part of *King Henry the Fourth*, II, 2], than to be Nothingness. What is Honor? It may lead to Nothingness, therefore it, too, is only a shade:

What is that Honour? Ayre. A trim reckoning! Who hath it? He that dy'de o' Wednesday. Doth he feele it? No. Doth he heare it? No. 'T is insensible then? Yea, to the dead. But will it not live with the living? No. Why? Detraction will not suffer it. Therefore Ile none of it. Honour is a meere Scutcheon, and so ends my Catechisme.
First Part of King Henry the Fourth, V, 1

[8]

The Hymn to Life

. . . A scutcheon, a "ghost in marble," or a shadow. What is Honor to a "honeysuckle villain," in a world that must have seemed to him, as to the Archbishop in *King Henry the Fifth*, one of "Singing Masons building roofs of gold"?

Falstaffe, in his instinctive life, is like "the old noontide sleeping. It moves its mouth. Doth it not drink a drop of happiness, an old brown drop of golden happiness, golden wine? . . ." He is "a well of eternity . . . the joyous, awful noontide abyss." [5]

[5] Nietzsche, *Thus Spake Zarathustra*.

II. Of the Clowns and Fools

"Music," said Wagner, "blots out our entire civilization, as sunshine does lamplight."

This is true of the giant harmonies of Shakespeare. In another kind, his poetry is a sun whose light does not blot out a civilization, but fuses it into a single being.

In the Comedies, the Sun forgives and remakes the shape of evil, dances, laughing and loving the world, over stupidity.

We see the nettle-dull Dogberry and Verges. Shakespeare reduces their sheer nonsense, their incomprehension and rustic fears, into Chaos; and then from Chaos he produces a dancing star.

When Dogberry inquires (at the beginning of the Second Scene of the Fourth Act of *Much Ado about Nothing*):

> Is our whole dissembly appeared?

or says:

> Write down, that they hope they serve God: and write God first; for God defend but God should go before such villains! Masters, it is proved already that you are little better than false knaves, and it will go near to be thought so shortly . . .
>
> [IV, 2]

— or when Bottom the Weaver declares that the ballad about his dream "shall be called 'Bottom's Dream,' because it hath no bottom" [*A Midsummer Night's Dream*, IV, 1] — we feel as if we were suddenly made conscious of "a deformation

[10]

undergone by all bodies carried forward by the earth's motion," or, going still further, had found ourselves in a universe reigned over "by any deformation whatsoever, — in accordance with any laws, as complicated as we liked," — "these laws ruling over our bodies also, and the rays of light emanating from the different objects." [1]

Outraged by being called "an Asse," Dogberry cries: "Dost thou not suspect my place? Dost thou not suspect my yeeres? O that hee were here to write me downe an asse! But masters, remember that I am an asse; though it be not written down, yet forget not that I am an asse." [*Much Ado about Nothing*, IV, 2] And from the word "yeeres" we see the long ears of the Ass growing.

("O Dionysos divine, why dost thou pull mine ears?" Ariadne asks her philosophical lover in one of the celebrated dialogues on the Isle of Naxos. [Nietzsche] "I find there is something agreeable, something pleasant about thine ears. . . . Why are they not still longer?") [2]

We are, in short, in the Fourth Dimension, — "offering itself to the intellect from the plastic point of view, — the immensity of space eternalising itself in all directions at a determined moment. It is space itself, the dimension of the infinite; it is this which endows objects with plasticity. It gives them, in a word, the proportions that they desire." [3]

Sometimes, amid the Titanic dust, the Titanic heat, a strange figure is thrown, that of the ancestor of Ancient Pistol and the Capitano of Italian Comedy. This shadow has drifted down the ages to us, escaped from the campaigns of Alexander, — retaining still his bluster, his tragic bombast, and with his tremendous crest of plumes (or "boastard's feathers," as an

[1] Henri Poincaré, *Science and Method*.
[2] Guillaume Apollinaire, *Les Peintres Cubistes*.
[3] *Ibid*.

enemy, Dikaiopolis, called that crest) still erect on his helmet.[4]

This being turns towards us, and we see, under the crest of feathers that is the mark of the soldier of fortune, a stock mask of Comedy, with empty eyes and open mouth — and, through these apertures, gain a glimpse of the face of Aeschylus.[5] Sometimes, again, some being turns, and we see, not the "Silenus-like figure and countenance, with its prominent eyes and snub nose"[6] of the true Socrates, but the lean black shadow, with hooked nose, "the pretended Comedy Mask of this philosopher,[7] affixed to the stock figure of the learned Doctor, ancestor of Il Dottore in Italian Comedy, and of the schoolmaster Holofernes, to whom, with his friend the Parson Sir Nathaniel, Goodman Dull, the Constable, plays buffoon."[8]

These faces, that of Aeschylus and of Socrates, as they were seen by Aristophanes, strangely wried by the Comedy masks into which they were thrust, are seen by us for a moment, brought into fresh life by the greatest of all human creators. Then the Titanic dust of all the summers that have passed since their birth, drifts round them again: and the high voice of the Clown is heard — the Ritual Laughter.

The Ritual Laughter

There are various kinds of the greater Laughter — of the Ritual or Sacred Laugh. We may study the origin and the

---

[4] See F. M. Cornford, *The Origin of Attic Comedy*, Chapter 8, "The Stock Mask of the Old Comedy."

[5] Descended to us from Aristophanes's *The Frogs*.

[6] F. M. Cornford, *op. cit.*

[7] Polonius is, in some sense, a descendant of this mock philosopher. — E. S.

[8] "When you see Socrates brought upon the stage, you are not to imagine him made ridiculous by the imitation of his actions," said Dryden, in *Dramatic Poesy*, "but rather by making him perform something very unlike himself, something so childish and absurd, as by comparing it with the gravity of the true Socrates, makes it a ridiculous object for the spectators."

nature of these, in Salomon Reinach's *Cultes, mythes, et réligions.*

There is the laughter inspiring fear — the braying of the world of asses following the army of Darius, which, causing terror (because of the unknown, uncouth quality of the sound) among the horses of the Scythian hordes, who heard it for the first time, led to the flight of the horses and the defeat of the Scythians. — There is the laughter of those who have escaped from an earthquake and find themselves in known fields. — There is the laughter which represents the return to life of the Goddess of Vegetation. — And there is the pure laughter of the God, the manifestation in sound of his presence.

"It was said," wrote Reinach, "that Caligula wished to transport to Rome the Zeus of Phidias, from the Olympia: the scaffoldings, the machinery, were already erected, when the statue broke into loud laughter, so that the terrified workmen took to flight. This laughter of Zeus was not caused by the attempted sacrilege of Caligula . . . but it was the solemn affirmation, the manifestation in sound, of the presence of God." [9]

The terrible laughter of Hamlet seems akin to that of the young men during the Rites of the Roman Lupercalia, — who, after they had been sacrificed by proxy, were obliged, as a part of the ceremony, to break into laughter, to show that their sacrifice was completed, and that they had passed beyond death.

It is this laughter that we hear, perhaps, in certain of Hamlet's speeches.

Sometimes the laughter of Hamlet is of this kind — some-

[9] "O the rich contrast between the Clown and Hamlet, as two extremes! You see in the former the mockery of logic, and a traditional wit valued, like truth, for its antiquity, and treasured up, like a tune, for use." — Coleridge, *Lectures, 1818.*

times of the sort of which Baudelaire wrote in *Curiosités esthétiques:* "Il est certain . . . que le rire humain est intimement lié à l'accident d'une chute ancienne, d'une dégradation physique et morale. Le rire et la douleur s'expriment par les organes où résident le commandement et la science du bien ou du mal: les yeux et la bouche. Dans le paradis terrestre . . . (c'est-à-dire dans le milieu où il semblait à l'homme que toutes les choses créés étaient bonnes), la joie n'était pas dans le rire. Aucune peine ne l'affligeant, son visage était simple et uni, et le rire qui agite maintenant les nations ne déformait point les traits de sa face. . . . L'Etre qui voulut multiplier son image, n'a point mis dans la bouche de l'homme les dents du lion, mais l'homme mord avec le rire.

.   .   .   .

"Le rire est . . . essentiellement contradictoire, c'est-à-dire qu'il est à la fois signe d'une grandeur infinie et d'une misère infinie, misère infinie relativement à l'Etre absolu dont il possède la conception, grandeur infinie relativement (. . .) aux animaux. C'est du choc perpétuel de ces deux infinies qui se dégage le rire."

Then, too, there is the grosser, more earthy laughter:

> . . . broad as ten thousand beeves at pasture
> Thunders of laughter, clearing air and heart.[10]

— the laughter of fertility at the thought of unfertility, — the laughter of life and growth arising out of the earth that hides the dead.

And over and through the laughter sounds the "tuneful planetting" of the verse.

*   *   *

[10] Sir Arthur Quiller-Couch's foreword to *All's Well that Ends Well,* Cambridge Edition Shakespeare.

Of the Clowns and Fools

Foolery Like the Sun

"Foolery, sir, does walke about the Orbe like the Sunne; it shines every where" — said Feste.

And all the characters of the Fools have "dimensions that are half-way between those of an atom and those of a star."

When John Ray, the great seventeenth-century naturalist, was asked, "What is the use of butterflies?" he replied, "To adorn the world and delight the eyes of men, to brighten the countryside, serving like so many golden spangles, to decorate the fields." And he added, "Who can contemplate their exquisite beauty and not acknowledge and adore the traces of divine art upon them?"

The Watteau Gilles, Pierrot, is of this kind . . . ("Je vécus, étincelle d'or de la lumière nature") . . . a simple creature adorning the world, and soon to die. The Fool in *King Lear* was once such a being.

It was Coleridge's opinion (reported by Crabb Robinson) that the Fools of Shakespeare supplied the place of the ancient Chorus. . . . "In *Hamlet*," he added, "the Fool, as it were, is divided into several parts, dispersed through the play."

The ancient wisdom, disguised as laughter, dances like the light of a great summer sea. So it is with Feste. Or it rises, in rustic disguise, like some bearded god of the ripe fig trees, from the very earth of Death:

> I wish you all joy of the Worme.
>
> *Antony and Cleopatra*, v, 2

Or it turns black and terrible, as if lightning-struck, as in *Hamlet:*

FIRST CLOWN: Come, my Spade: there is no ancient gentlemen but Gardiners, Ditchers, and Grave-makers; they hold up Adam's profession.

[15]

.   .   .   .   .

What is he that builds stronger than either the Mason, the Shipwright, or the Carpenter?

.   .   .   .   .

A Grave-maker: the Houses that he makes last till Doomesday.

Hamlet, v, 1

Or again, we have "the true man, the bearded satyr, shouting joyfully to his god." [11] Such is Dromio of Syracuse, invoking the comfort of his master, because he is pursued by Nature, by the Earth in the shape of a kitchen wench: "No longer from head to foot than from hippe to hippe: she is sphericall, like a globe: I could find out Countries in her."

*   *   *

ANTIPHOLUS OF SYRACUSE: Where Spain?
DROMIO OF SYRACUSE: Faith, I saw it not: but I felt it hot in her breath.
ANTIPHOLUS OF SYRACUSE: Where America, the Indies?
DROMIO OF SYRACUSE: O, sir, upon her nose: all ore embellished with Rubies, Carbuncles, Sapphires, declining their rich Aspect to the hot breath of Spaine, who sent whole Armadoes of Caracks to be ballast at her nose.

The Comedy of Errors, III, 2

Round these beings, the air sparkles like a sea. And indeed, Dromio of Syracuse and Dromio of Ephesus seem like two strange sea-creatures, shining with the sea-jewelry. But they come alive as we watch them and listen to them.

"When I had taken up what I had supposed to be a fallen star," wrote Dryden, in the Epistle Dedicatory to *The Spanish*

---

[11] Nietzsche, *The Birth of Tragedy.*

Friar, "I found I had been cozened with a jelly; nothing but a cold, dull mass, which glittered no longer than it was shooting; a dwarfish mass, dressed up in gigantic words."

He spoke of the disappointment experienced when reading certain plays, which he had enjoyed upon the stage. But with Shakespeare, every shooting star remains a star, no matter whence it is seen.

Other clowns, such as poor Pompey, the bawd's tapster, in *Measure for Measure*, have a strange animal character — that of the beast of burden turned prophet or soothsayer.

Dr. C. G. Jung, in *Psychology of the Unconscious*, speaks of legends in which "the Horse acquires the significance of the Animal Unconscious, which appears domesticated and subjected to the will of Man."

It is this "Animal Unconscious" which speaks through the lips of Pompey, when, all unknowing, he utters words which tell us of the great mercy of Christ.

The giant dances, and grandeur is the air, the climate, through which the storm of his footsteps sounds:

BOY: Do you not remember, a saw a Flea sticke upon Bardolph's Nose, and a said it was a Blacke Soul burning in Hell-fire?

BARDOLPH: Well, the fuel is gone that maintain'd that fire: that's all the Riches I got in his service.

King Henry the Fifth, II, 3

And Falstaffe:

Doe thou amend thy Face, and Ile amend my Life: thou art our Admirall, thou bearest the Lanterne in the Poope, but 'tis in the Nose of thee; thou art the Knight of the Burning Lampe.

BARDOLPH: Why, Sir John, my Face does you no harme.

FALSTAFFE: No, Ile be sworne; I make as good use of it as many a man doth of a Death's Head or a Memento Mori: I never

[17]

see thy Face, but I think upon Hell-fire, and Dives that lived in Purple; for there he is in his robes, burning, burning. If thou wert any way given to vertue, I would sweare by thy Face; my oath should bee "By this Fire, that's God's angel": but thou art altogether given over; and wert indeede, but for the Light in thy Face, the Sonne of utter Darknesse. When thou ran'st up Gads Hill in the Night to catch my Horse, if I did not thinke thou hadst beene an Ignis Fatuus or a Ball of Wild-fire, there's no Purchase in Mony.

First Part of King Henry the Fourth, III, 3

Gold is inherent in all natures. We see the buried, undreamt-of treasure in the smile of gravity.

"He doth smile his face into more lines than are in the new Map, with the augmentation of the Indies," said Maria of Malvolio.

III. *Comedy and Tragedy*

(Coleridge: *Lectures*, *1818*)

". . . In the old comedy the very form itself is whimsical; the whole work is one great jest, comprehending a world of jests within it, among which each maintains its own place without seeming to concern itself as to the relation in which it may stand to its fellows. In short, in Sophocles the constitution of tragedy is monarchical, but such as it existed in early Greece, limited by laws, and therefore the more venerable — all the parts adapting and submitting themselves to the majesty of the heroic sceptre: — in Aristophanes, comedy, on the contrary, is poetry in its most democratic form, and it is a fundamental principle with it, rather to risk all the confusion of anarchy, than to destroy the independence and privileges of its individual constituents — place, verse, characters, even single thoughts, conceits and allusions, each turning on the pivot of its own free will.

*   *   *

"The comic poet idealises his characters by making the animal the governing power, and the intellectual the mere instrument.

*   *   *

"The sportive ideal . . . consists in the perfect harmony and concord of the higher nature with the animal, as with its ruling principle and its acknowledged regent.

*   *   *

[19]

"An old critic said that tragedy was the flight or elevation of life, comedy (that of Menander) its arrangement or ordonnance.

* * *

"The old tragedy moved in an ideal world, the old comedy in a fantastic world."

IV. *Some General Notes on the Tragedies*

"All is indiscriminately stamped with grandeur," as Fuseli said of Michelangelo. "A beggar rose from his hand the patriarch of poverty; the hump of his dwarf is impressed with dignity" . . . "the hump and withered arm of Richard are engines of terror and persuasion in Shakespeare" as "the crookback of Michelangelo strikes with awe."

Thus, when Richard the Third says

> Shine out, faire Sunne, till I have bought a glasse,
> That I may see my Shadow as I passe   [I, 2]

although he is speaking only of his image in a mirror, we feel, not only Richard's indifference to darkness or light, excepting inasmuch as they enhance his being, or aid him in his purpose: but we feel, also, that in the end the shadow of his hump, the shade of his withered arm, will blot out the sun.

Shakespeare knew all differences in good and evil — that between the evil of Iago, who, though a subterranean devil, is also "Prince of the Power of the Air" ("as the air works upon our bodies, this Presence works upon our minds"), and that of Titus Andronicus, the kind of being of whom Donne, in his 41st Sermon, said, "He is a devil in himself, that could be, and would be, ambitious in a spital, licentious in a wilderness, voluptuous in a famine, and abound with temptations in himself, though there were no devil." (This is not one of Shakespeare's greatest plays, but has, as Swinburne said of Chapman, "passages of a sublime and Titanic beauty, rebellious and excessive in style as in sentiment, but full of majestic and massive harmony.")

Certain characters in Shakespeare have the grandeur and loneliness of a pariah sun in a heaven of evil, casting down disastrous rays upon all alike, breeding new forms of life from primeval mud.

For the mud exists, but so does Beauty, "a lively harmony, a glittering brightness, resulting from effused good by ideas, seeds, reasons, shadows, stirring up our minds that by this good they may be united and made one." [1]

Darkness fell because of Helen, and yet she is seen as

> . . . a Grecian queen, whose youth and freshness
> Wrinkles Appolloe's, and makes stale the morning.
>
> *Troilus and Cressida*, II, 2

The faults of the hero have a planetary splendor:

> LEPIDUS: I must not think there are
> Evils enow to darken all his goodnesse;
> His faults in him seeme as the Spots of Heaven,
> More fiery by night's Blacknesse.
>
> *Antony and Cleopatra*, I, 4

Old age in Shakespeare is of a profound grandeur, though the kiss of Age brings winter even to the lips of Beauty:

> Ile take that winter from your lips, faire lady

says Achilles to Cressida, after the kiss of Nestor. [*Troilus and Cressida*, IV, 5]

Beside the life of one of these beings, almost all other characters that ever lived seem but

> As is the morn-dew on the myrtle leafe
> To his grand sea.
>
> *Antony and Cleopatra*, III, 12

[1] Plato, quoted by Burton, *The Anatomy of Melancholy*.

Some General Notes on the Tragedies

Their griefs, their joys, are vast as those of the elements, of the universe, of the heavens.

> Will Caesar weepe?
>> He has a cloud in's face.
>>> *Antony and Cleopatra*, III, 2

Cleopatra's passions "are made of nothing but the finest part of pure love. We cannot call her winds and waters sighes and teares; they are greater stormes and tempests than Almanackes can report. This cannot be cunning in her; if it be, she makes a showre of rain as well as Jove." [*Antony and Cleopatra*, I, 2]

The passions of these beings are great and irresistible as the rising of the sap in spring — as in the wild and unlawful springtime love of these lines:

PANDARUS: . . . he will weepe you, an 'twere a man borne in Aprill.

CRESSIDA: And Ile spring up in his tears, an 'twere a nettle against May.

> *Troilus and Cressida*, I, 2

Iras, looking at the hand of her fellow waiting-woman, Charmian, says:

> There's a Palme presages Chastity, if nothing else.

Charmian replies:

> E'en as the ore-flowing Nylus presageth Famine.
>> *Antony and Cleopatra*, I, 2

And we see the veins of the hand changed to long rivers in that fruitful earth.

A narrow bed is changed to the Indies with all its splendors:

Her bed is India; there she lyes, a Pearle:
Betweene our Ilium and where she resides
Let it be cald the wild and wandring flood,
Ourselfe the merchant, and this sayling Pandar
Our doubtfull hope, our convoy and our Barke.

Troilus and Cressida, I, 1

It is great morning,

So said Paris in the opening of the Third Scene of the Fourth Act of *Troilus and Cressida*. And, by the light of that great morning, even the beings whom we see passing in the common street are transformed for us, for evermore, into the epitome of all beauty, or all sorrow. We ask

Who were those went by? [I, 2]

and the answer comes:

Queen Hecuba and Helen.

*   *   *

In the Tragedies the themes are these: the struggle of Man against the gigantic forces of Nature, or of Man brought face to face with the eternal truths. . . . The King made equal with the beggar at the feast of the worm, the King whose will had never been combated, finding that his hand "smelles of mortalitie." The King who

Strives in his little world of Man to outscorne
The to-and-fro conflicting wind and rain.

King Lear, III, 1

(When the rain came to wet me once and the wind to make me chatter, when the Thunder would not peace at my bidding, there I found 'em, there I smelt 'em out. Go to, they are not men o'

[24]

their words: they told me I was everything: 'tis a Lie: I am not
Agu-proofe.)

King Lear, IV, 6

Macbeth and Lady Macbeth, hunted through the days and
nights by the Furies their crime has summoned from the
depths of their own souls — those Furies who drag down the
days and nights upon them, until light is as darkness, darkness as light:

MACBETH: What is the night?
LADY MACBETH: Almost at odds with morning, which is which.

[III, 4]

Death quenching the light of beauty and of youth, quenching
love:

> The jawes of darknesse do devoure it up:
> So quick bright things come to confusion.

A Midsommer-Night's Dream, I, I

Timon of Athens digging with his nails in the wilderness to
unearth the most humble root wherewith to appease his hunger, and finding, at first, not a root, but uneatable gold, the
source of all evil. The world of Hamlet, that "distracted
globe" that holds his brain, ruled over by a small star.

These are the themes. The night of King Lear would seem
to blot out all life. Here the great creator of these Hymns to
Life has given us a work that is largely a diatribe against procreation — uttered, perhaps, at a time when darkness had en-
gulfed his own soul.

Yet even here, Lear, cursing his daughter, Goneril, calls
upon Nature to

> Dry up in her the organs of increase [I, 4]

as the most appalling curse that may fall.

[25]

And here, as throughout the Tragedies, Man may rise to such a height that he can speak, as an equal, with Fate, although he is in her power:

KENT: Fortune, good night, smile once more, turn thy wheel!

[II, 2]

Man speaks with the gods, though the answer of the gods sounds through strange mouths . . . the voice of the Oracle speaks through the lips of three passers-by in the market-place:

"'Tis verie like he hath the Falling sicknesse."

"No, Caesar hath it not; but you and I And honest Casca, we have the Falling sicknesse."

"I know not what you meane by that, but I am sure Caesar fell downe. If the rag-tagge people did not clap him and hisse him, according as he pleas'd and displeas'd them, as they use to do the players in the theatre, I am no true man."

Julius Caesar, I, 2

But those passers-by, through whose lips the Oracle spoke, were to be the murderers of Caesar.

The voice of Fate sounds through the lips of Macbeth's porter. As the knocking on the Castle gate changes to the noise of the Damned knocking at the gate of Hell, so that voice changes to that of the porter at Hell's gate — the Castle is no longer the Castle, but the place of the Damned, of that "Farmer that hang'd himselfe on th' expectation of Plentie" (the woman to whom the harvest was of the physical world, — who sowed, who reaped, and who, in the end, hanged herself when the reaping was done, and she knew the work of the harvest) — and the man "who committed Treason enough for God's sake, yet could not equivocate to Heaven: O, come in, Equivocator."

Some General Notes on the Tragedies

Throughout the Tragedies there are strange mutterings, as of a sibyl prophesying Doom:

".. . There was such laughing. Queen Hecuba laught that her eyes ran Ore."
"With millstones."
"And Cassandra laught."

Troilus and Cressida, I, 2

Or a ghost turns prophet:

BRUTUS: Why comst thou?
GHOST: To tell thee thou shalt see me at Philippi.
BRUTUS: Well, then I shall see thee againe?
GHOST: I, at Philippi.
BRUTUS: Why, I will see thee at Philippi then.

Julius Caesar, IV, 3

And from the lips of another ghost sounds this prophecy:

> And duller shouldst thou be than the fat weede
> That roots itself in ease on Lethe Wharfe,

Hamlet, I, 5

* * *

The beating of these greater hearts, the pulse of this vaster humanity, seem energized by the rhythms, which are like the "active principles" of which Newton wrote.

Shakespeare's immense benevolence and love, and the dooms which are shadows cast by these huge characters — shadows bearing their shape, moving in accordance with their movements — are conveyed through the world of sound. Through rhythm, which is "the mind of dance and the skeleton of tone," and through tone, "which is the heart of man," "this organic being clothed with the flesh of the world." [2]

[2] Richard Wagner, *Opera and Drama.*

[27]

At moments in the very sound of the verse or the prose is heard the tread of Doom. The beating of Macbeth's heart changes, suddenly, to the knock of Fate's hand upon the door, in the passage quoted above, where the Porter hears the Damned knocking at the gate of Hell.

PORTER: Here's a knocking indeede! If a man were Porter of Hell-gate he should have olde turning the key. Knock, knock, knock . . . But this place is too cold for Hell.

[II, 3]

And why is it too cold for Hell? Because of the coldness of the will that planned the deed? Because the upper circles of Hell are warmed by some human passion, and the Porter knew nothing, as yet, of the utter darkness? Or was it, not the tread of Doom, the knocking of the damned souls, that was heard, but (as Sir Arthur Quiller-Couch suggested, in *Shakespeare's Workmanship*) "the sane, clear, broad, ordinary workaday world asserting itself, and none the more relentingly for being workaday, and common and ordinary, and broad, clear and sane"?

*   *   *

And what of Shakespeare's "tuneful plannetting"? [3]

If we consider the celestial and terrestrial mechanics of Shakespeare's vast music, at times the movement of the lines is like the slow astronomic rhythm by which the northern and southern atmospheres are alternately subject to greater extremes of temperature. So it is, I think, with *Othello*. Sometimes the verse is frozen into an eternal polar night, as in certain passages of *Macbeth*. Sometimes it is like the sun's heat, as in *Antony and Cleopatra;* sometimes it is the still-retained heat of the earth, as in *King Henry the Fourth*

[3] Leigh Hunt's description of poetry.

and *King Henry the Fifth* (works of a very different order from that of the Tragedies). It moves like Saturn in the Dorian mode, like Jupiter in the Phrygian.

Sometimes the gigantic phrases, thrown up by passion, have the character of those geological phenomena, brought about in the lapse of cosmical time, by the sun's heat, by the retained internal heat of the earth, — or they seem part of the earth, fulgurites, rocky substances fused or vitrified by lightning, as in *Timon of Athens*. Or, as in *King Lear*, the words seem thunderbolts, hurled from the heart of heaven. *King Lear, Timon of Athens*, seem the works of a god who is compact of earth and fire, of whom it might be said that he is a fifth element.

The immense differences in shape and character between the caesuras in his verse, and between the pauses that end the lines, have much to do with the variation of sound, rhythm, and movement.

Sometimes the pause is like a whirlpool or vortex, as in the first line of Othello's

> Excellent wretch! Perdition catch my Soule,
> But I do love thee. And when I love thee not,
> Chaos is come againe.   [III, 3]

Here, between "wretch" and "perdition," the caesura has a swirling movement. But the most wonderful of all uses of the caesura occurs in *Macbeth*, as we shall see.

V. "Macbeth"

The events in the life of a character, as well as the personality, even the appearance, of Shakespeare's men and women, are suggested by the texture, the movement of the lines. In *Macbeth*, for instance, we find, over and over again, schemes of tuneless dropping dissonances:

FIRST WITCH: When shall we three meet againe?
                 In thunder, lightning, or in raine?
SECOND WITCH: When the hurly-burly's done,
                 When the battle's lost and won.
THIRD WITCH: That will be ere set of Sun.
FIRST WITCH: Where the place?
SECOND WITCH: Upon the heath.
THIRD WITCH: There to meet with Macbeth.   [I, I]

"Done" is a dropping dissonance to "raine," "heath" to the second syllable of "Macbeth," and these untuned, dropping dissonances, falling from the mouths of the three Fates degraded into the shapes of filthy hags, have a prophetic and terrible significance. — So do Macbeth and Lady Macbeth, slow step by step, descend into Hell.[1]

Charles Lamb said of these witches: ". . . The hags . . . have neither child of their own, nor seem to be descended from any parent. They are foul anomalies, of whom we know not whence they are sprung, nor whether they have begin-

---

[1] "When the battle's lost and won . . . ." Could anything be more significant of the absolute stony indifference of the three hags — seeing all things alike, seeing evil in all things?

ning or ending. . . . Except Hecate, they have no names —
which heightens their mysteriousness."

Has not Macbeth himself brought them into being? . . .
The first speech of these three Fates ends thus:

> Fair is foul, and foul is fair:
> Hover through the fog and filthy air.

The first words spoken by Macbeth are, as Bradley has pointed
out, nearly an echo of this:

> So foul and fair a day I have not seen.   [I, 3]

. But that great critic omitted to call attention to the fact
that sometimes the Apparitions' voices sound with the very
tone of Lady Macbeth's voice:

> Be bloody, bold, and resolute.   [IV, 1]

Might this not have come from the lips of Macbeth's loving
Fury? And does not Lady Macbeth, herself, apostrophizing
her absent husband, say:

> Hie thee hither,
> That I may pour my spirits in thine ear.   [I, 5]

Here, as is usual with Shakespeare, a phrase does not bear
its obvious meaning alone.

Sir Arthur Quiller-Couch has said "the whole play, as
it were a dark corridor of Inverness Castle, resounds with . . .
echoes."

These echoes fall because Time (as has been pointed out
by two distinguished poets and critics,[2] working independ-
ently and from quite different points of view) "has become
inoperative," no longer means anything. Mr. Stephen Spender
says:

[2] Mr. Stephen Spender and Mr. Mark Van Doren.

"One often hears quoted:

> Come what may
> Time and the hour run through the roughest day.

Actually, the tragedy of Macbeth is in his discovery that this is untrue.

.   .   .   .   .   .

"In the minds of Macbeth and Lady Macbeth there are, after the prophetic meeting with the weird sisters, three kinds of time: the time before the murder of Macbeth, the time of the murder of Duncan, and the enjoyable time afterwards, when they reap the fruits of the murder. Their problem is to keep these times separate, and not to allow them to affect each other."

Quoting Macbeth's soliloquy before the murder,

> If it were done — when 'tis done — then 'twere well
> It were done quickly: if the assassination
> Could trammel up the consequence, and catch
> With his surcease, success: that but this blow
> Might be the be-all and the end-all here,
> But here upon this bank and shoal of time
> We'ld jump the life to come. But in these Cases
> We still have judgement here: that we but teach
> Bloody instructions, which, being taught, return
> To plague the inventor.   [1, 7]

Mr. Spender remarks: "Macbeth certainly has good reason to fear even-handed justice. . . .

"The real fear is far more terrible. It is a fear of the extension into infinity of the instant in which he commits the murder. The bank and shoal of time is time that has stood still; beyond it lies the abyss of a timeless moment."

Later, Mr. Spender refers to Lady Macbeth's

"Macbeth"

             . . . Nor time, nor place,
Did then adhere, and yet you would make both.
They have made themselves, and that their fitness now
Does unmake you.   [I, 7]

In this, I see that Time and Place have become active principles, — a part of Destiny.

This illuminated criticism explains, of course, both Lady Macbeth's insistence on the *hour* in the sleepwalking scene, and the repetition in a speech of Macbeth's — the perpetual return to:

             Shall sleepe no more.

               *   *   *

"The words of Banquo to the witches:

    If you can look into the seeds of Time,
    And say which grains will grow and which will not,
                                          [I, 3]

plant early in the play," says Mr. Van Doren,[3] "a conception of time as something which fulfills itself by growing — and which, the season being wrong, can swell to monstrous shape. Or it can find crannies in the mold, and extend secret sinister roots into dark soil that never has known them. Or it can have no growth at all; it can rot and fester in its bed and die. The conception wavers, like the courage of Macbeth, but it will not away. Duncan welcomes Macbeth to Forres with the words:

    I have begun to plant thee, and will labour
    To make thee full of growing.   [I, 4]

"But Macbeth like Time itself, will burgeon beyond bounds."

[3] Mark Van Doren, *The Plays of Shakespeare.*

[33]

I think it means this — but has, also, another meaning. We plant our death in the man who will be the means of it. Not only his deformity, but the looks and taunts of his fellow men planted evil in the nature of Richard the Third. As for Edmund — such speeches as that made by his father to Kent were responsible for his nature.

Perhaps the good Duncan had planted ambition — which was to be the cause of his own death — in Macbeth.

In this vast world torn from the universe of night, there are three tragic themes. The first theme is that of the actual guilt, and the separation in damnation of the two characters — the man who, in spite of his guilt, walks the road of the spirit, and who loves the light that has forsaken him — and the woman who, after her invocation to the "Spirits who tend on mortall thoughts," walks in the material world, and who does not know that light exists, until she is nearing her end and must seek the comfort of one small taper to illumine all the murkiness of Hell. — That small taper is her soul.

These beings have the force, the vastness of Nature.

Dr. Caroline Spurgeon has already, in her book *Shakespeare's Imagery and What It Tells Us*, called attention to "the *unnaturalness* of Macbeth's crime," being like "a convulsion of nature." This, she says, "is brought out repeatedly and emphasised by imagery, as are also the terrible results of going against nature." Macbeth says that Duncan's wounds

> . . . look'd like a breach in nature,
> For ruin's wasteful entrance.   [II, 3]

Again, the doomed Queen's malady is "a great perturbation in nature."

This, I think, has reference to the crime. But it shows Macbeth and his Queen, also, as figures of the same vastness and eternity as Michelangelo's "Night and Day."

The second tragic theme of the play is the man's love for the woman whose damnation is of the earth, who is unable, until death is near, to conceive of the damnation of the spirit, and who in her blindness therefore strays away from him, leaving him forever in his lonely hell.

The third tragic theme is the woman's despairing love for the man whose vision she cannot see, and whom she has helped to drive into damnation.

The very voices of these two damned souls have therefore a different sound. His voice is like that of some gigantic being in torment — of a lion with a human soul. In her speech invoking darkness, the actual sound is so murky and thick that the lines seem impervious to light, and, at times, rusty, as though they had lain in the blood that had been spilt, or in some hell-born dew. There is no escape from what we have done. The past will return to confront us. And that is even shown in the verse. In that invocation there are perpetual echoes, sometimes far removed from each other, sometimes placed close together.

For instance, in the line

And fill me from the Crowne to the Toe, top-full

"full" is a darkened dissonance to "fill" — and these dissonances, put at opposite ends of the line, together with the particular placing of the alliterative *f*'s of "fill" and "full" and the alliterative *t*'s, and the rocking up and down of the dissonantal *o*'s ("Crowne," "Toe," "top"), show us a mind reeling on the brink of madness, about to topple down into those depths, yet striving to retain its balance.

Let us examine the passage for a moment. The manner in which the stressed assonances are placed is largely responsible for the movement, and the texture is extremely variable —

murky always, excepting for those few flares from the fires
of Hell, but varying in the thickness of that murk.

> The Raven himselfe is hoarse
> That croakes the fatall entrance of Duncane
> Under my Battlements. Come, you Spirits
> That tend on mortall thoughts! unsex me here,
> And fill me from the Crowne to the Toe, top-full
> Of direst Cruelty! Make thicke my blood;
> Stop up the accesse and passage to Remorse,
> That no compunctious visitings of Nature
> Shake my fell purpose, nor keepe peace betweene
> The effect and it. Come to my Woman's Brests,
> And take my Milke for Gall, you murthering Ministers,
> Where-ever in your sightlesse substances
> You waite on Nature's Mischiefe. Come, thicke Night,
> And pall thee in the dunnest smoake of Hell,
> That my keene knife see not the Wound it makes,
> Nor Heaven peepe through the Blanket of the darke
> To cry Hold, Hold.   [1, 5]

Throughout the whole of this speech, an untuned and terrible effect is produced by these discordant, dissonantal *o*'s,
used outwardly and inwardly — "hoarse" echoed by "croakes"
(I am assuming, from the evidence of other words, that the
oa of "croakes" was then pronounced as an assonance to the
oar of "hoarse") — these thickening to "come," darkening
again to "mortall thoughts" and then — supreme example —
making the line rock up and down, and finally topple over, in

> And fill me from the Crowne to the Toe, top-full.

"Blood," "Stop," "Remorse," "Come" — each of these dissonantal *o*'s has a different height or depth, a different length
or choked shortness.[4]

[4] Dissonantal: but in the case of "Stop" and "Come" hardly so; for in the

[36]

There is a fabric, too, of dull and rusty vowels, thickened *m*'s, and unshaping *s*'s (these latter are unshaping because they are placed close together, and so deprive the line of form, to some extent, as in

> Stop up the accesse and passage to Remorse,
> That no compunctious visitings of Nature

or

> Where-ever in your sightlesse substances.

Throughout the passage, the consonants are forever thickening and then thinning again — perhaps as the will hardens and then, momentarily, dissolves. In the lines

> That croakes the fatall entrance of Duncane
> Under my Battlements. Come, you Spirits

"Come" is a thickened, darkened assonance (almost a dissonance) to the "Dun" of Duncane and of the first syllable of "under." And in the line

> That no compunctious visitings of Nature

the first syllable of "compunctious" is a kind of darkened, thickened reverberation of the word "Come" (darkened or thickened because what follows throws a shade backward); the second syllable is a thickened echo of the first syllable of "Duncane."

As the giant shuttles of Fate weave, closing and opening, so do the lines of this speech seem to close and open, and to change their length. But this change is in appearance only, and not real. By this I mean that there are no extra syllables to the line. The apparent change is due to the lightening and

---

pronunciation of that line the sound of these particular *o*'s was almost identical — only the end *p* and *m* distorted them slightly.

lengthening of the vowel sounds. For though, as I have said already, the words are frequently dull and rusty in this passage, at times they stretch out into a harsh shriek, which sometimes is sustained, sometimes broken, — as with the broken echoes "Raven," "fatall."

There are moments, too, when the line is prolonged for other reasons than that of the changing vowel lengths:

> And take my Milke for Gall, you murthering Ministers

is an example. Here, in spite of the fact that all the vowels are dulled (with the exception of the high *a* of "take" and the dark *a* of "gall"), the *l*'s prolong the line slightly, the thick, muffled reverberations of the alliterative *m*'s, placed so close together, produce a peculiar effect of dull horror. In

> Stop up the accesse and passage to Remorse

we shall find that instead of the line being slowed (and therefore, in appearance, lengthened) by the *s*'s, the dull assonantal *a*'s, a more powerful factor when placed close together, actually shorten the line, which, again, is thickened by the *p*'s ending words that are placed side by side. The effect produced in a line by *p*'s *ending* a word, and by *p*'s *beginning* a word, is completely different. A *p* beginning a word does not necessarily thicken the line.

Sometimes the particular placing of the assonances produces a sound like that of a fevered, uneven pulse, — an example is the effect brought about by the drumming of the dull *un . . . om* sounds in the lines

> Duncane
> Under my Battlements. Come

This terrible drumming sound is heard over and over again throughout the passage, and is due not only to the placing of the assonances, but also to the particular placing of double-syllabled and (this has a still stronger effect) treble-syllabled words and quick-moving, unaccented one-syllabled words. In the line

> And fill me from the Crowne to the Toe, top-full

"to the" gives an example of the effect of those quick-moving, unaccented one-syllabled words:

> That no compunctious visitings of Nature

as an example of the use of three-syllabled words, disturbing, purposely, the movement of the line.

This march towards Hell is slow, and has a thunderous darkened pomp. It is slow, and yet it has but few pauses (for that march is of her own will, she is driven by that will as by a Fury) and these pauses are not long, but deep, like fissures opening down into Hell. There is, however, a stretching pause after the word "Gall."

In the Second Scene of Act Two, while the sleeping King is being sent to his death, Lady Macbeth's voice has a different tone:

> That which hath made them drunke hath made me bold,
> What hath quench'd them hath given me fire.
> > Hearke!
> Peace!
> It was the Owle that shriek'd, the fatall Bell-man,
> Which gives the stern'st good-night.[5]

Here we actually feel the silence of the night, broken by that long flame of a voice, like a torch held by a Fury before the destruction of a world is begun. That voice, pausing, as it seems forever, on the long sound of "Peace" (a word that

---

[5] So it is printed in the Oxford edition. The Second Folio has it thus:
"Hark! Peace!"
in one line, instead of two. This seems to me fatal to the splendor of the passage.

has the high doom-haunted tone of the owl's shriek), echoes, in a straight line, down all the corridors of the Dead.

The speeches of Macbeth have a different sound. He, at least, would retreat from the path, if only it were possible. But he is a prisoner, bound forever to his first hell-born deed, and he must go where his deed drags him.

The dark and terrible voice of Macbeth is not covered by a blood-dewed rust, is not like a black and impenetrable smoke from Hell, or the torch of a Fury — as is the voice of the woman who, to him, is Fate. It is hollow like the depths into which he has fallen, it returns ever (though it, too, has discordances) to one note, dark as the Hell through which he walks with that sleepless soul. The sound is ever "no more."

> Cawdor
> Shall sleepe no more, Macbeth shall sleepe no more.
>
> [ii, 2]

Dr. Bradley, in *Shakespearean Tragedy*, calls attention to the three beings in one that must suffer damnation. "What he [Macbeth] heard was the voice that cried 'Macbeth does murder sleepe,' and then, a minute later, with a change of tense, denounced him, as if his three names gave him three personalities to suffer in the doom of sleeplessness:

> Glamis hath murder'd Sleepe, and therefore Cawdor
> Shall sleepe no more, Macbeth shall sleepe no more."

The despair of Macbeth, hearing the voice that cries these words, his sense that there is no escape, is brought home to us by the dark, hollow, ever-recurrent echoes of the *ore . . . aw* sounds. That is the keynote of the whole speech.

As with Lady Macbeth's speech quoted above, the magnificence is largely brought about and controlled by the particular places in which the alliterations and assonances are placed (though in the two speeches they are used completely differently, and have an entirely different effect).

MACBETH: Me thought I heard a voyce cry "Sleepe no more,
Macbeth does murder Sleepe," — the innocent Sleepe,
Sleepe that knits up the ravell'd sleave of Care,
The death of each daye's Life; sore Labour's Bath,
Balme of hurte mindes, Great Nature's second Course,
Chiefe Nourisher in Life's Feast —

LADY MACBETH: What doe you meane?

MACBETH: Still it cry'd "Sleepe no more!" to all the house:
Glamis hath murder'd Sleepe, and therefore Cawdor
Shall sleepe no more, Macbeth shall sleepe no more.

The hollow vowels are like "Burrows, and Channels, and Clefts, and Caverns, that never had the comfort of one beam of light since the great fall of the Earth." [6]

Twice, a word shudders in that dark voice. The first time, it is the word "innocent" — that word which must henceforth fly in terror from the voice that uttered it, but that will yet sound again from those guilty lips, bringing with it a renewed agony of soul.

Sometimes an awe-inspiring, drum-beating sound is heard. Once it is slow, and is caused by placing alliterative *b*'s, with near-assonantal vowel sounds — "Bath," "Balme" (these being pronounced at that time "Bawth," "Baulme") — at the end of one line and the beginning of the next. (There is a strong pause between these words.) These dark *a*'s are not an exact assonance, because of the difference in thickness between the *th* and the *lme*. Then, for a second time, two *a* sounds are placed together, "Great Nature's," and here the beat is less emphatic; there is no pause between the sounds.

But above all, the quickened beat of a terror-stricken heart is heard, in "therefore Cawdor" — "fore" being a darkened

[6] Burnet, *The Theory of the Earth.*

dissonance to "there," and the two other syllables being as nearly as possible assonances to "fore," to "Balme" and to "Bath," though all have different degrees of darkness.

This is followed by the long, stately, and inexorable march of Doom:

>Shall sleepe no more, Macbeth shall sleepe no more.

It is in this scene that we first become aware of the different paths of damnation, — the path of the spirit that sees not all great Neptune's ocean will wash his hand clear of blood, — and that of the earth-bound Fate who, until she is near her end, dreams that

>A little water cleares us of this deede,

and who, when the voice cries

Cawdor

>Shall sleepe no more, Macbeth shall sleepe no more

hears only the small voice of the cricket — or a dark, but yet human voice:

MACBETH: I have done the deed. Didst thou not heare a noyse?
LADY MACBETH: I heard the Owle screame, and the Crickets cry. Did not you speake?
MACBETH: When?
LADY MACBETH: Now.
MACBETH: As I descended?
LADY MACBETH: Aye.
MACBETH: Hearke!
 Who lyes i' the second chamber?
LADY MACBETH: Donalbaine.   [II, 2]

*   *   *

"Did not you speake? . . ." Often, in this drama, Fate takes to herself, and uses, the voice of one of the protagonists.

[42]

. . . And, as Macbeth must hear the voices of the three Sisters
and the Apparitions speaking through the lips of his wife, and
her voice through theirs ("Be bloody, bold and resolute."
Who spoke those words: "who was it thus that cry'd?" as
Lady Macbeth asked) — so, here, in the words "As I descended," it may be that the descent was into Hell, and that
his doom spoke through his unknowing lips.

Doom and he were one.

Macduff, discovering the murder of the King, shouts:

> Banquo and Donalbain! Malcolm! Awake!
> Shake off this downy sleepe, Death's counterfeit,
> And looke on Death itselfe! — up, up, and see
> The great Doome's image! — Malcolm! Banquo!
> As from your graves rise up, and walk like sprights
> To countenance this horror! [ii, 3]

These words, that have a strange echoing sound like that
of a boulder being thrown into deep water, must have struck
the soul of the guilty man with terror.

. . . Malcolm, who must fly, if he would escape his father's fate, Banquo, who must soon die, are called as from
their graves, — and to look on what? The great Doome's
image. Duncan? Or *Macbeth*. For so he must have seen himself — as the great Doome.

Before the first murder was accomplished, the act that was
to be done had slain the half of Nature — in the world, and
in the hearts of Macbeth and Lady Macbeth:

> Now o'er the one-halfe world
> Nature seemes dead. . . . [ii, 1]

So the innocent Night and its peacefulness seemed to Macbeth. As Johnson says: "over our hemisphere all action and
motion seem to have ceased."

From now onward, only blood, and the road that he must tread, exist for Macbeth in the tangible world.

Who lyes i' the second chamber?   [II, 2]

. . . Who must be the next to fall under his bloodstained hands, upon that road? . . . But to Lady Macbeth, he is speaking, not of a grave that must be dug, and of a man about to die, but of one sleeping in his bed — Donalbain.

Here, then, in these few lines, the two guilt-stricken souls say farewell, forever. The immense pause after Lady Macbeth's "Aye" is a gap in time, like the immense gap between the Ice Age and the Stone Age, wherein, as Science tells us, "the previously existing inhabitants of the earth were almost wholly destroyed, and a different class of inhabitants created." On the other side of that gap in time, Macbeth rises as the new inhabitant of a changed world — and alone in the universe of eternal night, although the voice of Lady Macbeth, his Fate, his loving Fury, still drives him onward.

Here we have one stupendous use of the pause. After the words that follow Lady Macbeth's "Donalbaine," Macbeth looks at his hands.

MACBETH: This is a sorry sight.

The four beats falling upon the silence before Macbeth speaks thus, seem like the sound of blood dropping, slowly, from those hands —

What hands are here! Hah! they plucke out mine Eyes.

Those hands are the hands of Murder. They are no longer the hands of the living man who was once Macbeth — hands made to caress with, hands made to open windows on to the sun and air, hands made to lift the life-giving . . . food to the mouth. These hands have now given him . . . darkness forever — a darkness surrounded by a terrible and all-seeing light, that mars every action, and that yet has no part in him.

> "Io venni in luogo d'ogni luce muto." [7]

And yet these beings, and those who surround them, speak ever of the light.

How may the sun have appeared to them? Seeming, at noon, "as blank as a clouded moon," and shedding "a rust-coloured ferruginous light on the ground and the floors of rooms," [8] as at a time of earthquake? — Surely, to them, the sun must often hide his head, or appear "with a discoloured face, pale like so many ghosts, with a dusty or bloody countenance," or, "as in some foggy days, hang in the firmament like a lump of blood." [9]

Though these souls are separated forever, yet sometimes the appalling necessities arising from their crime leash them together for a moment . . . as in the scene (Act iii, Scene i) where, with a sort of crouching, horror-inspiring quietness, like that of a tiger about to lap blood, Macbeth says

> Heere's our chiefe Guest.

And, stretching beyond him, straining even more eagerly towards the doomed Banquo, Lady Macbeth continues:

> If he had been forgotten,
> It had beene as a gap in our great Feast
> And all-thing unbecomming.

— the sound of the word "forgotten" being like that of a beast lapping.

[7] "I came into a place of all light dumb."
[8] Gilbert White, *The Natural History of Selborne.*
[9] Et seq. *Theory of the Earth.* Burnet, *Concerning the Conflagration.*

Macbeth then says:

> To-night we hold a solemne Supper, Sir,
> And Ile request your presence.

(Here, as always, drawing down his own doom upon himself.)

Banquo murmurs:

> . . . Let your Highness
> Command upon me; to the which my duties
> Are with a most indissoluble tye
> For ever knit.

. . . That tie is the shedding of his own blood. From the moment of his death he is indeed knit to Macbeth, — he is a part of his Hell.

So did Iago say to Othello:

> I am your owne for ever.   [iii, 3]

But, in *Macbeth*, the victim is speaking to the slayer.

A moment later, he says:

> I must become a borrower of the Night
> For a darke houre or twaine.

and Macbeth replies:

> Faile not our Feast.

Says the man who is already half ghost — the ghost who is still a man:

> My lord, I will not.

And Macbeth bids him:

> Adieu, till you returne at Night.

The invited guest was faithful to his promise. The night he must borrow could not hide him long from sight.

"*Macbeth*"

Once, and once only, from the lips of the man who would sleep no more, sounds a voice so stilled, so drowsy, so furred, that it would seem the Conscience itself had begun to fall into an animal slumber:

> There's comfort yet; they are assaileable;
> Then be thou jocund. Ere the Bat hath flowne
> His cloyster'd flight, ere to black Hecate's summons
> The shard-borne Beetle with his drowsie hums
> Hath rung Night's yawning Peale, there shall be done
> A deed of dreadful note.

LADY MACBETH: What's to be done?
MACBETH: Be innocent of the knowledge, dearest Chuck,
> Till thou applaud the deed. Come, Seeling Night,
> Skarfe up the tender Eye of pittiful Day,
> And with thy bloody and invisible Hand
> Cancell and teare to pieces that great Bond
> Which keepes me pale! Light thickens, and the Crow
> Makes Wing to the Rookie Wood:
> Good things of Day begin to droope and drowse,
> Whiles Night's black agents to their Preys doe rowse.
> Thou marvell'st at my words: but hold thee still,
> Things bad begun, make strong themselves by ill.

> [III, 2]

". . . Which keepes me pale"? . . . What, exactly, does he mean? Pale from the horror of his own deed? Or does he mean that he is not yet reddened once more by freshly spilt blood?

In this passage, the words "innocent," "invisible," "pittiful," shudder as if the guilty man's voice hardly dared utter them. Here, although the sounds of

> Makes Wing to the Rookie Wood:
> Good things of Day

seem huddling together as if for comfort — the discordances, the reversals of "summons," "hums," "done," "Hand," "Bond," all show that his soul is falling into the frightful pattern of his new life — that this life has begun to take shape . . . the settling of the pattern is like the cooling of a dead sun.

When we come to the scene where the ghost of Banquo keeps his tryst, we shall hear again the terror-maddened drum-beat of Macbeth's heart:

MACBETH: Avaunt! and quit my sight! let the earth hide thee:
Thy bones are marrowless, thy blood is cold:
Thou hast no speculation in those eyes
Which thou dost glare with.

LADY MACBETH: Thinke of this, good Peeres,
But as a thing of Custome: 'tis no other,
Only it spoyles the pleasure of the time.

MACBETH: What man dare, I dare:
Approach thou like the rugged Russian Beare,
The arm'd Rhinoceros, or the Hircan Tiger;
Take any shape but that, and my firm Nerves
Shall never tremble. Or be alive againe,
And dare me to the Desart with thy Sword;
— If trembling I inhabit then, protest me
The Baby of a Girle. Hence, horrible shadow!
Unreall mockery, hence!
                          Why, so; being gone,
I am a man againe. Pray you, sit still.[10]   [III, 4]

---

[10] "If trembling I inhabit then, protest me." It is a moot point whether the line should run thus, or whether it should be

"If trembling I inhibit thee, protest me."

Pope changed it to the latter. "Inhabit" may have seemed to him vague, though it has been used by Shakespeare, elsewhere, in the meaning of "staying indoors," without a noun attached: as, in *As You Like It:* "O knowledge ill-inhabited! Worse than Jove in a thatched house." (In this sense, it means "lodged.") This has been pointed out by Steevens.

"Macbeth"

In these lines, the terror-stricken heart-beat is produced, as before, by the varying use of alliteration of assonances and near-assonances placed close together within the lines: "firm," "Nerves," "never tremble," "rugged Russian," "Take any shape." The feeling of unendurably tautened, sharpened nerves is produced by the particular use of vowels in the preceding word: "Hircan Tiger," for instance. The change from "firm Nerves" to the higher discordances of "Hircan Tiger" is another example. "Sight" is a rising dissonance to "quit," — rising as terror rises. "Hide" is an assonance to "sight" but is longer because of the *d*. Further on in the passage there are the dissonances "Girle," "Unrealle" — the latter being, as it were, a crumbling shadow of the sound of "Girle" — and the rising dissonances "gone," "againe." All these general discordances add to the impression of a nature alternately sharpened and untuned by fear.

Internally and externally in these lines, there are far-separated, but still insistent, echoes, and these help in part to keep the slow sound together. ("Glare," "dare," "Beare," and Lady Macbeth's lower "Peeres.")

On the other hand, "inhibited" has been used by Shakespeare, in the exact sense in which it is used in the debatable line:

"A practiser of arts inhibited"   [*Hamlet*]

To "inhibit" is to forbid.

The original reading is

"If trembling I inhabit, then protest me,"

and my own feeling is that, in changing it, the eighteenth-century precise mind of one of the greatest of all technicians in poetry (and one to whom we owe emendations in Shakespeare of the greatest beauty, and the most subtle beauty) has, for once, won the battle over his ear. If we say

"If trembling I inhibit thee, protest me"

the line shambles, because of the rhyming "thee" and "me" being so close together, but unevenly in the line. The deadly pomp of the march through Macbeth's lonely desert is destroyed, and the sense that comes through sound. This is how it appears to me: but I may be wrong.

[49]

In the last line:

> I am a man againe. Pray you, sit still

the doom-haunted man has lost even the sound of his own heart-beat. There is no pulse to be heard. There is practically no shape in that line, excepting that given by the caesura, which in this case is a chasm dividing the line. . . .

For it seems as if all the blood had fled from the heart of Macbeth, to join the blood that had been shed. Blood will haunt his spirit forever, but will leave the veins like that "most ghastly thing in Nature," the bed of the ocean from which the ocean has fled.

After this scene, the gulf separating the two beings is impassable. Not only the change of the world in which they live, but the whole depth of the soul, separates them. They are divided in all but love. . . . She will love him forever: but he has gone beyond love.

> This Avarice

says Macduff

> Stickes deeper, growes with more pernicious roote
> Than Summer-seeming Lust: and it hath bin
> The Sword of our slain Kings. . . . [IV, 3]

Ambition, Avarice, had no stronger root than love in Macbeth. But now there is no room for her in that Hell.

He asks her

> What is the night?

and she replies

> Almost at oddes with morning, which is which.
>   [III, 5]

Here, I think, Macbeth is asking if the night is blacker for this fresh crime. But Lady Macbeth is speaking of the physical universe.

Macbeth then utters these words:

> How sayst thou, that Macduff denies his person
> At our great bidding?

He is speaking to the invisible beings who now, with the past and future victims of his guilt, alone inhabit his world. His wife, surprised by the question, replies:

> Did you send to him, Sir?

And Macbeth, from his polar solitude, answers this being of another universe, who is separated from him by the whole darkness of her spiritual blindness:

> I heare it by the way: but I will send.   [III, 4]

From that moment, I think that the appearance of Macbeth must have inspired terror, as if he were no longer a mortal man, but one of those giant comets whom Pliny named Crinitas, "shaggy with bloody locks . . . having the appearance of a fleece surmounted with a kind of crown, — or one that prognosticates high winds and great heat . . . they are also visible in the winter months, and about the South Pole, but they have no rays proceeding from them."

And Lady Macbeth — how changed is she, in that pitiful scene when she, who had cried to "thicke Night" to envelop the world and her soul, she who had rejected light, seeks the comfort of one little taper, — the small candle-flame of her soul, to light all the murkiness of Hell! Yet still, in the lonely mutterings of one who must walk through Hell alone, save for the phantom of Macbeth, we hear that indomitable will that pushed him to his doom, rising once more in the vain hope that she may shield and guide him.

There is, in these two beings, the faithfulness of the lion and his mate. It is not their fault that never more can she be his companion.

To speak of this scene from a technical point of view, the extremely interesting theory was propounded by Mr. M. A. Bayfield, in *A Study of Shakespeare's Versification*, that "Lady Macbeth's speeches, which have always been printed in prose, are really verse, and very fine verse too. The reader" (he continues) "will see how enormously they gain by being delivered in measure, and that the lines drawn out in monosyllabic feet are as wonderfully effective as any that Shakespeare wrote.

"But for the retention of the iambic scheme, the recognition would doubtless have been made long ago, but editors recognise no monosyllabic foot and would hesitate to produce lines with initial 'Trochees.'"

The speeches in the sleepwalking scene, if spoken as verse, have a great majesty: they drag the slow weight of the guilt along as if it were the train of pomp. But they have not the infinite pathos of the speeches when they are in prose, they do not inspire the same pity for this vast being, her gigantic will relaxed by sleep, trying to draw that will together, as she wanders through the scenes of her crime. The more relaxed sound of the prose produces that effect. The beat of the verse should be felt rather than heard, underlying the speeches.

Again, there will come one of those reminiscent whispers — the words of Macbeth when he hears of her death. . . .

Out, out, brief candle. . . .   [v, 5]

And we see again that lonely being, wandering through Hell with the help of one small light. But to Macbeth the weak light of the candle was not to be treasured, as a hope in the midst of the increasing darkness.

Macbeth, like that lonely sleepwalker, had changed. That change began when he, alone, heard the voice that cried "Macbeth has murdered Sleepe," — and knew that he was alone forever. He, who, in the midst of the darkness in that universe his soul, could yet love the light, is about to turn from it, for he must undergo the Mesozoic Age, the Age of Stone:

> I gin to be aweary of the Sunne.

And after the piteous human longing of

> Cure her of that.
> Canst thou not Minister to a minde diseas'd
> Plucke from the Memory a rooted Sorrow,
> Raze out the written troubles of the Braine,
> And with some sweet oblivious Antidote
> Cleanse the stufft bosome of that perilous stuffe
> Which weighs upon the heart?   [v, 3]

the words

> She should have dy'd hereafter;
> There would have beene a time for such a word
>   [v, 5]

in their very quietness, their slowness, seem tears shed in the soul by those lidless eyes: an oblation, the wasting of a rock or glacier by water-dropping, by melting.

Those two beings have passed even from the darkness of a world in which it was possible to ask

> Is't Night's predominance, or the Daye's shame,
> That darknesse doth the face of Earth intombe,
> When living Light should kiss it?   [ıı, 4]

[53]

— a darkness of which they have become so much natives that night and day are one:

MACBETH: What is the night?
LADY MACBETH: Almost at oddes with morning, which is which —

but that yet is illumined by the vision of a lost heaven — a heaven that lives yet in spite of their fall:

Angels are bright still, though the brightest fell.

[IV, 3]

VI. "King Lear"

As flies to wanton boyes, are wee to the Gods:
They kill us for their sport.

King Lear, IV, I

"Here," wrote Swinburne, "is no need of the Eumenides, children of Night everlasting, for here is very Night herself. The words just cited are not casual or episodical, they strike the keynote of the whole poem, lay the keystone of the whole arch of thought. . . . We have heard much and often from the theologians of the light of revelation: and some such thing indeed we find in Aeschylus: but the darkness of revelation is here.

"For in this, the most terrible work of human genius, it is with the very springs and sources of nature that her student has set himself to deal. The veil of the temple of our humanity is rent in twain."

"To see the true light," said Meister Eckhart, "one must become blind and strip God naked of things."

Here, in this play in which the cry sounds always "Poor Tom's a-cold!" (Man going bare to Death, or Man under "the extremitie of the skies"), unrolls before us the history of a great King powerful and ancient as the heavens, who must learn that his hands "smelle of mortalitie" — and who, through the darkness of the mind, reaches the Night of the Soul (but not that which is known by the Saints) — and, through the Night of the Soul, reaches the light. And this

[55]

history is mirrored by that of the great King's lesser counter-part, his servant Gloucester — the lusts of the heart in Gloucester taking the place of the pride of the will.[1]

Cries the mad Lear to his blinded servant:

> O, ho! are you there with me? No eyes in your head, nor money in your purse. Your eyes are in a heavy case, your purse in a light: yet you see how this world goes.

GLOUCESTER: I see it feelingly.
LEAR: What! Art mad? A man may see how this world goes
with no eyes.   [IV, 6]

One of the keynotes of the play, I suggest, is the phrase spoken by the supposed madman, Edgar:

> . . . Nero is an angler in the lake of Darknesse.
>
>   [III, 6]

In Book II, Chapter 37, of Pausanias's *Description of Greece* occurs this passage:

"I saw also a spring, called the spring of Amphiaraus, and the Alcyonian Lake. Through this lake, the Argives say, Dionysus went to Hell to fetch up Semele; and they say that Polymnus showed him the way down to Hell. The lake is bottomless. I never heard of any one who was able to sound the depth. Nero himself made the experiment, taking every precaution to ensure success. He had lines made many furlongs long: these he joined together and weighted with lead, but he could find no bottom. I was told, too, that smooth and still as the waters of the lake look to the eye, it yet has the property of sucking down any one who is rash enough

---

[1] "What could better point the transcendent issues Shakespeare has developed . . . than this encounter of the sensual man robbed of his eyes, with the wilful man, the light of his mind put out." — Granville Barker, *Prefaces to Shakespeare.*

to swim in it. The water catches him, and sweeps him down into the depths."

The meaning of this line of Edgar's, taken in conjunction with the above passage (to which, I would suggest, it must refer), is of an appalling greatness and terror.

"The lake of Darknesse" — the bottomless depths of human nature, in which the mad Lear, the blinded Gloucester (in that world in which child turns against parent, Nature against Man), and the ghost of Nero the matricide, find blackness after blackness, depth beneath depth.

Nor is this all. In many a line of Shakespeare's there is a second meaning, — and this lake through which Dionysus went to Hell to fetch up Semele, may also be the lake of human sorrows through which (in this world of transpositions) Lear and Gloucester, the fathers, went to recover the beloved Cordelia, the beloved Edgar.

Higden, as translated by Trevisa, uses this appalling phrase: ". . . he [Nero] let kerve his own moder wombe, for he wolde see the place that he was conceyved in."

And Shakespeare evidently regarded Nero as the pattern of all matricides.

In *King John* (v, 2) occur the lines:

> Yon bloody Neros, ripping up the wombe
> Of your deere Mother England.

There is a reference to Nero as a matricide in *Hamlet*, and one to his cruelty in the Third Part of *King Henry the Sixth* (III, 1).

I ask myself, therefore, if the image of Nero angling in the lake of Darknesse may not, in addition to those meanings I have suggested, be an image of Lear, who, in his prayer to Nature to kill the sources of life in his daughter, struck at the very heart of Nature, disturbing that lake of Darknesse, the original chaos from which all being arose.[2]

The old King, the events of the play, have the hugeness of Nature's forces. With the "waters of old fond eies"

. . . poor old heart, he holp the heavens to raine.

[III, 7]

Those tears have the mightiness of the heavens in dissolution, that would "temper clay" — the cold clay of the earth, and of Goneril's and Regan's hearts. The clay of his own nature.

At one moment, the King who had left humanity to its wickedness, as Lot's wife left Sodom, cast a glance over his shoulder at the abandoned and abandoning — moved by an instance of kindness, a redeeming pity in the heart of Man.

In answer to the words of the Messenger sent by Cordelia,

You shall have anything,

Lear, the humble, replies:

No seconds? All myself?
Why this would make a man a man of salt,
To use his eyes for garden water-pottes,
Ay, and laying Autumne's dust,   [IV, 6]

— a man of tears, laying the dust that the fullness of life, the ripeness, has laid upon the heart.

Lear knows, now, that he is Nothing. But with that knowledge of Nothingness comes Patience. "Nothing." "Patience."

---

[2] There is a foreshadowing of that lake of darkness that has no bottom, in Edgar's "Fathom and half, fathom and half" (III, 4), a speech not given in the quartos. Of this line, Steevens says: "He gives the sign used by those who are sounding the depths at sea." And may not some light be cast upon the passage (some light upon the first meaning I have suggested) by these words spoken by Isabella about Angelo, in the First Scene of the Third Act of *Measure for Measure:*
"His filth within being cast, he would appeare
A pond as deepe as hell."

"King Lear"

These two words, and the words "Good Night," echo through the play.

At first, powerful and ancient as the heavens, the great King calls upon them, as upon an equal, to avenge him upon his unnatural offspring:

> O heavens,
> If you do love olde men, if your sweet sway
> Allow obedience, if yourselves are old,
> Make it your cause, send downe and take my part!
>
> [II, 4]

And Nature, his mother, having heard the appalling curse he pronounces upon his child:

> Dry up in her the organs of increase,   [I, 4]

— seeing in this prayer a crime against her holiest laws, an unnatural abomination, turns the prayer

> All the stor'd vengeances of heaven fall
> On her ingrateful top!   [II, 4]

against him, pours "the extremitie of the skies" upon his uncovered head.

"How many Oceans of Water would be necessary to compose this great Ocean, rowling in the Air without bounds or banks?" . . . "Some great violence has been offered to Nature, such as we suppose to have been in the General Deluge when the frame of the Earth was broken.[3] Certainly there had been some change in Nature, or some violence offered her.

"How else," said Nietzsche, writing of the Oedipus myth, "could one force Nature to surrender her secrets, but by victoriously opposing her . . . i.e. by means of the unnatural.

[3] Burnet, *The History of the Earth.*

It is this intuition I see imprinted by the awful riddle of the destiny of Oedipus. . . . The man who solves the riddle of Nature . . . that double-constituted Sphinx . . . must also, as the murderer of his father, the husband of his mother, break the holiest laws of Nature."

In this play, we see the upheaval of all Nature, the reversal of all histories.

In the beginning of the legend, Cronos devoured his own offspring. In *King Lear* the brood devours the parent, in whom Age had become Time, and Time a fifth element. In the myth of Oedipus, son of Laius, King of Thebes, the Theban King, having learned from the oracle that he was doomed to die by the hand of his own son, exposed that son upon Mount Cithaeron immediately after his birth, with his hands and feet tied together. Here it is Lear, the father, who having first cast from his bosom his child Cordelia, is then shut from the gates to wander under the "extremitie of the skies," as an outcast. The eyes, not feet, of Gloucester (the father of Edmund, and the smaller echo of the great King) are pierced, and he is thrust outside the gates, to wander in blindness.

In the Fourth Scene of the Third Act, when Lear says "I'll talk with this same learned Theban," the outcast King has reversed his rôle. He is no longer Oedipus, but is the Sphinx, who must ask the great question. . . . And it is the naked man exposed upon the mountains — one more naked even than the questioner — one who has nothing but his bare humanity — who is now Oedipus the Theban, who can give an answer to the Riddle. No longer does the Sphinx, as in the ancient legend, put an oblique question, to which the answer is: "This is Man!" Instead, bare and terrible, the question is put. Lear, the Sphinx, asks: "Is Man no more than this?"

But in this work of Night, no answer comes from the Naked Man, — no direct answer, only a few meaningless

[60]

words, like dust from the ruins. But behind that huddle of meaningless words lies the true answer: "Man is nothing."

The sounds of the words "Nothing" and "patience" reverberate through the play.

Almost at the beginning, Lear and his daughter Cordelia reply to each other with this word:

LEAR: Speak.
CORDELIA: Nothing, my lord.
LEAR: Nothing!
CORDELIA: Nothing.
LEAR: Nothing will come of nothing: [I, I]

There are echoes of this in the Fourth Scene of Act One:

FOOL: Can you make no use of nothing, nuncle?
LEAR: Why no, boy, nothing can be made out of nothing.

And again:

FOOL: Now thou art an O without a figure. I am better than thou art now; I am a Fool, thou art nothing.

This is Man, with his "lendings" off — and before the light came through darkness, through being blind and having stripped God naked of things.

Lear says:

No, I will be the patterne of all patience,
I will say nothing. [III, 2]

When, in the Second Scene of the First Act, Gloucester, asking to see the letter Edmund pretends to have received from his brother, says "The quality of nothing hath not such neede to hide it selfe," — it seems like one of those strange echoes, or sibylline utterances, which abound in Shakespeare.

Nothing. Nothingness, — and yet in Shakespeare there is no waste, no barrenness. All is of some use.

A Poet's Notebook

In *Hamlet*, the world of the all-seeing, universal light, where there is no healing, comforting darkness, but only the shattering darkness that precedes revelation, — in one of the most terrible aeon-moments of the play, Hamlet asks:

Dost thou think Alexander looked o' this fashion in the earth?

HORATIO: E'en so.

HAMLET: And smelt so? Pah!

HORATIO: E'en so, my lord.

HAMLET: To what base uses we may return, Horatio! Why may not imagination trace the noble dust of Alexander, till he find it stopping a bung-hole?

HORATIO: 'Twere to consider too curiously, to consider so.

HAMLET: No, faith, not a jot: but to follow him thither with modesty enough, and likelihood to lead it; as thus: Alexander died, Alexander was buried, Alexander returneth into dust; the dust is earth; of earth we make loam, and why of that loam, whereto he was converted, might they not stop a beer-barrel?

> Imperious Caesar, dead and turn'd to clay,
> Might stop a hole to keep the wind away:
> O! that that earth which kept the world in awe,
> Should patch a wall to expel the winter's flaw.
>
> [v, 1]

All things are put to some use. Is there here *only* despair? Or is it but contempt for the trappings of glory? Is there here utter annihilation?

So, in *King Lear*, as in other of the plays, tears seem, not a barren waste overflow, but a sign of the quickening spirit of redemption. They are a life-giving wonder.

> All you unpublish'd virtues of the earth
> Spring with my tears!   [IV, 4]

[62]

"Be your tears wet?" Lear asks Cordelia. "Yes, faith. I pray, weep not." Yet by those tears, he knows that she lives yet, and is not a phantom returned to him from the grave.

There is a foreshadowing of the tears of the old humbled King, "laying Autumn's dust," in these lines spoken by Titus, in *Titus Andronicus*:

> O earth! I will befriend thee more with raine
> That shall distill from these two ancient urnes,
> Than youth full Aprill shall with all his showres:
> In sommer's drought Ile drop upon thee still;
> In winter with warme teares Ile melt the snow,
> And keepe eternall spring-time on thy face
> So thou refuse to drinke my deare sonne's blood.
>
> [III, 1]

Even when the growth is an evil one, as from the unlawful springtime tears of Troilus, — still it is life that arises from the tears, and not barrenness.

Through the night of the soul, a terrible wisdom comes to the mad King, and his blind and lesser prototype. Gloucester says:

> I have no way, and therefore want no eyes;
> I stumbled when I saw.   [IV, 1]

The lust of the eyes, the pride of the heart, are gone.[4]

As I said at the beginning of the book, this play would seem to be largely a diatribe against procreation.

EDGAR: The gods are just, and of our pleasant vices
　　Make instruments to plague us:
　　The dark and viteous place where thee he got
　　Cost him his eies.   [V, 3]

---

[4] Here, as elsewhere, we are reminded of certain pages in the *Phaedo Dialogue*.

GLOUCESTER *to* LEAR: Dost thou know me?
LEAR *to the* EYELESS GLOUCESTER: I remember thine eyes well
    enough.
    Dost thou squiny at me? No, doe thy worst, blind Cupid!
    Ile not love.   [IV, 6]

LEAR (*crying*):   No, they cannot touch me for coyning:
    I am the King himselfe,   [IV, 6]

— the coining to which he refers is, I think, the procreation of
his two elder daughters, that base metal.[5]
The lusts of the heart and of the flesh will not keep the
body warm in the face of death.

FOOL: . . . Now a little fire in a wide field were like an old
    Letcher's heart; a small sparke, all the rest on's body cold.
    Look! (*as Gloucester approaches*) here comes a walking fire!
                                      [III, 4]

Were it not, however, for the baseness of mankind, procreation would seem to be the greater good, and the giving
of life the purpose behind all Nature. And at first, they seem
to be so. As the most appalling of all curses, Lear calls upon
his mother and goddess, Nature, to curse Goneril with
sterility.

    Heare, Nature, heare! deere Goddesse, heare!
    Suspend thy purpose, if thou didst intend

[5] In support of this theory, I would remind the reader of the following
lines from *Measure for Measure:*

ANGELO: Ha! fie, these filthy vices! It were as good
    To pardon him that hath from nature stolne
    A man already made, as to remit
    Their sawcie sweetnesse that doe coine Heaven's image
    In stamps that are forbid! 'tis all as easie
    Falsely to take away a life true made
    As to put mettle in restrained meanes
    To make a false one.   [II, 4]

"King Lear"

To make this Creature fruitefull!
Into her Wombe convey sterility!
Dry up in her the organs of increase,
And from her derogate body never spring
A Babe to honor her! If she must teeme,
Create her child of Spleene, that it may live
And be a thwart disnature'd torment to her!
Let it stampe wrinckles in her brow of youth;
With cadent teares fret Channels in her cheekes,
Turne all her Mother's paines and benefits
To laughter and contempt, that she may feele
How sharper than a serpent's tooth it is
To have a thankless childe! Away, away.   [I, 4]

Here, the second and third lines — it must be remembered that the third line was then pronounced with each syllable sounding: "To make this Cre-a-ture fru-ite-full" have no pause — move with the slow irresistible power and horror of a tidal wave. There are pauses of uneven lengths, as if the earth had been worn into chasms by the retreating flood of passion. Sometimes, there seems to be an upheaval of the earth itself, as in the sounds of the words "sterility," "derogate."

At one moment of his madness, the voice of Lear, the great King, pardoning the life of a man who should die for the sin of adultery, changes to that of Nature herself, blessing the procreation of all life:

Thou shalt not dye: dye for Adultery! No:
The Wren goes too't, and the small gilded Flye
Do's letcher in my sight.
Let Copulation thrive: for Gloucester's bastard Son
Was kinder to his father than my Daughters
Got 'tweene the lawful sheets.
Too't Luxury, pell-mell! for I lacke Souldiers.   [IV, 6]

The first part of this speech is beneficent but unseeing, like the sun whose warmth brings into being the life hidden in insect's egg, in chrysalis, on a garden wall.

After this, the voice that speaks is no longer that of Nature alone, but is also, once again, the voice of the King who may condemn. The two voices are fused into one, as, in uncaring tones, the true reason for the procreation of life is divulged: that there may be struggle and destruction:

For I lacke Souldiers!

This is followed by the Stygian, smirching darkness of Lear's invective against Woman, the lustful, the life-giving. This darkness at first has shape, but then crumbles, falls at last into that Chaos in which the world will end.

It is not without a reason that the vastly formed verse of the first lines, blessing the procreation of life, gutters down, gradually, into an unshaped prose, whose very words seem "the grosser parts of Chaos falling down toward the centre of the earth." [6]

Behold yond simpering Dame,
Whose face between her Forkes presageth snow;
That minces virtue, and does shake the head
To heare of pleasure's name;
The Fitchew nor the soyled horse goes too't
With a more riotous appetite.
Downe from the waist they are Centaures,
Though Women all above:
But to the Girdle doe the gods inherit,
Beneath is all the fiends'.
There's hell, there's darkness, there is the Sulphurous pit,
Burning, scalding, stench, Consumption: Fie, fie, fie!
    pah! pah! Give me an Ounce of Civet, good Apothecary,
    to sweeten my imagination: there's Money for thee.

[6] Burnet, *op. cit.*

GLOUCESTER: O! let me kisse that hand.
LEAR: Let me wipe it first:
    It smelles of Mortality.   [IV, 6]

*   *   *

"Are not all things generated out of their opposites? I mean such things as good and evil, just and unjust. . . . And I want to show that in all opposites there is, of necessity, a similar alternation. I mean to say, for example, that anything which becomes great must become greater after being less."

Thus spoke Socrates, just before his death; and the words were reported in the *Phaedo Dialogue*, which I believe may possibly have been in Shakespeare's mind at the time of the creation of certain passages in *King Lear*.

I advance this suggestion with the greatest humility, since I do not wish to exhibit such a spirit as that of "the late Mr. Simpson," to whom Swinburne paid tribute in *A Study of Shakespeare*, as one "who must have had beyond all other sane men — most assuredly beyond all other fairly competent critics — the gift bestowed on him by a malignant fairy, of mistaking assumption for argument and possibility for proof. He was the very Columbus of mares' nests; to the discovery of them, though they lay far beyond the pillars of Hercules, he would apply all shifts and all resources possible to an Ultra Baconian process of unphilosophical induction."

But it is certain that from Lear (the element of fire, the will, the pride, the passion, which are the essence of fire) generated the endless cold of Goneril and Regan. To become greater, Lear became less. Out of his madness was born his wisdom.

In the first scene of the play, we see the ancient King take coldness to his heart, for all his denial:

[67]

LEAR: So young, and so untender?
CORDELIA: So young my Lord, and true.
LEAR: Let it be so: thy truth then be thy dower:
 For, by the sacred radiance of the Sunne,
 The mysteries of Hecate and the night
 By all the operations of the Orbes,
 From whom we do exist and cease to be,
 Here I disclaime all my Paternall care,
 Propinquity and property of blood,
 And as a stranger to my heart and me,
 Hold thee from this for ever. The barbarous Scythian,
 Or he that makes his generation messes
 To gorge his appetite, shall to my bosome
 Be as well-neighbour'd, pitied, and reliev'd
 As thou my some-time daughter!

At that moment, he lays his heart bare to the cold. While shuddering at the barbarous Scythian,

  Or he that makes his generation messes

(he that devours those of his own begetting), Lear lays his heart open to the mercy of the brood that tear and devour their begetter.

 So he moves into the universe of the cold.

 When Lear says to his daughter:

  Your name, fair Gentlewoman? [I, 4]

this is as quiet as Death, or as Goneril's death-dealing words. But the quiet of this sentence of Lear's is like that of a volcano before an earthquake. Regan's words

  I pray you, father, being weake, seeme so, [II, 4]

might be the cry of the Furies in the 9th canto of the *Inferno:*

  "Vegna Medusa, si 'l farem di smalto." [7]

[7] "Let come Medusa, and change we her to stone."

[68]

For this Fury, too, would petrify Medusa. Stone, herself, she changes all to stone. Even the cry of the Fury is no more a cry: the cold has frozen it to a whisper.

Her voice seems dying away in the cold, at the end of each phrase:

> O sir! you are old;
> Nature in you stands on the very Verge
> Of her confine: You should be rul'd and led
> By some discretion that discernes your state
> Better than you your selfe. Therefore, I pray you,
> That to our sister you do make returne:
> Say you have wrong'd her, sir.   [II, 4]

Goneril's answer to Lear's cry:

> How sharper than a Serpent's tooth it is
> To have a thanklesse Child! . . .

> Never afflict your selfe to know the cause;
> But let his disposition have that scope
> That dotage gives it,   [I, 4]

is uncaring as the heavens.

*   *   *

In this play, of which the beings are gigantic as phantoms from Thebes or Cyclopean cities, but yet have tides of blood beating in their veins, one theme is that of the war between the ordinary nature and the King-nature, the sacred madness that is genius; — the war of the waking workaday world, the "world of appearance, with its exceeding distrust of the Titanic powers of Nature," against "the rapture of the Dionysian state, the annihilation of the ordinary bounds and limits of existence."[8]

[8] Nietzsche, *The Birth of Tragedy*. The phrases have a universal application, and are not describing King Lear.

At first, Goneril and Regan are not, in their own view, nor from the world's point of view, wicked. Their practical natures, the nature of the waking world, must protect the old mad genius-King against himself and his fires.

Indeed, at one moment, the voice of Regan, the evil daughter, seems that of the discerning Fate that will bring the old man wisdom.

> O! sir, to wilful men,
> The injuries that they themselves procure
> Must be their schoolmasters. [II, 4]

At first, these daughters tell themselves that they are but doing their duty towards their father, and towards the world. The sane workaday world, the world of Appearance, must be protected against him. Economies must be effected, a quiet life ensured. But, with power, their coldness hardens, and the evil takes shape.

Of the two sisters, Goneril is the greater, in force, in coldness. The difference between them appears when Regan says of Gloucester:

> Hang him instantly.

The colder, infinitely greater Goneril says:

> Plucke out his eyes. [III, 7]

Then Regan, from the low horror of her nature, conceives the idea, more frightful even than that of Goneril:

> Goe thrust him out at gates, and let him smell
> His way to Dover.

Gloucester, the sensual man, is to be reduced to the most animal of the senses . . . that in which Man is most deficient, but which is most powerful in, and makes the greatness of, the Beast.

"*King Lear*"

"I have found," said Leonardo da Vinci in his *Notebooks*, "that in the composition of human bodies as compared with the bodies of animals, — the organs of sense are duller and coarser. Thus it is composed of less ingenuous instruments, and of spaces less capacious for receiving the faculties of sense. I have seen in the Lion Tribe, that the sense of smell is connected with the part of the substance of the brain which comes down from the nostrils."

The blind man is to smell, not feel, his way to Dover. The sense of touch is what separated Man from the beasts, and gave him reason.

Gloucester is to become one of the company of the Lion.

"He [Shakespeare] seems to have been asking himself [said Bradley] whether that which he loathes in man, may not be due to some strange wrenching of the frame of things, through which the lower animal souls have found a lodgement in human forms, and there found, to the horror and confusion of the thinking mind — brains to forge, tongues to speak, and hands to execute, enormities which no mere brute can conceive or execute. He shows us in *King Lear* these terrible forces bursting into monstrous life and flinging themselves upon these human beings who are weak and defenceless, partly from old age, partly because they are human and lack the dreadful energy of the beast."

"Thou chang'd and self-cover'd thing, for shame," says Albany to Goneril. And constantly Lear refers to the covering of Man. It is as if these beings wished to hide their evil souls, taking upon themselves the covering of the beast.

There are references to the "detested kite," or to the "false of heart, light of eare, bloudy of hand; Hog in sloth, Fox in stealth, Wolfe in greedinesse, Dog in madnesse, Lyon in prey."

A Poet's Notebook

And in this world of the cold, thinking of Lear's "dogge-hearted daughters," we see another circle of Hell, where

> Poscia vid' io mille visi cagnazzi,
> Fatti per freddo; onde mi vien riprezzo,
> E verrà sempre, de' gelate guazzi.[9]
>
> — DANTE: *Inferno*

There is a passage relating to the transference of the baser souls into the bodies of certain animals, in the *Phaedo Dialogue:*

SOCRATES: . . . The souls, not of the good, but of the evil . . . are compelled to wander about . . . in payment of the penalty of their former evil way of life; and they continue to wander until through the craving after the corporeal which never leaves them, they are imprisoned finally in another body. And they may be supposed to find their prisons in the same natures which they had in their former lives. . . . Those who had chosen the portion of injustice and tyranny and violence, will pass into wolves, or into hawks and kites; — whither else can we expect them to go?[10]

The book, *A Declaration of Egregious Popish Impostures to withdraw Her Majesty's Subjects from their Allegiance,* etc., written by Dr. S. Harsnet (afterwards Archbishop of York) by order of the Privy Council, and printed in 1603, is referred to more than once in the scenes with Edgar the supposed madman. Frateretto, who brought the news about Nero, was one of the devils mentioned in the *Declaration:*

[9] "There saw I countless visages, alas!
   Dog-like with cold, that made me shudder, and still
   The shudder comes when frozen pools I pass."
   Trans. L. Binyon

[10] However, there is also much to suggest that Harsnet's *Declaration* was referred to. For in that work there is a scene in which the Jesuits cast out of the possessed Mainy the seven deadly sins, in the shape of animals, — Mainy, with each casting-out, acting that particular sin.

"Fraterreto, Fliberdigibet, Hoberdidance, Tocobalto, were four devils of the round or morrice. . . . These four had forty assistants under them, as themselves doe confesse."
As for

> The prince of darkness is a gentleman
> Modo he's call'd, and Mahu.

we find, in Harsnet, in the deposition of the possessed Richard Mainy:

"Furthermore it is pretended . . . that there remaineth still in mee the prince of all other devils, whose name should be *Modo*." (He is referred to, elsewhere, as "the prince Modo.") *Mahu* was the chief devil possessing Sarah Williams, and Richard Mainy, in his deposition, says, "When the said priests had dispatched theire business at Hackney" (where they had been exorcising Sarah Williams), "they then returned towards mee, upon pretence to cast the great Prince *Modo*. . . ."

* * *

When, in Act Two, Scene Four, Lear says of the supposed madman Edgar, "I'd talke a word with this same learned Theban" — may not the Theban have been at once Oedipus, son of the King of Thebes, — he who could answer the question of the Sphinx, — and one of those two Thebans who were the last companions of Socrates when, released from his chains, he awaited Death? We read of their conversations with Socrates in the *Phaedo Dialogue:*

"The execution of Socrates having been deferred, Socrates talks with two Thebans, Simmias and Cebes, whom by his enchantments he has attracted from Thebes."

In the *Dialogue*, after a long discussion about the evils of the body and of the senses and the lusts of the body, and of the vain nature of the clothing of Man, it is asked: "Have

[73]

sight and hearing any truth in them?" "He [who] has got rid, as far as he can, of eyes and ears and of the whole body, which he conceives of only as a disturbing element, hindering the soul from the acquisition of truth and knowledge . . . is not this the sort of man who, if any man, is likely to attain to the knowledge of true being?"

Later, Socrates says to the two Thebans, "Like children, you are haunted with a fear that when the soul leaves the body, the wind may really blow her away, and scatter her, especially if a man should happen to die in a great storm, and not when the sky is calm."

To which Cebes answers: "Then, Socrates, you must argue us out of our fears — and yet, strictly speaking, they are not our fears; but there is a child within us to whom Death is a sort of hobgoblin: him too we must persuade, not to be afraid when he is alone in the dark."

In *King Lear,* we have one to whom the darkness of the mind brought a wisdom greater than that of Socrates (one who, like Socrates, is soon to cast off the chains of the body) — enduring the utmost rigors of a storm such as might blow the soul away, speaking of the vain nature of the clothing of man, then comforting one who is alone in the dark through the blindness of the eyes, but who had stumbled when he saw.[11] The great King who has known all splendors, all the richness of life, and their true worth, comforts the destitute — him from whom even the sight of the world has been taken.

[11] SOCRATES: And were we not saying, long ago, that the soul when using the body as an instrument of perception, that is to say, when using the sense of sight or hearing or some other sense (for the meaning of perceiving through the body is perceiving through the senses) — were we not saying that the soul too, is then dragged by the body into the region of the changeable, and wanders, and is confused; the world spins round her, and she is like a drunkard. . . .
GLOUCESTER: I stumbled when I saw.

Thou must be patient; we came crying hither:
Thou know'st the first time that we smel the ayre
We waul and cry. I will preache to thee: Marke.

.   .   .   .   .   .

When we are borne, we crie that wee are come
To this great stage of fooles.   [IV, 6]

And the young man who has worn the rags and known the
nakedness of the beggar, comforts those who must live, speaks
of the sweetness of living:

EDGAR: O! our lives' sweetness,
   That we the paine of death would hourely die
   Rather than dye at once! — taught me to shift
   Into a madman's ragges, to assume a semblance
   That very dogges disdain'd: [V, 3]

— or speaks of patience, almost with the tones of the King,
since endurance has taught him wisdom:

                . . . Men must endure
   Their going hence, even as their coming hither:
   Ripenesse is all.   [V, 2]

"Are not all things generated out of their opposites?" Patience
from madness, the richness of the spirit from the destitution
of the body.

An agonized human heart "cries sleepe to death" throughout the play. His heart, I think, was the Drum of which Lear
speaks when summoning Regan and Cornwall:

   . . . bid them come forthe and heare me,
   Or at their chamber doore Ile beat the Drum
   Till it cry sleepe to death,   [II, 4]

— for next, he cries,

   O me! my heart, my rising heart! But, downe!

It is on our hearts, also, that he beats. Not all the agonies even of Othello can pierce our hearts like those of this old man, with his weeping fond eyes — the great outcast King whose hand "smells of mortalitie."

How shall it be explained by what sublime genius this old King, so willful, so terrible in his passions, is yet so near to our hearts that we would cradle him in our arms like a child? And cradled he is, for all his greatness, like the child whom we must persuade not to be afraid when he is alone in the dark. So did these few loving beings who remained to him — Kent for instance, and Gloucester, see him:

Gloucester says:

> Come hither, friend, where is the King my master?
> KENT: Here, sir; but trouble him not; his wits are gone.
> GLOUCESTER: Good friend, I prithee take him in thy armes.
>
> [III, 6]

And later, Kent says:

>   . . . I am come
> To bid my King and master aye good night.   [V, 3]

Here the great King is seen once more as a child who must be comforted before the darkness of the night.

Sometimes, all becomes a lullaby:

> LEAR: Make no noise, make no noise; draw the Curtains:
>   so, so, so. We'll goe to supper i' the morning. So, so, so.
> FOOL: And Ile go to bed at noon.   [III, 6]

This has been taken, by some commentators, as referring to the Fool's approaching death. Mr. John Gielgud thinks (and with great kindness allows me to quote him as saying so) that the mystery of the Fool's death is explained by the fact that at the time when the play was first produced, Cordelia and

the Fool were in all probability acted by the same boy. The
audience, therefore, on hearing of Cordelia's death, would be
conscious, also, of the death of Lear's "poor boy."

It is a beautiful explanation — that these two heavenly in-
nocences, — the warmth at the old King's heart, should be one
and the same in the eyes of the beholders.

It is to be remembered, also, that Lear says:

> *And* my poor Foole is hang'd. [v, 3]

As if he referred, not only to Cordelia, but also to a second
being — to his "poor boy."

*　　　*　　　*

After the piteous humility of the moment when the King
proclaims himself no higher than a beggar at whom the dogs
bark:

> . . . the little dogges and all,
> Trey, Blanch, and Sweet-heart, see they barke at me, [III, 6]

and:

> You must bear with me.
> Pray you now, forget and forgive: I am old and foolish. [IV, 7]

(although there are moments when he thinks that the mortal
wound to his brain was gained in battle, as if he were young
and great and still acknowledged to be a King:

> . . . Let me have surgeons:
> I am cut to the braines), [IV, 6]

the two beings, Cordelia, from whose sorrows

> All you unpublished virtues of the earth
> Spring with my teares! [IV, 4]

and the old King whose eyes are

> . . . Garden water-pottes,
> Ay, and laying Autumn's dust,

await the coming darkness.

*   *   *

When Lear says:

> Pray you, undoe this Button: thank you, sir,   [v, 3]

— he is, I think, asking to be released from his outworn life
. . . from his "lendings." . . . So little a thing, now, is
Death to him — only the undoing of a button, then the casting-
off of mortality.

*   *   *

That world of night, *King Lear*, contains all degrees of darkness, from the lines spoken by Goneril:

> . . . Where's thy drum?
> France spreads his banners in our noiseless land,   [IV, 2]

(where, by the use of the word "noiseless" we are given a
land of night where all the sounds of life are quenched in
darkness) — to the advance into a still darker night of

> Childe Rowland to the darke tower came.   [III, 4]

Both the quartos print this alternative:

> Childe Rowland to the dark *towne* came.

It is not for me to pronounce on the rightness or wrongness
of this, when men who are learned have judged it better not
to do so. But my instinct (and this, alone, can guide me) tells
me that "towne" may have been in that giant mind, and that
certain reasons have led to the change to "tower."

If he wrote "towne," originally, then we know, beyond

any doubt, what he meant. The "dark towne" is Death (and the passage was so understood by Byron). But the reasons for the change may have been these. In the dark *towne* the roofs are low: our house is our coffin. We are huddled together, are one of a nation, are equal.

If we come to the dark *tower*, we are alone with our soul. The roof is immeasurably high, — as high as heaven. In that eternal solitude there are echoes.

* * *

Consider the change from the anguish of:

> You doe me wrong to take me out o' the grave:
> Thou art a soule in blisse; but I am bound
> Upon a wheele of fire, that mine own teares
> Doe scald, like molten lead,   [IV, 7]

to the gentleness, the consoling and tender darkness of these lines, spoken by one to whom a world-wide ruin has, in the end, taught wisdom and resignation:

> No, no, no, no! Come let's away to prison;
> We two alone will sing like Birds i' the Cage:
> When thou dost aske me blessing, Ile kneele downe
> And ask of thee forgivenesse. So we'll live,
> And pray, and sing, and tell old tales, and laugh
> At gilded Butterflies, and heare poore Rogues
> Talke of Court newes, and we'll talke with them too,
> Who loses, and who wins; who's in, who's out;
> And take upon's the mystery of things,
> As if we were God's spies: and we'll weare out
> In a wall'd prison, packs and sects of great ones,
> That ebbe and flowe by the moone.   [V, 3]

Here, part of the gentleness, the moving sweetness, is given by the fact that in the double-syllabled and treble-syllabled words, in every case excepting in two ("gilded Butterflies"), every hard consonant there may be is softened by an internal *s* — "prison," "blessing," "forgivenesse," "mystery."

The passages which come immediately before the death of Cordelia have all this heartbreaking sweetness. Is there another poet in the world who would have dared the use of that five-times repeated trochee in the line quoted below?

> . . . Thou'lt come no more,
> Never, never, never, never, never,   [v, 3]

— trochees that with each repetition seem dropping further into darkness. Is there another poet in the world who could have wrung from the simple repetition of one word, such tears?

*   *   *

The sound of the verse is, now of an unparalleled grandeur, now of an equal sweetness and tenderness.

Consider the raging darkness, the furious whirlwind sweep of the second Scene on the Heath, — those gigantic lines in which Lear defies the whole heaven, cries to it to blot out the world:

> Blow, windes, and cracke your cheeks! Rage! Blow!
> You Cataracts and Hyrricanos, spout
> Till you have drench'd our Steeples, drown'd the Cockes!
> You Sulphurous and Thought-executing Fires,
> Vaunt-couriers to Oake-cleaving Thunder-bolts,
> Sindge my white head! And thou, all-shaking Thunder,
> Strike flat the thicke Rotundity o' the world!
> Cracke Nature's moulds, all germaines spill at once
> That make ingratefull Man.   [III, 2]

The verse has variety as vast as the theme. The first line is an eight-syllabled one; then, under the sweep of this enormous rage, stretching from pole to pole, the lines rush forward into decasyllabics and even hendecasyllabics (and this is not always, though it is sometimes, the result of pretended elision).

The movement is hurled backward and forward. In the first line, for instance, of those strong monosyllables "Rage," "Blow," the first sweeps onward across the world into infinity, the second is hurled backward.

In "You Sulphurous and Thought-executing Fires" the vowel sounds mount, like a rising fury, then the word "Fires" (with its almost, but not quite, double-syllabled sound) gives again, though with a different movement, the effect of stretching across the firmament.

Part of the immensity of this vast primeval passage is due to the fact that in the line

> Vaunt-couriers to Oake-cleaving Thunder-bolts,

the only word that does not bear an accent is "to." And part, again, is due to the contrast between the stretching one-syllabled words of the first line and the three-syllabled "Cataracts" and four-syllabled "Hyrricanos" of the second. Added vastness is given by the balance of the high *a* of "Rage" and that of "Hyrricanos," and by the huge fall from the *a* in this latter word, to that word's last syllable. Variety in this ever-changing world-tempest is given, too, by the long menacing roll, in the midst of those reverberating thunder-claps, the *c*'s and *ck*'s of the whole passage, the roll, gradually increasing in sound, of the first three words in

> And thou, all-shaking Thunder,

rising and stretching to the long first syllable of "shaking" and then falling from that enormous height to the immense, long, thickened darkness of the word "Thunder."

In such lines as Lear's

Detested kite, thou liest!

and

Beat at this gate that let thy folly in,   [1, 4]

the single-syllabled words take on the hugeness of those new-made stones that Deucalion and Pyrrha, the Deluge being over, found and cast behind their backs, — the bones of their mother Earth, which were broken into pieces in that great ruin.

ADDITIONAL NOTES: *King Lear* and the *Phaedo Dialogue*

NOTE I. Thomas Taylor's Notes to the *Phaedo Dialogue*

"According to Orpheus, there are four governments: the first, that of Heaven, which Saturn received, cutting off the genitals of his father. After Saturn, Jupiter reigned, who hurled his father into Tartarus."

The father of Saturn was Cronos. . . . Time. . . . In Lear, Age had become Time, and Time a fifth element. I see the fundamental maiming of the life-springs of the parent in the fate of Lear, — reflected in the diatribes of Lear against procreation. — E. S.

NOTE II. The *Phaedo Dialogue*

SOCRATES: Is not Evenus a philosopher?

SIMMIAS: I think he is.

SOCRATES: Then he, or any man, who has the spirit of philosophy, will be willing to die; but he will not take his own life, for that is held to be unlawful!

[82]

Consider the raging "Off, off, you lendings; come, unbutton here" of the unregenerate Lear (tearing off his clothes being a symbol of his wish to tear, violently, the soul from the body) — and the later, humble, gentle resignation of

> Pray you, undoe this Button: thank you, sir.

Note III. Lear and the "learned Theban"

Mr. Edmund Blunden, in *Shakespeare's Significances*, has the following passage:

"Lear, from the first, is portrayed as a little inclined to remember his school education. His reply to Cordelia's unhappy 'Nothing' is exactly a thesis of the old natural philosopher's 'An Aliquid producatur et Nihilo?'"

Nothing will come of nothing!

Soon after, with a reference to "the barbarous Scythian," he appears to have Horace in mind. He breaks into Latin — "Hysterica passio" — where describing his physical trouble, "a fit of the mother"; he compares himself to Prometheus with a vulture at his heart.

. . . Presently he refers to poor Tom as "this philosopher," and propounds to him a question, not solely suitable to the war of elements all round, but familiar among the ancient philosophers: "What is the cause of thunder?" Even in this is involved, not only the academic interest of Lear, his notion of poor Tom and the weather, but some allusion to the clash of hot and cold, of his own ardent love confronted with the marble-hearted ingratitude of his daughters. We proceed. "Riding over four-inched bridges" and other visions raised by poor Tom's autobiography have stirred Lear's recollections of a famous passage. "Modo is he called and Mahu" chances to rhyme with that. The next title he gives poor Tom is "learned Theban" and after a while that is changed to "good

[83]

Athenian." In short, fascinated by Tom's amazements, Lear is all the time contemplating the position through the First Epistle of the Second Book of Horace, and particularly through those lines:

> Ille per extentum funem mihi posse videtur
> Ire poeta, meum qui pectus inaniter angit,
> Irritat, mulcet, falsis terroribus implet,
> Ut magus; et modo me Thebis, modo ponit Athenis.

"That is the poet for me, the man who can walk the whole tightrope of his art, the man who distresses me with imaginings, who angers, comforts, fills with unreal horror like a wizard, who makes me be at Thebes one minute and the next at Athens."

* * *

Towards the end of that scene, he reverts to his caprice of quoting Horace, and orders poor Tom to find some other "garments" — he had only a blanket; "You will say they are Persian attire, but let them be changed." This witty stroke is fully appreciated if we see that it plays on the last Ode of Horace, Book First, "Persicos odi, puer, apparatus" ("my boy, Persian attire and I don't agree").

* * *

This seems to me to prove, conclusively, that Horace was in Shakespeare's mind: but I hold, also, that so was the *Phaedo Dialogue*. Over and over again, in Shakespeare, are short sentences which hold several vast meanings.

NOTE IV. *King Lear* and the *Phaedo Dialogue*

SOCRATES: Ought the philosopher to care about the pleasures . . . if they ought to be called pleasures, of eating and drinking?

"Certainly not," answered Simmias.

"And what about the pleasures of love — shall he care for them?"

"By no means."

"And will he think much of the other ways of indulging the body — for example, the acquisition of costly raiment or sandals, or other adornment of the body? Instead of caring about them does he not rather despise anything more than nature needs?"

Compare the last paragraph of this, with Lear's

> O! reason not the need; our basest Beggars
> Are in the poorest thing superfluous:
> Allow not Nature more than Nature needs:
> Man's life is cheape as Beastes. Thou art a Lady;
> If onely to go warme were gorgeous,
> Why, Nature needs not what thou gorgeous wear'st,
> Which scarcely keeps thee warm. But, for true need,
> You heavens, give me patience. Patience I need! [II, 4]

As for the worth of "the pleasures of love" — that theme resounds through the play.

NOTE V

SOCRATES: Many a man has been willing to go to the world below, animated by the hope of seeing there an earthly love, a wife or son, and conversing with them. And will he who is a true lover of wisdom, and is strongly persuaded in like manner that only in the world below he can worthily enjoy her, still repine at death? Will he not depart with joy?

LEAR: Thou'lt come no more,
Never, never, never, never, never!
Pray you, undoe this Button: thank you, sir.
Doe you see this? Looke on her, looke, her lips,
Looke there, looke there!

Note VI. Shakespeare and the *Phaedo Dialogue*

In Sir John Edwin Sandys's Address to the Academy (read May 27, 1914), he said that Roger Bacon (who was born, probably, in 1214) refers to Plato's *Phaedo*, firstly for its witness to immortality, and secondly, for its commendation of detachment from temporal causes. "In the case of the *Phaedo*," adds the Lecturer, "he may easily have used the current Latin translation."

According to the same authority, Roger Bacon had explained that "Plato was better known to the Fathers than Aristotle, because Plato had been translated into Latin."

This is one way in which Shakespeare may have become acquainted with the *Phaedo Dialogue*. — E. S.

Note VII

". . . Plato was accessible only in Shakespeare's time through the Latin version, namely, the complete works translated by Ficino, published at Bâle in 1551, or in another edition of Ficino's version, published at Venice in 1581, in Colophon, dated 1570, or in the translation by Janus Cornarias, published at Bâle in 1561." — J. CHURTON COLLINS.

Note VIII. The Fool's Songs and "And my poore Foole is hang'd"

In the Fourth Scene of the First Act, the Fool's strange and apparently meaningless snatches of song concentrate, in a few words, the story of the King and his servant Gloucester:

> Mum, mum.
> He that keepes nor crust nor crum,

> Weary of all, shall want some.
> That's a sheal'd Peascod.   (*pointing to Lear*)

and

> The Hedge sparrow fed the Cuckooe so long,
> That it had it head bit off by it young.
> So, out went the Candle, and we were left darkling.

The sanity of Lear, the head that had worn the crown, destroyed, devoured, that the crown might be taken. . . . The Cuckooe . . . one who should not have been in the nest — the bastard Edmund . . .

These songs show the fate of both Lear and Gloucester; the third song shows, perhaps, in a distorting mirror, the Fool's own end:

> A Fox, when one has caught her,
> And such a daughter,
> Should sure to the slaughter,
> If my Cap would buy a Halter;
> So the Foole follows after.

The Fox . . . the fox whom the Spartan youth bore close to his heart, until his heart was devoured . . . Goneril or Regan.

The halter was for himself in the end. Or so I understand it. Before, he had said to the King, "Tarry, and take the Fool with thee." He may have meant into the darkness.

NOTE IX

From time to time, in *King Lear*, the symbol of a wheel is used — culminating in Lear's words:

> Thou art a Soule in blisse, but I am bound
> Upon a wheele of fire, that mine owne teares
> Doe scald, like molten lead.   [IV, 7]

It has been suggested that Lear's reference was to Ixion and his wheel, since the ingratitude of Ixion was the reason for his punishment.

But I believe the wheel, also, to be the Wheel of Being.

NOTE X

LEAR: 'Tis a good blocke!
It were a delicate stratagem to shooe
A Troope of horse with felt: Ile put it in proofe,
And when I have stolne upon these Sonnes-in-Lawe,
Then, kill, kill, kill, kill, kill, kill. [IV, 6]

"This 'delicate stratagem' had actually been put in practice about fifty years before Shakespeare was born, as we learn from Lord Herbert of Cherbury's *Life of Henry the Eighth*, p. 41. 'And now,' says that historian, 'having feasted the ladies royally for divers dayes, he [Henry] departed from Tournay to Lisle (Oct. 13, 1513) whither he was invited by the Lady Margaret, who caused there a juste to be held in an extraordinary manner; the place being a fore-room raised high from the ground by many steps, and paved with black square stones like marble, while the horses, to prevent sliding, *were shod with felt* or flocks (the Latin words are *feltro sive tormento*): after which the ladies danced all night.' " — MALONE.

Then, kill, kill, kill, kill, kill, kill.

"This was formerly the word given in the English army when an onset was made on the enemy. So in *Venus and Adonis*,

Gives false alarms, suggesteth mutiny,
And in a peaceful hour doth cry '*kill, kill.*' " — MALONE

This latter gives additional meaning and poignance to Lear's

I am cut to the braines.

uttered almost immediately after.

[88]

VII. "Hamlet"

Who and what is the ghost?
Hamlet, on seeing him beckon, says:

My fate cries out . . .   [1, 4]

and the ghost *is* Hamlet's fate. He would speak only to the appointed vessel. When Francisco cried "hey, answer me; stand, and unfold yourself" — in the opening scene, there was no reply.

But, from the moment when the message was given, the world turns to a ghost for Hamlet. Nothing remains but the ghost, the deed that should be done, and never will be, and himself.

There seems to be a certain connection between *Hamlet* and *Othello,* which comes next, in time, to *Hamlet;* because the otherwise entirely opposed characters of Hamlet and Iago live *by* the mind, *in* the mind.

There seems to be a connection, also, in one sense, between *King Lear* and *Hamlet.* One theme of *King Lear,* as I have said already, is the war between the ordinary nature and the King-nature, between the sacred madness that is genius, and the world of Appearance.

The King and Queen in *Hamlet* belong to the world of Appearance — crime or no crime. All the beings in *Hamlet,* excepting the Prince, and Ophelia (who is a Fertility-ghost), live in a waking world of action.

And yet theirs is a world of make-believe. Even the Prince,

[89]

at moments, finds in it a refuge. But this man who lives by thought alone, half deceived by the faults of his own nature, sees the truth, though at moments he denies it. These ordinary beings, living by the body, see the truth never. Truth shines (or, turned black and terrible, rages) round them, over them, under them — cries from under the earth, tries to invade their minds.

But they ever "lay the flattering unction to their souls."

The Prince says:

. . . there is nothing either good or bad, but thinking makes it so

[II, 2]

and earlier in the same scene, Polonius comforts himself for his straying wits by saying "How pregnant sometimes his Replies are! A happinesse that often Madnesse hits on, which Reason and Sanity could not so prosperously be deliver'd of."

In *King Lear* is "the darkness of Revelation," as Swinburne said. In *Hamlet* is the light of Revelation — but not the light seen by the Saints.

Over the world of *Hamlet*, unlike the worlds of *Macbeth* and *King Lear*, reigns a perpetual and terrible light — the light of truth, dissolving all into its element.

In this world of terrible light in which even the dead cannot rest in the peace of the grave, Time does not exist: the beat of the verse sometimes loses its pulse, dissolves in the light, changes to the shadowless, timeless clime of prose.

But Hamlet himself is wasted, not only by the ghost returned from the tomb, but by a shadow — the little Spring-ghost, the fertility daemon, the vegetation spirit that was Ophelia, who, like the fertility daemons of all time, would be dressed in flowers and cast into a stream, — Ophelia, a shade that at first gave him refreshment and oblivion from the all-seeing light. For a little, but not for long. Then she betrays him to the workaday world, — she shuts out him and his terrible dreams:

OPHELIA: He rais'd a sigh so piteous and profound
That it did seeme to shatter all his bulke,
And end his being. That done, he lets me goe,
And with his head over his shoulder turn'd,
He seem'd to find his way without his eyes;
For out o' doores he went without their helpe,
And to the last bended their light on me.   [II, 1]

We may note, here, how pulseless is the verse. A shadow is speaking. When the Ghost speaks — he who had lived a full and rich life, dying at the height of that richness — there is a pulse about his speech that Death could not destroy. He speaks with a dark voice that has gathered resonance from the metals that shared the darkness in which he has lain. . . . But Ophelia is disembodied as a shade, — for all those impulses of Spring which found their way at last into the scattered words of her madness.

*   *   *

When Rosencrantz and Guildenstern say, "We'll wait upon you," Hamlet, the man who could not tell the Dream from the Reality (and that was part of his tragedy), replies, "No such matter; I will not sort you with the rest of my servants; for to speake to you like an honest man, I am most dreadfully attended." [II, 2]

Here is a double meaning, already noted by commentators: i.e. the obvious physical meaning, and the meaning that the "bad dreames" ("I could be bounded in a nutshell, and count myselfe a King of infinite space, were it not that I have bad dreames" [II, 2]) are his servants, his dreadful attendants.

But there is a second meaning. "Truepenny" was a contemporary word for a faithful servant. . . . Hamlet addressed the ghost as "Truepenny." . . .

When Guildenstern, during this conversation, says "which dreames, indeed, are Ambition, for the very substance of the Ambitious is meerely the shadow of a Dreame" — in the first part of the sentence he said more than he knew. Hamlet's "bad dreames," his dreadful attendants, were indeed Ambition — the ambition to perform an action, dallied with, dwelt on, in the place of Reality.

But when Hamlet, in reply to Guildenstern, says

> A dreame itselfe is but a shadow

he is giving the dream more reality than Guildenstern knew. A shadow must be cast by something — it cannot exist otherwise.

Of Hamlet's strange phrase:

> Then are our Beggers bodies, and our Monarchs and outstretch'd Heroes the Beggers' Shadowes.   [II, 2]

Coleridge said, "I do not understand it. And Shakespeare seems to have intended the meaning not to be more than snatched at:

> By my fey, I cannot reason."

But are there not very deep meanings? i.e. that the beggars, alone among all the things of this world, have, through their sufferings, their destitution, become real? (Let us remember certain passages in *King Lear*.) And that the outstretched hero is but an *idea*, a dream, sprung from out of the being of suffering humanity, — a shadow, of a giant size, in appearance greater than the being that cast it, — a thing that cannot be seized, but that changes with the changing of the light. Kings and outstretch'd Heroes are cast by — brought into being by — beggars' necessities.

These shades are cast, in the all-seeing light, upon a world of dust. For to this, the world has now been changed — the dust which can be kneaded into crumbling shapes by Fate or, so Hamlet tells himself, by his own will. By dust is he persecuted. The speeches of Polonius drift round and round, generally slowly, upon his point, always returning again to the place whence they started, like a swirl of dry dust in a little air.

"Old men and Comets have been rever'd for the same Reason: their long Beards, and Pretences to foretel Events."[1]

Yet Polonius has a dry and worldly wisdom — one which is the antithesis of the dream-world of Hamlet (erected in a world of dust).

All things are equal — the dream and the reality. But, yet, amid the very dust of Death, some form of life survives, however poor; even with dead clay there is no waste:

A man may fishe with the Worme that hath eat of a King, and eat of the fishe that hath fed of that Worme.
KING: What dost thou meane by this?
HAMLET: Nothing, but to show you how a King may goe a
Progresse through the guts of a Begger.   [IV, 3]

*   *   *

Alexander dyed, *Alexander* was buried, *Alexander* returneth into dust; the dust is earth; of earth we make Lome, and why of that Lome, whereto he was converted, might they not stop a Beere barrell?
Imperious Caeser, dead and turn'd to clay,
Might stop a hole to keepe the wind away;
O! that that earth which kept the world in awe,
Should patch a Wall to expell the Winter's flaw. [V, 1]

Dust, dust, and Man turning to dust. And yet, in that dust, there is the seed of some use.

[1] Jonathan Swift, *Thoughts on Various Subjects.*

VIII. "Othello, the Moor of Venice"

"The heart," wrote William Harvey, in a dedication to King Charles the First, "is the beginning of life, the sun of the microcosm, even as the sun in his turn might well be designated the heart of the world."

The tragedy of Othello is that of the overthrow of a heart that was a sun, a sun that was a world — "a fountain of light, rich in fruitful heat . . . called King of Planets for his motion, heart of the world for his power, its eye for his beauty." [1] Though this ruled over a night-black body.

When Othello said (to Cassio and others):

> The goodnesse of the night upon you, friends! [I, 2]

it might have been his own goodness that he was bestowing upon them.

But this noble nature must be brought to ruin for no reason but that his grandeur offended the baseness of a cloud born from foul vapors.

The greatness and simplicity of Othello are those of Nature before it was altered by civilization, and his utterances have in them, sometimes the noble heat of the sun under which he was born, sometimes a grave and planetary splendor, sometimes a sonorous and oceanic strength of harmony. They have, as Swinburne said the verse of Homer has, "the innumerable music of luminous motion, the simplicity and equality of pas-

[1] Kepler, of the sun, in one of his earlier lectures, quoted by Sir Arthur Eddington, *The Expanding Universe*.

sion and of power; the majestic monochord heart of (the) verse has the multitudinous measures of the epic sea."

This is equally true of the *Othello*-verse.

Othello says of the handkerchief which was one of the engines of his ruin:

> 'Tis true; there's Magicke in the web of it;
> A Sibyll, that had numbred in the world
> The sun to course two hundred compasses,
> In her prophetic furie sew'd the worke;
> The Wormes were hallowed that did breed the Silke,
> And it was dyede in Mummey which the skilful
> Conserv'd of Maidens' hearts.   [iii, 4]

The whole of this play is dipped in the dyes of the heart. And the rich light from Othello's being seems to color the sayings of his satellites; as when the Second Gentleman exclaims:

> The wind-shak'd Surge, with high and monstrous Maine,
> Seems to cast water on the burning Beare
> And quench the Guards of the ever-fixed Pole.   [ii, 1]

In this world of physical splendor, at the moment of the overthrow of his heaven, Othello says:

> Had she been true,
> If heaven would make me such another world
> Of one entyre and perfect Chrysolite,
> I'd not have sold her for it.   [v, 2]

Nor would he have been surprised at the existence of such a world.

His love is great as the cause of gravity "that penetrates to the very centre of the Sun and Planets, without suffering the least diminution of its force. . . . So may the gravitation of the earth be caused by the combined condensation of some other like ethereal spirit." [2]

The love of Othello was such a spirit, "conserving the shining of the sun," his heart.

Here is no low jealousy. When Emilia asks:

> Is he not jealous?

Desdemona replies:

> Who? he? I think the Sun where he was born
> Drew all such humors from him.

But he believes that his heaven is turned to earth — all the planetary music then is discordant.

> But there, where I have garner'd up my heart,
> Where either I must live or bear no life,
> The Fountaine from the which my current runnes
> Or else dries up; to be discarded thence!
> Or keep it as a Cisterne for foule Toads
> To knot and gender in! Turne thy complexion there,
> Patience, thou young and rose lipp'd Cherubim;
> Ay, there, look grim as hell!

DESDEMONA: I hope my noble lord esteems me honest.
OTHELLO: O! ay; as Sommer flies are in the Shambles,
> That quicken even with blowing. O thou Weed!
> Who art so lovely faire and smellst so sweete
> That the Sence aches at thee, would thou hadst ne'er been
> born!   [IV, 2]

His love, young and golden-haired as Proserpine, has changed to

> . . . that cunning whore of Venice
> That married with Othello. You, Mistris,
> That have the office opposite to Saint Peter,
> And keepe the Gate of Hell.   [IV, 2]

[2] Sir Isaac Newton.

From the moment of doubting, Othello speaks of himself, often, as if the Othello he had once known, the Othello whom the world had known, were a person divided from him; or he speaks as a dead man might speak, watching the intolerable anguish of the living — he does not say "I," he says "Othello." [3]

Othello's Occupation's gone!   [III, 3]

He utters this terrible cry:

Where should Othello goe?   [v, 2]

But, a little later, in

That's he that was Othello; heere I am,

he seems to have taken farewell of himself forever. Only in the extremity of anguish will that dead man become the living man again. Even in the quieter, less terrible

> Then, must you speake
> Of one that loved not wisely but too well;
> Of one not easily jealous, but being wrought,
> Perplex'd in the extreme; of one whose hand,
> Like the base Indian, threw a Pearle away
> Richer than all his Tribe; of one whose subdu'd Eyes,
> Albeit unused to the melting moode,
> Drop teares as fast as the Arabian Trees
> Their med'cinable gumme.   [v, 2]

* * *

When not goaded by that gadfly Iago into some hurried utterance, even in the depths of his misery, his speeches have that grave and planetary measure, that unhurried splendor of utterance, which seems a part of his nature.

---

[3] This habit appears elsewhere in Shakespeare. But in the case of Othello, it has a particularly agonizing effect.

It is the Cause, it is the Cause, my soule; —
Let me not name it to you, you chaste Starres!
It is the Cause. Yet I'll not shed her blood,
Nor scarre that whiter skin of hers than Snow,
And smooth as monumental Alabaster.
Yet she must dye, else she'll betray more men.
Put out the Light, and then put out the Light:
If I quench thee, thou flaming Minister,
I can againe thy former light restore,
Should I repent me; but once put out thy Light,
Thou cunningst Patterne of excelling Nature,
I know not where is that Promethean heate
That can thy Light relume. When I have pluck'd the Rose
I cannot give it vitall growth againe,
It needs must wither: I'll smell it on the tree.
O balmy breath, that dost almost persuade
Justice to breake her Sword! One more, one more,
Be thus when thou art dead, and I will kill thee,
And love thee after. One more, and this the last:
So sweet was ne'er so fatall. I must weepe,
But they are cruell Teares; this sorrow's heavenly;
It strikes where it doth love.   [v, 2]

Othello had said, kissing his love,

>   And this, and this, the greatest discords be
>   That e'er our hearts shall make!   [ii, 1]

It is this harmony that must be broken by Iago:

> O! You are well tun'd now
> But Ile set downe the pegges that make this Musicke,
> As honest as I am.

  In the more noble passages of Othello's anger, the torture appears, in the very sound of the verse:

> If I do prove her Haggard,
> Though that her Jesses were my deere heart-strings,
> I'd whistle her off and let her downe the winde,
> To prey at Fortune. Haply, for I am blacke,
> And have not those soft parts of Conversation
> That Chamberers have, or, for I am declin'd
> Into the vale of years — yet that's not much —
> She's gone, I am abus'd; and my releefe
> Must be to loathe her. O Curse of Marriage!
> That we can call these delicate Creatures ours,
> And not their Appetites! I had rather be a Toad
> And live upon the Vapour of a Dungeon,
> Than keepe a corner in the thing I love
> For others' uses. Yet 'tis the plague of Great Ones;
> Prerogativ'd are they lesse than the Base;
> 'Tis destiny unshunnable, like death;
> Even when this forked plague is Fated to us
> When we do quicken.
> Look! Where she comes.
> If she be false, O! then heaven mocked itself.
> Ile not believe it! [III, 3]

("Mocked," is right, I think, and not "mocks" as appears in modern editions. The meaning, surely, is that Heaven mocked itself in the making of Desdemona.)

"This forked plague" means at once the horns of the deceived . . . the forked tongue of the serpent who brought about the Fall of Man . . . the serpent tongue of Iago. . . .

We have seen, already, that in the earlier lines:

> Excellent wretch! Perdition catch my Soule,
> But I do love thee! And when I love thee not,
> Chaos is come againe! [III, 3]

the pause between "wretch" and "Perdition" is like a whirlpool or vortex. In the first line of the passage quoted above,

[99]

the word "Haggard" swirls round on itself; the feeling has found words, found reality — the feeling which was unspoken and terrible in the swirling movement of the caesura to which I have just referred. The word "Appetites" is like something broken into bits, and tossed, at the end, into the empty air.

With the *a*-sounds echoing each other, of "plague of Great Ones," "Even then this forked plague is Fated to us" — fires seem breaking from the nature of Othello, those fires of the African which had long been covered by civilization — like "the Sun's advance towards the Earth, or such a rupture of the Earth as will let out the Central Fires."

This was now the fate of Othello. His complete disintegration is echoed and mirrored in the very sound of the verse.

High *a*-sounds occurred previously in the speech, in "prey" (where the *e* takes on the sound of *a*), in "Conversation" and "Chamberers." But later, these had a different effect, were, perhaps, even more terrible. The muttering sounds of "Conversation," "Chamberers," are like dust gathering itself into shape. For Othello is slowly being changed by the forked plague, into the likeness of that being of the 24th canto of the *Inferno:*

> Nè *o* sì tosto mai nè *i* si scrisse,
> Com' el s'accese ed arse, e cener tutto
> Convenne che cascando divenisse;
> E poi che fu a terra si distrutto,
> La polver si raccolse per sè stessa,
> E'en quel medesmo ritornò di butto.[4]

[4] Never "O" nor "I" was written in such a gust
Of speed as he took fire with, all allumed,
And then must needs drop into ash and dust,
When down to the very ground he was consumed
Of its own motion re-combining there,
The dust straightway its former shape resumed.
Trans. L. BINYON.

"Othello, the Moor of Venice"

As Othello speaks the words "the plague of Great Ones" his torture touches all extremes.

OTHELLO: O blood, blood, blood.
IAGO: Patience, I say, your minde, perhaps, may change.
OTHELLO: Never, Iago. Like to the Ponticke Sea,
Whose icie current and compulsive course
Ne'er feeles retiring ebbe, but keepes due on
To the Proponticke and the Hellespont,
Even so, my bloody thoughts, with violent pace,
Shall ne'er looke backe, ne'er ebbe to humble love,
Till that a capable and wide Revenge
Swallow them up.
　　　　　　Now, by yond Marble Heaven,
In the due reverence of a Sacred vow,
I heere engage my words. 　　　　　　　　　[III, 3]

The pause following "Never, Iago" is like a solar cyclone, and its center, as with that phenomenon, seems of an appalling coldness and darkness. (The central region of a solar cyclone [5] "must be a region of refrigeration." "Just where there would exist a . . . prolongation of the cyclonic cloud down towards the sun's body, the darkness is greater than elsewhere. . . .

". . . In a whirlwind, as in a whirlpool, the vortex will be below the general level, and all around the surface of the medium will descend towards it.")

We have met a pause like a cyclone before, in Shakespeare. But that was not cold, nor did it suck all down into its depth. Once, when the fires from his own nature, the mineral poison of Iago, have reduced him to dust, — the dust that was Othello, as it re-forms, takes on almost the likeness of Iago, speaks almost with his voice, — as in the speech: "Handkerchief — Confessions — Handkerchief! To confess, and be hanged for

---

[5] Herbert Spencer.

[101]

his labour. First, to be hanged, and then to confess: I tremble at it. . . ." Here, and through this passage, his very speech is shrunken, corroded, shriveled by that poison, — is dwindled down into shapeless prose. But elsewhere, almost always, in this agony, there are the glorious dyes of the heart, the light from that world which might have been "of an intire and perfect Chrysolite."

Only at the end, when all the blood from Othello's heart has flown, knowing the being he loved and has slain was innocent, are all the bright dyes gone.

> . . . O ill-starr'd wench!
> Pale as thy Smocke! When we shall meet at Compt,
> This looke of thine will hurle my soule from Heaven,
> And fiends will snatch at it. Cold, cold, my Girle!
> Even like thy Chastity.   [v, 2]

But even then, before his death, the richness and the grandeur return to

> . . . one whose subdu'd Eyes,
> Albeit unused to the melting moode,
> Drop teares as fast as the Arabian Trees
> Their med'cinable gumme.

Iago has killed this world for him, but not the next. In the lines:

> When we shall meet at Compt,
> This looke of thine will hurle my soule from Heaven,
> And fiends will snatch at it,

he is still Iago's property: he blackens Desdemona's heavenly love. But in the last lines:

> I kist thee ere I kill'd thee; no way but this,
> Killing myselfe, to dye upon a kisse,

he has gone to join her, in a world of which Iago's mind could have no conception.

*   *   *

Ludovici, apostrophizing Iago, cried

O Spartan dog!
More fell than Anguish, Hunger, or the Sea!

and almost all commentators have written of Iago's "greatness" — Swinburne saying that "Desdemona was between the devil and the deep sea." There he is right, and Mr. Wilson Knight speaks with equal truth when he calls Iago "the spirit of negation." [6]

Iago appears in a shrunken shape, with a dulled and hooded eye, as the first tempter appeared in Eden. With the exception of two earth-shaking sentences, and one speech of great beauty in which his voice has taken on the sound of Othello's, Iago never speaks "above a mortal mouth." For the rest, there is in his verbal intercourse with others, the terrible "deadness" that Dr. Bradley noted in the *feeling* of Iago.

He is a subterranean devil. . . . His voice comes to us muffled by the earth of the world and of his nature. It comes to us from underground, like that of the "old mole" that Hamlet knew. That is why it sounds so small. But it is none the less deadly. Iago is a million miles beneath the surface of our nature. Though ineffably tainted by the world's evil, he is so shut off from the world of ordinary men — he who is yet shaping their lives — that he cannot reach them by any words save those with a jet of poison in them. Though he can overthrow them with a touch, it hardly seems to be *his* touch.

He cannot express himself. "Do not weep, do not weep!

[6] *The Wheel of Fire.*

[103]

Alas the day!" [IV, 2] he says to Desdemona after the scene when she first realizes that night is falling.

Indeed, he does not need her tears. They give him no particular pleasure: if anything, they disturb him in his intellectual pride at what he has done.

In one gigantic phrase (as Bradley and other commentators have pointed out) Iago acknowledges the race from which he has sprung — his birthplace, and home. In answer to Othello's

> I looke downe towards his feet; but that's a fable.
> If that thou beest a divell, I cannot kill thee.   [V, 2]

comes Iago's

> I bleed, sir; but not kill'd.

Bradley writes: "He is saying, you see, he is right, I am a devil."

But it goes even further than that. He seems surprised, almost, at that one signal proof that he is man as well as devil: his blood.

This gigantic avowal is equaled by the earlier

> I am your owne for ever—   [III, 3]

echoing the still more appalling words of Othello's

> I am bound to thee for ever.   [III, 3]

Othello saw in those words no particular significance. Now, as Iago echoed that avowal, Othello, going through the door, did not hear the words telling him that through the rest of eternity they will be companions in Hell, as tormented and tormentor — that Othello has come down to Iago, and that Iago is attached to him as the serpent is to the heel of the first man.

Before these world-shaking acknowledgments of Iago's

devilship, there has been a subterranean hint of the race from
which he sprang:

OTHELLO: O misery!
IAGO: Poore and Content is rich, and rich enough,
    But riches finelesse is as poore as Winter
    To him that ever feares he shall be poore.
    Good heaven, the Soules of all my Tribe defend
    From jealousie!   [III, 3]

Here, perhaps, he is saying that the devils are not so forsaken
by Heaven that Heaven will not defend them from the worst
of all miseries.

Once, and once only, Iago speaks with the voice of a free
man:

      Not Poppy, nor Mandragora,
    Nor all the drowsy Syrups of the world,
    Shall ever medicine thee to that sweete sleepe
    Which thou ow'dst yesterday.   [III, 3]

This, in its profound beauty, its heart-shaking simplicity, is
almost like a foreshadowing of Othello's

        O! now, for ever
Farewell the Tranquill minde; farewell Content!
Farewell the plumed Troope and the bigge Warres
That make Ambition Virtue! O, farewell!
Farewell the neighing Steed, and the Shrill Trumpe,
The spirit-stirring Drum, the eare-piercing Fife,
The Royall banner, and all Quality,
Pride, Pomp, and Circumstance of glorious Warre!
And, O you mortall Engines, whose rude throates
The immortal Jove's dread clamours counterfeit,
Farewell! Othello's Occupation's gone!   [III, 3]

In the speech of Iago there was no exultance, — only the
freedom of one whose task is done. A human voice is speaking:

[105]

for once Iago has understood suffering, and the blood which has given him the semblance of a living being voices itself.

In nearly all other passages, even in

> Witnesse, you ever-burning Lights above!
> You Elements that clip us round about!
> Witnesse, that heere Iago doth give up
> The execution of his wit, hands, heart,
> To wrong'd Othello's service,   [III, 3]

— his speech is shrunken and bloodless, like the slough cast by a snake.

Once he is frightened — when Othello warns him:

> If thou dost slander her and torture me,
> Never pray more; Abandon all remorse;
> On Horror's head Horrors accumulate;
> Doe deeds to make Heaven weepe, all Earth amaz'd;
> For nothing canst thou to damnation adde
> Greater than that.   [III, 3]

Then, Iago's speech becomes a dirty, small, and fluttering thing, like a poisonous insect:

> O grace! O Heaven forgive me!
> Are you a man! Have you a Soule or Sense?
> God be wi' you; take mine office. O wretched Fool!
> That liv'st to make thine Honesty a Vice,
> O monstrous world! Take note, take note, O world!
> To be direct and honest is not safe.
> I thanke you for this profit, and, from hence
> Ile love no friend, sith love breeds such offence.   [III, 3]

It is through the very deadness of his speech that his creator expresses him.

He scarcely cares whom he injures, so long as an injury is done, and by his hand. In the first scene of the play, he says

Call up her father;
Rouse him, make after him, poyson his delight,
Proclaime him in the streets, Incense her kinsmen,
And, though he in a fertile clymate dwell,
Plague him with Flyes; though that his joy be joy,
Yet throw such changes of vexation on't
As it may lose some colour.

"Plague him with Flyes." Indeed, he lives in a world of flies.

What is this hell, this world of flies, which he inhabits as the devil of his own pain? Is it pride — as almost every critic has held? Is pride his element, his climate, and his eternity?

"If, of that which this heart of mine is feeling, one drop were to fall into hell, hell itself would become all life eternal. . . ." Thus spoke St. Catherine of Genoa. . . . The "life eternal" is union with God. . . . One drop from the darkness of Iago would raise all hell to the rebellion against God.

For Iago does not feel (as Bradley has pointed out). . . . I would add the suggestion that this may be one reason why he wishes to injure mankind, which possesses the power to feel, to suffer — that power which he lacks.

For he must be first in everything, — and to lack anything, even the power of feeling, is to be inferior.

Roderigo says to him, of Othello,

Thou toldst me thou didst hold him in thy hate.

And Iago replies,

Despise me if I doe not.   [I, 1]

To be despised, is death.

Iago is, perhaps, too far under the earth for hatred. . . . But pride, he tells himself, must surely give him *some* feeling: he owes it to his pride to hate.

And he is filled with an immeasurable contempt: but this is scarcely a *feeling*.

To Roderigo he says [1, 3],

> What sayst thou, noble heart?

And by the very fact of applying the words to that despised being, he tells us what is his opinion of a noble heart.

He has a curiosity to see what will be the movements, under pain, of these extraordinary beings of an alien world — beings who have passions, nobilities, and are ruled by a power that is not that of the will.

Sometimes he even tries to emulate their feelings, the speech born from these, — as when he pretends to himself, and to Emilia, that he knows jealousy (but even then the pretense breaks down, and we see the face behind the mask: it is that of Pride) — or as when, in the first scene, he says:

> Though I doe hate him as I doe hell-pains.

But here, we feel that he is disguising from us that those pains are his climate — he is used to them, is a native of them; they do not touch him as they would those who have hearts to be consumed. He would, indeed, hardly know the difference between those pains and the pleasures of heaven. For he is not a damned soul. He is a devil.

He lives by the will — that self-will which, the saints tell us, causes our perpetual separation from God.

"Vertue! a figge! 'tis in ourselves that we are thus, or thus. Our Bodies are our Gardens, to the which our wills are Gardiners; So that if wee will plant Nettles or sowe Lettice, set Hyssope and weed up Time, Supply it with one Gender of Hearbes or distract it with many, either to have it sterril with idlenesse or manured with Industry, why the power and corrigible authority of this lies in our wills. If the balance [7] of our lives had not one scale of Reason to poyse another of

[7] *"Balance."* In the 1632 Folio, it is *"braine."*

Sensuality, the blood and baseness of our Natures would con-
duct us to most preposterous Conclusions; but wee have reason
to coole our raging Motions, our carnall Stings, our unbitted
Lusts, whereof I take this that you call Love, to be a Sect
or Seyen." [I, 3]

He seems, in his curiosity, to be asking for information
about this strange stirring in the being.

Once, he almost believes (coldly and curiously) that he
himself feels this stirring:

> . . . That Cassio loves her, I do well beleeve it;
> That she loves him, 'tis apt, and of great credite;
> The Moore (howbeit that I endure him not)
> Is of a constant, loving, noble Nature;
> And I dare thinke he'le prove to Desdemona
> A most deare husband. Now, I doe love her too;
> Not out of absolute lust — (though peradventure
> I stand accountant for as great a sinne) —
> But partly led to dyet my Revenge,
> For that I doe suspect the lusty Moore
> Hath leap'd into my seat; the thought whereof
> Doth like a poisonous Minerall gnaw my Inwards;
> And nothing can or shall content my Soule
> Till I am even'd with him, wife for wife;
> Or failing so, yet that I put the Moore
> At least into a Jealousie so strong
> That Judgment cannot cure.   [II, 1]

To him, the destruction of Hell is always cold — that of a
poisonous mineral — is never that of fire, since fire purifies:

> The Moore already changes with my poyson:
> Dangerous conceites are in their Natures poysons,
> Which at the first are scarce found to distaste,
> But with a little act upon the blood,
> Burne like the Mines of Sulphure.   [III, 3]

Even at that moment when his pride tells him there is a stirring in his nature, "not out of absolute lust" he does not know feeling.

When Othello, in the midst of his torture, falls into a coma, following the words "Confess — ! Handkerchief — ! O divell!" [IV, 1], Iago says: "How is it, Generall? Have you not hurt your head?" and Othello, from his mine of sulphur, replies "Dost thou mocke me?"

Iago is honestly surprised by the question.

> I mocke you? No, by heaven.

For how should he understand the agony of the soul?

Yet he knows there is a difference between himself and the common humanity who feel that "Sect or Seyen" of lust that they call love; he realizes even, in a numb way, that they do not recognize it as only a freak of nature, a sport of that greater parent:

CASSIO: She's a most exquisite Lady.
IAGO: And, Ile warrant her, full of Game.
CASSIO: Indeed, she is a most fresh and delicate Creature.
IAGO: What an eye she has! methinkes it sounds a parley of provocation.
CASSIO: An inviting eye: and yet methinkes right modest.
IAGO: And when she speakes, is it not an Alarum to love?
CASSIO: She is indeed perfection.   [II, 3]

This difference between their point of view was, perhaps the

> . . . daily beauty in his life
> That makes me ugly,   [V, 1]

— and the reason why Cassio must die.

For at one moment, Iago had thought it would not be worth while to kill Cassio. If he lived or died would be indifferent to Iago, who is not a murderer for the sake of murder, but "an intellectual following his philosophical tenets to their logical conclusion."

> Though in the trade of warre I have slaine men,
> Yet doe I hold it very stuffe o' the conscience
> To doe no contriv'd murder: I lack iniquitie
> Sometimes to doe me service.   [I, 2]

This is his one fault, perhaps, according to his own tenets: his one failure to serve his god: Himself.

Iago sees himself as good as any man. (For does he not follow the tenets of his religion, evolved from his own nature?) Or, at any rate, he believes that the "good heaven" may "the souls of all my tribe defend." Like the fallen angels, he tells himself that he has a right to heaven. But he is not a fallen being . . . he has never known either the Paradise of the first man, or the heavens of the angels.

When Cassio is drunk [II, 3] he says to Iago:

Well, God's above all; and there be soules must be saved, and there be soules must not be saved.

Iago, amused, answers:

>   It's true, good lieutenant.
> CASSIO: For mine owne part — no offence to the Generall nor any man of quality — I hope to be saved.
> IAGO: And so doe i too, lieutenant.
> CASSIO: Ay; but by your leave, not before me; the lieutenant is to be saved before the Ancient.

This speech with its reminder of injuries that Iago thought he had suffered, and the claim that Iago might not be first in heaven (as he was first in hell), acted on Iago like the poison from the mines of sulphur. Remembered at the moment of decision, it determined Iago that Cassio must die. These words came from a being whom Iago despised, but who had been put before him and had reminded him of that preferment.

To Montana, who had been watching Cassio, he said:

> You see this fellow that is gone before;
> He is a Soldier fit to stand by Caesar
> And give direction: and doe but see his vice;
> 'Tis to his vertue a just Equinox,
> The one as long as the other; 'tis pity of him.   [II, 3]

For he, Iago, has no vice. To have a vice would be to sink below the strength of his will. Pride is the virtue of the devils: and to be a villain in the ordinary sense is beneath the dignity of the Princes of Hell.

Indeed, to bring about his own ends, Iago can even assume a virtue:

> How poore are they that have not Patience!

he says to Roderigo [II, 3]. And his own patience is endless.

"His creed," says Bradley, "for he is no sceptic, he has a definite creed, is that absolute egoism is the only natural and proper attitude, and that conscience or honour or any other kind of regard for others is an absurdity."

"O villainous!" he exclaims, when Roderigo threatens to drown himself because of his unrequited passion for Desdemona. "I have looked upon the world for four times seven years, and since I could distinguish betwixt a benefit and an injury, I never found a man that knew how to love himselfe. Ere I would say I would drowne myselfe for the love of a Gynney Hen, I would change my humanity with a Baboone." [I, 3]

It is to be noted here, that whilst most men would say "Since I could distinguish right from wrong," Iago says "distinguish betwixt a benefit and an injury"!

And yet, for all his self-love, this creature who in spite of his shrunken speech has what Baudelaire called "la vraie grandeur des pariahs," in order to bring about damnation in the world is willing to forfeit his own life. He scarcely cares. "In more than one way," said St. Augustine, "do men sacrifice to the rebellious angels."

As commentators have pointed out, Iago is perfectly honest in many of his speeches about himself. "Men should be what they seem," he says of Cassio. Iago is what he seems: but nobody will believe him. It is impossible that a man should impute such a character to himself, did it exist.

Iago says to Othello: "My Lord, you know I love you." [III, 3] He does not say: "I love you. . . ." And there must have been laughter in Hell at those words.

Sometimes, however, as all writers on Shakespeare have discerned, Iago looks from behind a grave mask, swearing "By Janus," and smiling to think we do not see the two faces of the god who is his patron and pattern — the god of the door, the gateway. . . . We know whither that door led, in Othello's case. . . .

But Iago's speech, as I have said already, is no mask. "The degree and nature of a man's sensibility," said Nietzsche, in *Beyond Good and Evil*, "extends to the highest altitude of his spirit." — Iago's did not. He is slow and sluggish as the serpent. When he speaks in verse, there is scarcely a beat or pulse, excepting when he is speaking of himself. The movement of the verse is horizontal, never vertical.

In spite of this pulselessness, the caesura is at times so deep that we feel we are looking down into a chasm of Hell.

> I am glad of it; for now I shall have reason
> To show the Love and Duty that I beare you
> With franker spirit; therefore, as I am bound,
> Receive it from me; I speake not yet of proofe.

> Looke to your wife; observe her well with Cassio;
> Weare your eyes thus, not jealous nor Secure:
> I would not have your free and Noble Nature
> Out of selfe-Bounty be abus'd; look to 't.   [III, 3]

Down to "abus'd" all the caesuras are equal — moderately long, — the ordinary breaks of speech. But with that word, we look down into a hell-chasm, — but only for a moment. The pause, though of that depth, is scarcely longer than the others.

After this speech, for a while, the pauses are less deep, — and are quick, as if Iago were covering up something, as in

> He thought 'twas witchcraft; but I am much to blame.

In the following lines:

> I hope you will consider what is spoke
> Comes from my love. But I do see y'are moov'd,
>   [III, 3]

— after the huddled movement of the first line, comes, in the second, another deep chasm, — that, perhaps, of the Hell from which Iago was born. That dulled speech of his causes him to repeat "I see y'are moov'd" once again within the space of nine lines.

*   *   *

How strangely must Iago and Desdemona have looked into each other's eyes.

"For," as Jeremy Taylor said of a gaze, "as from the eyes of some persons, there shoots forth an evil influence, and some have an evil eye and are infectious, some look truthfully as a friendly planet, and innocent as flowers."

Desdemona, this young being who said of her hand

> It yet has felt no age nor knowne no sorrow,
>   [III, 4]

— she whose "sins" were "loves she bore" Othello; she who was "a child to chiding," and who must go into the darkness alone — saw no treachery in Iago.

*   *   *

"An eye," said Jeremy Taylor, "that dwells too long upon a starre must be refreshed with lesser beauties, and strengthened with greens and looking glasses, lest the sight become amazed with too great a splendour."

The beauty is no less, but the ineffable drooping swanlike dying music of Desdemona is in contrast to the planetary magnificence of Othello's gait in verse:

> I cannot weepe, nor answer have I none,
> But what should go by water. . . .   [IV, 2]

and

> Sing all a greene willough shall be my garland.
>   [IV, 3]

— these are in the same tones.

> It is the wind.

— a dropping and dying fall, bringing memories of sweetness. Yes. "It is the wind." Only that, and as swiftly gone. Her words were always few, and always had the sound of a wind among trees.

Sometimes the very sound of her voice will bring a faint echo of that of her beloved Othello:

OTHELLO: Ah! Desdemona; away, away, away!
DESDEMONA: Alas, the heavy day! — Why do you weepe?
                                              [IV, 2]

An echo, more than a rhyme; and one deep in her heart, as the echoing sound lies deep in the line.

[115]

NOTE to *Othello*

Act I, Scene I

And, though he in a fertile Clymate dwell,
Plague him with Flyes. . . .

Johann Wier, pupil of Agrippa, gives the following names as being among the Powers and Principalities of Hell:

BEELZEBUB: Supreme Chief of the Infernal Court and Empire, And Founder of the Order of the Fly.
LEONARD: Grand Master of the Sabbath, Knight of the Fly.
CHAMOS: Knight of the Fly.

(Johann Wier — "Des prestiges des démons." Cinq livres de l'imposture et tromperie des diables, des enchantements et sorcelleries. Fait français par Jacques Grévin de Clermont. Paris, 1569.)

IX. "Timon of Athens"

Swinburne, writing of Chapman's translation of Homer, said, "His [Homer's] fiery and turbid style has in it the action rather of earthquakes and volcanoes than of the oceanic verse. . . . It can show but the huge movements of the heaving earth, inflated and inflamed with unequal and violent life, for the innumerable unity and harmony, the radiant and buoyant music of luminous motion, the simplicity and equality of passion and of power, the majestic monochord of single sound and underlying as it were the multitudinous measures of the epic sea."

This passage might equally be applied to the difference between the splendors of *Othello* and the turgid magnificence of *Timon of Athens*, where the earth-shaking rumblings seem to come from the deepest heart of Nature.

> That Nature, being sicke of man's Unkindnesse,
> Should yet be hungry! Common Mother, thou
>
> *(digging)*
>
> Whose Wombe Unmeasurable, and infinite breast,
> Teemes and feedes all; whose selfe-same Mettle
> Whereof thy proud Child, arrogant man, is puft,
> Engenders the blacke Toad and Adder blew,
> The gilded Newt and eyelesse venom'd Worme,
> With all the abhorred Births below crispe Heaven
> Whereon Hyperion's quickening fire doth shine;
> Yeald him, who all thy human Sonnes doth hate,
> From foorth thy plenteous bosome, one poore roote!
>
> [IV, 3]

[117]

Here, in the third, fourth, and eighth lines, the sound is turgid and rumbling as if it preceded an earthquake.

This play of

> . . . Fools of fortune, trencher-friends, Time's flies,
>
> [III, 6]

and of one who came to this change

> As the Moone doe's, by wanting light to give:
> But then renew I could not like the Moone;
> There were no Sunnes to borrow of,   [IV, 3]

bears a prophetic coloring of the present age, — of

> Flinty mankinde; whose eyes do never give,
> But thorough Lust and Laughter. Pittie's sleeping:
> Strange times, that weepe with laughing, not with weeping.
>
> [IV, 3]

In this poem "inspired at once," as Swinburne said, "by the triune Furies of Ezekiel, of Juvenal, and of Dante," — in the Fifth Act, as Swinburne thinks (and, I would suggest, in the Fourth also, beyond any reasonable doubt), the presence of Shakespeare "predominates generally over the sullen and brooding atmosphere, with the fierce imperious glare of a 'bloody sun' like that which the wasting seamen watched at noon 'in a hot and copper sky.' "

But even here the noble man does not descend to the company of the beasts; the difference is shown between the man who hates through his excess of love, shattered in his breast, and the man whose hatred is a negation of life.

TIMON: What wouldst thou do with the world, Apemantus, if it lay in thy power?

APEMANTUS: Give it to the Beasts, to be rid of the men.

TIMON: Wouldst thou have thy selfe fall in the confusion of men, and remaine a Beast with the Beasts?

APEMANTUS: Ay, Timon.
TIMON: A beastly Ambition, which the Goddes grant thee to
   attaine to.

.   .   .   .   .

What Beast couldst thou bee, that were not subject to a
Beast? And what a Beast art thou already, that seest not thy
losse in transformation!   [IV, 3]

Nothing is wasted, excepting Time's flies, that vanish like
the vapors to which they are compared. The very fires of
Timon's hatred weld weak evil into a strong and active good:

TIMON (*to the thieves*): The Sunne's a Theefe, and with his
      great attraction
   Robbes the vast Sea; the Moone's an arrant Theefe,
   And her pale fire she snatches from the Sunne;
   The Sea's a Theefe, whose liquid Surge resolves
   The Moon into Salte teares; the Earth's a Theefe,
   That feeds and breeds by a composture stolne
   From general excrement. . . .   [IV, 3]

But in answer to this, and to Timon's exhortation to continue
in their Roguery, the thieves reply thus:

THIRD THIEF: He has almost charmed me from my Profession
   by persuading me to it.
FIRST THIEF: 'Tis in the malice of mankinde that he thus ad-
   vises us; not to have us thrive in our mystery.
SECOND THIEF: I'll beleeve him as an Enemy, and give over my
   Trade.
FIRST THIEF: Let us first see peace in Athens; there is no time
   so miserable but a man may be true.

I do not understand the last sentence. Did the First Thief
mean that he would resign his "mystery," in order to do his
duty to the city that bred him? Or was Shakespeare speaking,

[119]

through the thief's lips, with a terrible irony? Did the thief mean that he would be true to his own villainy?

But all comes to an end, and Nature, in her wisdom, forgives all.

In Alcibiades's words over the tomb of Timon, lies the epitome of the poem:

> Though thou abhorrd'st in us our humane griefes,
> Scornd'st our Braine's flow and those our droplets which
> From niggard Nature fall, yet rich Conceit
> Taught thee to make vast Neptune weepe for aye
> On thy low grave, on faults forgiven. . . .   [v, 4]

X. *"Measure for Measure"*

I place this play among the Tragedies, for that, in effect, is what it is.

Measure for Measure is, perhaps, the only generation born of the Cold to be found in the work of Shakespeare.

At first sight it appears cold as the brain of Justice, hard and perfect as a hailstone might be, were this not ephemeral and small, but vast and everlasting as a meteoric boulder.

But this is because the coldness of human justice is contrasted with the great mercy of God.

Excepting in Claudio, the condemned sinner, it is Sin that is cold — all the heat and marrow of youth are gone.

Lucio says:

  Thy bones are hollow: Impiety has made a feast of thee.

[I, 2]

In the scene where Barnardine the pirate is called to execution, the clown Pompey says:

He is comming, Sir, he is comming: I heare his straw rustle.

[IV, 3]

And we know that to these beings the whole of life is only a small ratlike rustling in straw, amid a thick and fetid darkness. Claudio, contemplating Death, says:

  To be imprisoned in the viewlesse windes
  And blowne with restlesse violence round about
  The pendant world.   [III, 1]

[121]

And we see the world hanging — swinging maybe, like a pendulum, from Man's Idea of Good to Man's Idea of Evil — over an abyss of Nothingness, or of Hell.

> Like doth quit like, and Measure still for Measure,

says the Duke [v, 1]. But this is not the only meaning of the play's title. In this work, all things are weighed against their apparent opposites — the coldness of virtue against the cold and calculating sin — the good against the evil in the heart of Man — the terrors against the peacefulness of Death — one against the other. The motive and the action, the good that lies in the one, the sin that lies in the other — these, too, are weighed.

ISABELLA: Save your Honor!
ANGELO: From thee; even from thy vertue!
    What's this? What's this? Is this her fault, or mine?
    The tempter or the tempted, who sinnes most?
    Ha!
    Not she; nor doth she tempt; but it is I,
    That, lying by the Violet in the Sunne,
    Doe as the Carrion do's, not as the flowre,
    Corrupt with vertuous season.[1]   [II, 2]

The play, with its corrupt shreds of flesh that cling about it, and with the hollow bone devoured by Impiety, seems, at moments, like the Night wherein the soul is alone with God. But still the soul hides from itself, though it cannot hide from God.

    The cold and repellent Isabella tells herself that her natural repulsion against the loathsome attempt of Angelo, is not a

---

[1] I find the meaning of this obscure, so add Dr. Johnson's note: "I am not corrupted by her, but by my own heart, which excites foul desires under the same benign influences that exalt her purity, as the carrion grows putrid by those beames which increase the fragrance of the violet."

natural repulsion, but a horror of sin as sin. Yet she does not scruple to lie and cheat. She, herself, acts as bawd for the very sin for which her brother is to die — and this, in order to save her own soul!

Claudio had said of Juliet:

> You know the lady; she is fast my wife   [1, 2]

and he explains that there is a true contract between them.

Mariana, also, had been troth-plight to Angelo; but whereas Claudio had committed a sin for which he must die, unless respited by mercy, there was, according to Isabella, no sin and no disgrace in what Mariana did — because, apparently, it was expedient.

Towards the end of the play, begging for Angelo's life, in order that he may be given over, an unwilling husband, to Mariana, she says:

> . . . My brother had but justice,
> In that he did the thing for which he di'd.

but, of Angelo,

> His act did not o're take his bad intent;
> And must be buried but as an intent
> That perish'd by the way. Thoughts are no subjects;
> Intents but meerely thoughts.   [v, 1]

Yes Isabella knows that fault was only not committed, because she had cheated him. She knew, also, that he, in sending Claudio to his death (for which she seems to care very little), had believed he cheated her — and by a hellish crime.

Isabella knew that Angelo was a hypocrite. But what was she?

At least, until the hellish horror of Angelo's final sin (that of ordering the execution of Claudio) — his fall from what he had believed himself to be was, to himself, a tragedy. He even saw himself as he was:

> . . . heaven in my mouth,
> As if I did but onely chew his name,
> And in my heart the strong and swelling evill
> Of my conception.   [II, 4]

And perhaps that final act which must plunge his soul into Hell was performed in order to cozen himself that though he had betrayed all else, he had not betrayed and broken the letter of the Law of which he was an engine.

He is tragic. But Isabella is one of the company of the

> Sanctimonious Pyrat, who went to Sea with the Ten
> Commandments, but scrap'd one out of the Table.   [I, 2]

"Thrown upon the terrible dilemma of the piece," says Pater (*Appreciations*), "called upon to sacrifice that cloistral whiteness to sisterly affection, become in a moment the ground of strong contending passions, she develops a new character and shows herself suddenly of kindred with those strangely conceived women, like Webster's Vittoria, who unite to a seductive sweetness something of a dangerous and tiger-like changefulness of feeling. The swift anger leaps, like a white flame, into this white spirit, and stripped in a moment of all convention, she stands before us, clear, detached, columnar among the tender frailties of the piece."

Well — no doubt that is how she saw herself! Just as the other characters may have seen themselves addicted to "tender frailties."

Isabella says to the Duke:

> You bid me seek redemption of the Divell.   [V, 1]

But, indeed, even goodness seems but the devil in disguise. In order to obtain possession of an unwilling mate, the forsaken Mariana lends herself to a cheating which is almost as loathsome as Angelo's design upon Mariana (excepting, of course, that Death was not a pawn in *this* game, and that she thought good — the saving of Claudio's life — would come out of evil).

Not only does the judge speak with the voice of the tempting devil:

> Might there not be a charity in sinne
> To save thy brother's life?   [II, 4]

but the supposed Man of God (the disguised Duke) in a passage of magnificent poetry, speaks, to the condemned who must die, of Death as if it were only a matter of the cold earth.

> . . . Thou art by no means valiant,
> For thou dost feare the soft and tender forke
> Of a poore worme. Thy best of rest is sleepe,
> And that thou oft provok'st; yet grossly fear'st
> Thy death, which is no more. . . .

And after speaking of the ills of life:

> . . . What's yet in this,
> That bears the name of life? Yet in this life
> Lie hid moe thousand deaths: yet death we feare,
> That makes these oddes all even.

But the sinner sees more clearly:

> I humbly thank you.
> To sue to live, I find I seeke to dye —
> And, seeking death, find life.   [III, 1]

Yet even in the midst of this filth, the miasma arisen from the hidden dirt of humanity — in this play where only the man condemned for sin has an innocent heart, Shakespeare

[125]

"judges not as the judge judges, but as the sun falling round a helpless thing." [2]

The Duke, in the speech about Death to which reference was made earlier, says

> . . . Thou art not noble:
> For all the accommodations that thou bear'st
> Are nurst by baseness.   [III, 1]

Of this, Johnson says: "Whatever grandeur can display, or luxury enjoy, is procured by *baseness*, by offices of which the mind shrinks from the contemplation. All the delicacies of the table may be traced back to the shambles and the dung-hill. All magnificence of building was hewn from the quarry, and all the pomps of ornament dug from among the damps of the mine."

In the same speech, the Duke says:

> . . . Thou art not thy selfe:
> For thou exist'st on many a thousand graines
> That issue out of dust.

We are no better than poor Pompey, to whom the Duke says:

> Canst thou believe thy living is a life,
> So stinkingly depending?   [III, 2]

We must have mercy upon other dust. And may there not be jewels among that dust of which we are made, as well as the gaudy shining of sin to which Angelo refers?

> . . . What's open made to Justice,
> That justice ceizes: What know the Lawes
> That theeves do pass on theeves? 'Tis very pregnant,

[2] Walt Whitman, writing of the poet's nature, in the Preface to *Leaves of Grass*.

"*Measure for Measure*"

> The jewel that we finde, we stoope and take it
> Because we see it; but what we doe not see,
> We tread upon, and never thinke of it.   [II, 1]

This is the sense that Pater finds in these lines. As for the pride of place that has been built upon such dust, while despising it:

> Respect to your great place! and let the Divell
> Be some time honour'd for his burning throne.   [V, 1]

The proud must stoop to see the jewel in the dust. For indeed, we are all equally in the need of mercy. As Imogen says:

> . . . If there be
> Yet left in heaven as small a drop of pitty
> As a wren's eye, fear'd gods, a part of it.
> *Cymbeline*, IV, 2

Instead, Man threatens his own image, in passing judgment.

> Could great men thunder
> As Jove himselfe do's, Jove would nere be quiet,
> For every pelting, petty officer
> Would use his heaven for thunder; nothing but thunder.
> Merciful heaven!
> Thou rather, with thy sharpe and sulphurous bolt
> Splitst the unwedgeable and gnarled oke
> Than the soft Mertill; But man, proud man,
> Drest in a little briefe authority,
> Most ignorant of what he's most assur'd —
> His glassie essence — like an angry Ape,
> Playes such phantasticke trickes before high heaven
> As makes the Angells weepe; who, with our spleenes
> Would all themselves laugh mortall.   [II, 2]

Says the wicked and heart-corrupted Judge, who had believed himself pure as the heaven:

It is the law, not I, condemns your brother. [II, 2]

The law of Man. Not the law of God, which is Mercy.

Pompey, no doubt, raised a gale of laughter amid the audience, by his words to Mistress Overdone:

Courage! there will be pitty taken on you; you, that have worne your eies almost out in the service, you will be considered.

[I, 2]

But there is a great truth, none the less. She was blind in her sinning. She and Pompey, like Claudio, had

    . . . but as offended in a dream — [II, 2]

And, no doubt, the heavenly mercy *will* consider blindness, the little or no light, the offense in a dream. So, in this play in which the brain rebukes the body, coldly, the soul in a blaze of glory speaks to brain and body of pity and redemption, speaks, sometimes, through strange lips.

And as from the lips of Claudio, whose love of life had been too fevered, comes this splendor:

    . . . If I must dye,
I will encounter darknesse as a bride,
And hugge it in mine arms. [III, 1]

So from the lips of the unconscious hypocrite Isabella — lips cold and perfect as the hailstone, comes this splendor, warm from the heart:

    . . . alas! alas!
Why all the soules that were, were forfeit once;
And He that might the vantage best have tooke,
Found out the remedy. How would you be,
If He, which is the top of judgment, should
But judge you as you are? O! thinke on that,
And mercy then will breathe within your lips,
Like man new made. [II, 2]

[128]

NOTE. The Song

Of this miracle, Swinburne, in *Studies of Shakespeare*, wrote, "Shakespeare's verse, as all the world knows, ends thus:

> But my kisses, bring againe,
>   Bring againe,
> Seales of love, but seal'd in vaine,
> Seal'd in vaine.   [IV, I]

The echo has been dropped by Fletcher, who has thus achieved the remarkable feat of turning a nightingale's song into a sparrow's. The mutilation of Philomela by the hands of Tereus is nothing to the mutilation of Shakespeare by the hands of Fletcher. . . ."

Part of the poignance of this marvelous song — I speak of the technical side — is due to the repetition, to the echoes which sound throughout the verse, and part to the way in which the imploring stretching outward of the long vowels in "Take" and its internal assonance "againe" (and other words with long high vowels) are succeeded in nearly every case, in the next stressed foot, by a word which seems drooping hopelessly, as with "lips" and "forsworne," for instance.

The third line, however:

> And those eyes, the breake of day,

is an exception. Here, all is hope. Indeed, the sound of "breake" and "day" rises after the sound of "eyes."

A singular beauty, too, is given by the variation in the length and depth of the pauses. Let us examine the song for a moment:

Take, oh take those lips away,
  That so sweetly were forsworne;
And those eyes, the breake of day,
  Lights that doe mislead the Morne!
But my kisses bring againe,
  Bring againe,
Seales of love, but seal'd in vaine,
  Seal'd in vaine.

Note the lightening dissonance of "lips" and "Lights," the way in which "breake of day" would echo, exactly, "take those lips away," but for the fact that "breake" and "day" are drawn more closely together by the space of one syllable. Note, too, the beauty of the assonances "eyes" and "Lights," and how the particular position in which they are placed gives additional poignancy.

XI. "*Antony and Cleopatra*"

"The world of *Antony and Cleopatra*," said Mr. Mark Van Doren, "is so immense that time yawns in it; and this is not because time is going to die, as in *Macbeth*, but because it luxuriates in a sense of perfect and endless health. The mandragora that Cleopatra wants to drink so that she may 'sleep out the great gap of time my Antony is away' [I, 5], needs scarcely be drunk in a universe already drugged with a knowledge of its own size." [1]

"La musique donne l'idée de l'espace," said Baudelaire (*Journeaux intimes*), and in the sound of this verse there is the grandeur of space.

When a Messenger says that a rival conqueror

> . . . hath with his Parthian force
> Extended Asia,   [I, 2]

— "extended," here, means seized. But the word brings before us all Asia's vastness.

The moments stretch forever:

> There's not a minute of our lives should stretch
> Without some pleasure now

says Antony. [I, 1]

Kings, drunken with time, with wine, with the noonday light, nod to each other across a universe of light over which

[1] *Op. cit.*

[131]

Antony reigns, like the Sun from which Cleopatra, the "day of the world," takes her light.

*   *   *

> . . . Think on me,
> That am with Phoebus' amorous pinches black,
> And wrinckled deepe in time.

said Cleopatra [I, 5]. Phoebus: the Sun, who is Antony. He was all gold — a "mine of bounty," with a generosity like that of the harvest —

> There was no winter in't, an autumn 'twas,
> That grew the more by reaping. . . .   [v, 2]

And the mood of this mature conqueror was that of the time of ripeness:

CLEOPATRA: What! Was he sad or merry?
ALEXAS: Like to the time o' the year between the extremes
     Of hot and cold.   [I, 5]

He

> With his tinct gilded   [I, 5]

the messenger who came from him — like medicinable gold — or like the autumn sun.
     And when Antony says:

> Unarm, Eros; the long day's task is done,
> And we must sleep,   [IV, 12]

it is as if the Sun were speaking.
     The play has a cosmic splendor, as though the whole of Nature's ripening Sun had changed, suddenly, to warm and mellow gold that one can hold in one's hands.
     But the Sun sinks, and after his death

[132]

> . . . there is nothing left remarkable
> Beneath the visiting moon.   [IV, 13]

Yet the darkness is not that of a night haunted by the Furies and lit by the flares of Hell, but is like the beauty of one who said:

> . . . Think on me,
> That am with Phoebus' amorous pinches black,
> And wrinckled deepe in time.

This night of death, to which the splendors of the day must sink, the night in which the warrior unarms, his task done, to find sleep by the side of his lover, is a smiling darkness.

> Finish, good lady; the bright day is done,
> And we are for the darke.   [V, 2]

This softness, this languor, this dark magnificence, shapes the movement, lies on the last scenes like the bloom on the fruit. Even Death is brought in a basket of figs, carried by a country clown with the earth about him.

> . . . a rurall Fellow,
> That will not be deny'd your Highnesse' presence:
> He brings you Figges.   [V, 2]

And lying on all that scene there is this strange and smiling bloom, the peacefulness of death that is no more fearful than the shining darkness that lies on the figs.

CLEOPATRA: Hast thou the pretty Worme of Nylus there,
   That kills and paines not?
CLOWN: Truly, I have him; but I would not be the partie that
   should desire you to touch him, for his biting is immortal. .

·   ·   ·   ·   ·   ·

> . . . I wish you all joy of the Worme.   [V, 2]

In the slow-moving pomp and splendor of the verse in the scene of Cleopatra's death, all the vowel-sounds, at the beginning of the passage, are dark and full, and these vowels are, in part, the cause of the movement, because they bring about the pauses:

CLEOPATRA: Give me my Robe, put on my Crowne; I have
Immortall longings in me; Now no more
The juyce of Egypt's Grape shall moyst this lip.
Yare, yare, good Iras; quicke. Me thinkes I heare
Antony call: I see him rowse himselfe
To praise my noble Act; I heare him mocke
The lucke of Caesar, which the gods give men
To excuse their after wrath: Husband, I come:
Now to that name my courage prove my Title!
I am Fire and Ayre; my other elements
I give to baser life. So; have you done?
Come then, and take the last warmth of my lippes.
Farewell, kinde Charmian; Iras, long farewell.
                              (*Kisses them. Iras falls and dies.*)
Have I the Aspicke in my lips? Dost fall?
If thou and Nature can so gently part,
The stroke of death is as a Lover's pinch,
Which hurts, and is desir'd. Dost thou lie still?
If thus thou vanishest, thou tell'st the world
It is not worth leave-taking.
CHARMIAN: Dissolve, thicke Cloud, and Raine; that I may say
The gods themselves doe weepe.
CLEOPATRA: This proves me base:
If she first meet the curled Antony,
Hee'l make demand of her, and spend that kisse
Which is my heaven to have. Come, thou mortall wretch
                    (*to the asp, which she places at her breast*),
With thy sharpe teeth this knot intrinsicate
Of life at once untie: Poore venomous Foole,
Be angry, and despatch. O! couldst thou speake,

That I might heare thee call great Caesar Asse
Unpolicied.
CHARMIAN: O Eastern starre!
CLEOPATRA: Peace, peace!
Dost thou not see my Baby at my breast,
That suckes the nurse asleepe?
CHARMIAN: O breake! O breake!
CLEOPATRA: As sweet as Balme, as soft as Ayre, as gentle, —
O Antony! — Nay, I will take thee too.
                    (*Applying another asp to her arm.*)
What should I stay —   (*Dies.*)
CHARMIAN: In this vile world? So, fare thee well!
Now boast thee, Death, in thy possession lies
A Lasse unparallel'd. Downy windowes, cloze;
And golden Phoebus never be beheld
Of eyes again so Royall! Your Crowne's awry;
Ile mend it, and then play . . .   [v, 2]

In the lines with which Cleopatra's speech begins:

> Give me my Robe, put on my Crowne; I have
> Immortall longings in me; Now no more

— the first line has the same two long dissonantal *o*'s as in
the first line of Lady Macbeth's

> And fill me from the Crowne to the Toe, top-full
> Of direst Cruelty! Make thicke my blood;   [I, 5]

— but the place of the dissonance is reversed, and the effect
is utterly different. This is due, in part, to the *t*'s of Lady
Macbeth's lines, and to the *k* and *ck* of "Make thicke." Also,
in the second line of Lady Macbeth's, the vowels are not
deep, dark, and rich as are those in the second line of Cleopatra's in

> Give me my Robe, put on my Crowne; I have . . .

[135]

Here the long magnificence of the *o*'s, the first being rich and deep, but not dark, the second effulgent with brightening jewels — these darken to the splendor of the *o*'s in the second line — that in "immortall" being the deepest; that in "longings," in spite of the *g* which gives it poignancy, is soft because of the *n*. The *o* of "Now" echoes (though the length is less) the *o* of "Crowne," "more" echoes the *or* of "immortall," and indeed throughout the first lines there are echoes, some lengthening, some dying away, some more air-thin than the sound of which they are a memory, because of the difference between the consonants that embody the vowels. And these echoes give the verse the miraculous soft balance of the whole.

For instance, "lucke" in the seventh line is a dulled dissonance to "quicke" in the fourth and is divided from this by the darker, more hollow dissonance of "mocke" in the sixth. "Praise" in the sixth line is a higher dissonantal echo of "rowse" in the fifth, and "Come," the first word of the twelfth line, is an echo of "done," the last word in the eleventh. In the lines

> . . . This proves me base:
> If she first meet the curled Antony,
> Hee'l make demand of her, and spend that kisse
> Which is my heaven to have.

the miraculous balance is due to the dissonances "base" and "kisse," and the alliterative *h*'s of "heaven" and "have."

In that wonder of poetry:

CHARMIAN: O Eastern starre!
CLEOPATRA: Peace, peace!
> Dost thou not see my Baby at my breast,
> That suckes the nurse asleepe?
CHARMIAN: O breake! O breake!
CLEOPATRA: As sweet as Balme, as soft as Ayre, as gentle, —

the Eastern starre is Venus, the star of the east, and is also Cleopatra, who is all Beauty; — it is, too, the rising star of death, — all three in one. — The beauty of the sound is due to the balance of the poignant *e*'s of "Eastern" and "Peace" — dimming to the *e* of "breast" — then brightening again; to the particular arrangement in which the brightening and dimming *e*'s are placed; and, also, to the placing and balancing of the two-syllabled words: the long *e* of "asleepe" is a reversed echo of the long *e* of "Eastern," the *e* of "gentle" is dimmed and softened. The arrangement of *s*'s throughout this passage gives a feeling of strange gentleness, and the fact that they are sometimes placed so that they are alliterative, gives balance.

The texture of the passage is forever darkening and softening, then brightening and becoming poignant once more: "breast," for instance, is a higher, slightly dissonantal echo of the dusky, softened "Dost," — "Ayre" is a softened, bodiless, wavering, dissonantal echo of the shorter, sharper "starre."

In the first three lines of that passage which begins with the words "In this vile world" there is a lovely pattern of *l*'s, gentle and languorous; the beauty of the dropping dissonances "vile," "well"; "lies," "Lasse," "cloze" is very great. And it is these, the occasional alliteratives ("world," "well"; "lies," "Lasse"), the occasional *o*'s, placed close together, of "Windowes," "cloze," "golden," and the perpetual ground-sound (if I may so express it) of *i*'s and *y*'s — "vile," "lies," "eyes," "awry" — together with the particular arrangement of assonantal dim *e*'s, — "well," "Death," "possession," "beheld," "mend," which give the passage its flawless balance.

An extraordinary beauty and strangeness is given in the last four lines of that passage, by the difference in balance and length of the double-syllabled words — the first syllable of

"Downy" and "Windowes" being not quite equal, for the *ow* of "Downy" is longer — the first syllables of "golden" and "Phoebus" being equal, and "Royall" being less a word of two syllables than a word of one and three quarters.

But the whole play is one of the greatest miracles of sound that have ever come into this world.

In the Second Scene of the First Act, for instance, we have this wonder, from the lips of Antony:

> . . . O! then we bring forth weeds
> When our quicke mindes lye still: and our illes told us
> Is as our earing. Fare thee well awhile!

Here, the strange beauty is due partly to the change from "weeds" to "mindes," from "still" to "illes."

XII. *"Julius Caesar"*

"The Earth," said de Quincey, "has one prerogative City, and that City was Rome. As was the City, such was its Prince, — mysterious, solitary, unique. Each was to the other an adequate counterpart, each reciprocally that perfect mirror which reflected, as in *alia materia*, those uncommunicable attributes of grandeur that under the same shape and determination never upon this earth were destined to be revived. Rome has not been repeated: neither has Caesar. . . . Caesar and Rome have flourished and expired together. Each, reciprocally, was essential to the other. Even the Olympian Parthenon needed Rome for its full glorification; and Jove himself first knew his own grandeur when robed and shrined as Jupiter Capitolinus. The illimitable attributes of the Roman Prince, boundless and comprehensive as the universal air, — like that also bright and apprehensive to the most vagrant eye, yet in parts (and those not far removed) unfathomable as outer darkness (for no chamber could shroud in more impenetrable concealment a deed of murder than the chambers of the air): these attributes, so impressive to the imagination, and which all the subtlety of the Roman wit could as little fathom as the fleets of Caesar could traverse the Polar Basin or unlock the gates of the Pacific, are best symbolised, and find their most appropriate exponent, in the illimitable City itself, — that Rome whose centre, the Capitol, was immovable as Teneriffe or Atlas, but whose circumference was shadowy, uncertain, restless, and advancing as the frontiers of her all-conquering empire."

As for that empire, "its range, the compass of its extent, was appalling to the imagination. Coming last among what are called the Great Monarchies of Prophecy . . . beyond it lay Parthia and the great fable of India." [1]

In this play, the great Caesar, bright as the Prince of the Powers of the Air, the fallen Angel whose sin was pride, says, almost at the moment of his death:

> I could be well mov'd if I were as you;
> If I could pray to moove, Prayers would moove me;
> But I am constant as the Northerne Starre,
> Of whose true fixt and resting quality
> There is no fellow in the Firmament.
> The skyes are painted with unnumber'd Sparkes,
> They are all Fire and every one doth shine:
> But there's but one in all doth hold his place:
> So, in the World; 'tis furnished well with Men,
> And Men are Flesh and Blood, and apprehensive.
> Yet in the number I do know but One
> That unassayleable holds on his Ranke,
> Unshake'd of Motion: and that I am he.   [III, 1]

But, in the end, the unshakeable star proved to be Fate — a disastrous planet hidden behind the gross mists of the breath of crowds, — "the stinking breath" of the crowd that "had almost choaked Caesar: for hee swoonded and fell downe at it." [I, 2]

The voice of Fate sounds not only through the lips of the Soothsayer who said but five words: "Beware the Ides of March," or amid the strange dreamlike mutterings of the Conspirators in the market place — one of whom had seen the swoon of Caesar:

[1] De Quincey, "Philosophy of Roman History," *Historical and Critical Essays.*

BRUTUS: 'Tis very like: he hath the Falling sicknesse.
CASSIUS: No, Caesar hath it not; but you, and I,
And honest Casca, we have the Falling sicknesse.
CASCA: I know not what you meane by that; but I am sure
Caesar fell downe. If the tag-ragge people did not clap him,
and hisse him, according as he pleas'd and displeas'd them,
as they use to doe the Players in the theatre, I am no true
man.   [I, 2]

Not these alone, but the Elements, speak of danger:

CASSIUS: . . . for now, this fearfull Night,
There is no stirre, or walking in the streets;
And the Complexion of the Element
In Favor's like the Worke we have in hand,
Most bloudie, fierie, and most terrible.   [I, 3]

                              . . . Never till now,

says Casca,

    Did I goe through a tempest dropping fire.

            .   .   .   .   .

    A common slave — you know him well by sight —
    Held up his left hand, which did flame and burne
    Like twentie torches joyn'd; and yet his Hand,
    Not sensible of fire, remain'd unscorch'd.
    Besides, — I have not since put up my sword, —
    Against the Capitoll I met a Lyon,
    Who glar'd upon me, and went surly by.   [I, 3]

  Calpurnia says to Caesar:

            A lioness hath whelped in the streets;   [II, 2]

— and this seems like the birth of Disaster, or of some terrible new-fallen Angel — half lion, half spirit, fallen before
his birth. But Caesar does not heed the complexion of the

elements. He remains deaf to the dream of his wife, as to the voice of the Soothsayer:

CAESAR: What say the augurers?
SERVANT: They would not have you to stirre forth to-day.
          Plucking the intrailes of an offering forth,
          They could not finde a heart within the beast.
CAESAR: The Gods do this in shame of Cowardice:
          Caesar should be a Beast without a heart
          If he should stay at home to-day for feare.
          No, Caesar shall not; Danger knowes full well
          That Caesar is more dangerous than he:
          We are two Lyons litter'd in one day,
          And I the elder and more terrible.   [II, 2]

Even Voltaire, in the midst of his caviling, was moved to exclaim that this is of an inconceivable elevation.

The play is amongst the most *pure* poetry written by Shakespeare. The theme is the greatness of Man pitted against the power of Fate. The poetry itself has the complexion of the elements. It moves with an incredible grandeur, as it tells of the bright Angel Caesar — the Angel, perhaps, of Death, who must fall from his place as Lucifer fell, because of pride, or because of the pride that his killers believed existed in him.

BRUTUS: It must be by his death: and, for my part,
          I know no personall cause to spurne at him,
          But for the generall. He would be crowned:
          How that might change his nature, there's the question:
          It is the bright day that brings forth the adder;
          And that craves warie walking. Crowne him? — that!
          And then, I graunt, we put a Sting in him.
          That at his will he may doe danger with.
          The abuse of Greatnesse is, when it dis-joynes
          Remorse from Power.   [II, 1]

There is a strange beauty in this scene, when Brutus, returning from his orchard to the closet, says:

> The exhalations whizzing in the Ayre
> Give so much light that I may reade by them.   [II, 1]

A few moments later comes the knock on the door. It is the knock of Fate. From that moment, there is only one road on which Brutus may travel.

This knocking on the door is only one of the several incidents which, as various commentators have pointed out, connect the play with *Macbeth*.

In *Julius Caesar*, however, the knocking foretold the deed. It did not, as in *Macbeth*, tell that the deed was done, and that the gates of Hell would soon close behind the doer.

Brutus, hearing of the death of his beloved wife Portia, says:

> Speake no more of her.   [IV, 3]

And, mourning over the death of Cassius:

> Friends, I owe more teares
> To this dead man than you shall see me pay.
> I shall find time, Cassius: I shall find time.   [V, 3]

Both these passages seem like forerunners of that wherein Macbeth hears of the death of his wife.

Then, too, there is the scene where the Ghost of Caesar confronts Brutus, and the living man says:

> How ill this Taper burns! Ha! who comes heere?
> I thinke it is the weaknesse of mine eyes
> That shapes this monstrous Apparition.
> It comes upon me. Art thou any thing?
> Art thou some God, some Angell, or some Divell,
> That makst my blood cold, and my haire to stare?
> Speake to me what thou art.

[143]

GHOST: Thy evill Spirit, Brutus.
BRUTUS: Why com'st thou?
GHOST: To tell thee thou shalt see me at Philippi.
BRUTUS: Well: then I shall see thee againe?
GHOST: Ay, at Philippi.
BRUTUS: Why, I will see thee at Philippi then.   [IV, 3]

The beginning recalls the moment when Macbeth sees the Ghost of Banquo. But to his questioning, that Ghost made no answer. The Ghost of Caesar speaks with the dark voice of an Augury.

The end of the play contains two supreme grandeurs:

TITINIUS: But Cassius is no more. O setting Sunne!
    As in thy red Rayes thou dost sinke to night,
    So in his red blood Cassius' day is set;
    The Sunne of Rome is set. Our day is gone;
    Cloudes, Dewes, and Dangers come: our deeds are done.
                                                      [V, 3]

And Brutus:

    Night hangs upon mine eyes; my Bones would rest,
    That have but labour'd to attaine this houre.   [V, 5]

*   *   *

"With polysyllabic and ample-sounding words" (to para-phrase a sentence by Gautier), "verses are made which seem immense, and in which these vibrating sounds prolong the measure."

And here, in *Julius Caesar*, are words whose vibrating sounds prolong the measure. But they are more often words of one syllable than polysyllabic. The voices sound, often, with the resonance of dark marbles, of bronze, of porphyry.

XIII. The Historical Tragedies

. . . The histories of our English kings — the events of their
reigns, I mean, — are like stars in the sky; whatever the real
interspaces may be, and however great, they seem close to
each other. The stars — the events — strike us and remain in
our eyes little modified by the difference of dates.

— S. T. COLERIDGE.

XIV. The Comedies

Shakespeare's Comedies, roughly, are of three kinds. In the first kind

> The Sommer still doth tend upon my state;

as the Queen of the Fairies said in *A Midsommer-Night's Dream*. And this is true even in tales of winter, and when

> . . . hoary-headed frosts
> Fall in the fresh lap of the crimson Rose.
>> *A Midsommer-Night's Dream*, II, 1

"There's sap in it yet" — in the world and in the heart.

In the second kind the strong force of life fights and overcomes a thin and meagre living death — as in *All's Well that Ends Well*.

In the third kind there is separation ending in reunion and in reconciliation, — in peace of heart.

Some of the Comedies, again, are like Beatrice, who "dreamed of unhappinesse and waked her selfe with laughing." [*Much Ado about Nothing*, II, 1]

Even anger is of the nature of the rose:

DON JUAN: I had rather be a canker in the hedge than a rose in his grace.
>> *Much Ado about Nothing*, I, 3

And through all the plays — comedies and tragedies — sound the songs — sometimes epitomizing the meaning of the play, sometimes hiding a strange, haunting wisdom — or coming to us only as "naked ear-delighting absolute Melody — Melody that is just Melody and nothing else; that glides into the ear, one knows not why . . . that sounds sad when we are merry and merry when we are sad.[1]

"A Musical thought," said Carlyle, "is spoken by a mind that has penetrated into the inmost heart of the thing; detected the inmost mystery of it, namely, *the melody* that lies hidden in it, the inward harmony of coherence which is its soul, whereby it exists."

*   *   *

The wisdom in these Comedies is "the divine understanding and knowledge, which shall blossom in the time of the lily." [2] For wisdom it is — flowering sometimes from what would seem to be the dry earth — or coming to us on a sudden wind of spring that brings whispers of immortality.

[1] Richard Wagner, *Posthumous Works.*
[2] Jacob Boehme, *The Signature of All Things.*

XV. "All's Well that Ends Well"

The second kind of Comedy, as I said in the general notes on the Comedies, is one in which the strong force of life fights against a thin and meager living death. In *All's Well that Ends Well*, Helena, a strong, bright, rank flower, forces her powerful roots, her living strength, her passion for life, through the bleak air by which she is surrounded, towards her sun, Bertram.

"It is from my influence," said Folly in Erasmus's *Panegyrick upon Folly*, "that the whole world receives her ferment of mirth and Jollity. . . ." Ferment, the saps and juices of the earth disturbed by Spring. But in this play even the Clown is thin and white like Winter, but with none of the sparkling bright quality of Jack Frost.

As Mr. Van Doren has pointed out, he is "as bleak and bitter as the air that blows through his old mistress's rooms. . . . Not only has she [the old Countess] hung her house with black in sign of her unfortunate widowhood; she oppresses it with her thin, cold way of speaking, which is like that of Lafeu, the old lord who haunts it with her, and who is as far from being a Polonius or a Menenius as the peeled stick is from a budded stem."

Lafeu is an aged bore, pleased with his withered platitudes: " 'Twas a good lady, 'twas a good lady. We may pick a thousand salads ere we light on such another herb — " he says of Helena.

[148]

And we see again the plant ruled by a sun, amid the general withering.

No wonder that, in such an air, Helena, loving the braggart Parolles for Bertram's sake, feels a liking for him, too, because of his strong growth, his will to live:

> And yet I know him a notorious Liar,
> Thinke him a great way foole, solie a coward;
> Yet these fixed evils sit so fit in him,
> That they take place, when Vertue's steely bones
> Looke bleake in the cold wind: withall, full oft we see
> Cold wisdom waiting on superfluous follie.   [I, I]

And here again, in the case of Parolles, we see a character pardoned for his faults, because of his force of life. Shown, at last, as what he is, he declares

> Simply the thing I am
> Shall make me live,   [IV, 3]

and, with this, attains a kind of grandeur.

But Helena's strength of life is greater still:

> I am undone: There is no living, none,
> If Bertram be away. It were all one
> That I should love a bright particular starre
> And thinke to wed it, he is so above me:
> In his bright radience and collaterall light
> Must I be comforted, not in his sphere.   [I, I]

"Everything," said Thomas Vaughan, "hath its character pressed upon it by its Star for some peculiar effect, especially by the Star which doth principally govern it: And these characters contain, and retain in them the peculiar natures, virtues, and roots of their Stars, and produce the like operations upon other things, on which they are reflected." [1]

[1] *Magica Adamica.*

[149]

He says, elsewhere (*Lumen de Lumine*), "There is not an Herb here below, but he hath a *star in Heaven above*, and the star strikes him with her *Beames* and sayes to him 'grow.'"

"The bright particular star," says Mr. Van Doren, "is not the only strong thing here. Helena speaks often of stars, and the fact that she does, symbolizes her solitary blazing brightness in the play. . . . One of her favourite words is 'Nature,' and there is much of it in her. She has body as well as mind. . . . There is nothing frail about Helena, whose passion is secret and unmeasured: and because her body is real her mind is gifted with a rank, a sometimes masculine fertility."

Helena is like Nature ruled by a planet.

"Virginity," says Parolles, "murthers it selfe, and should be buried in highwayes, out of all sanctified limit, as a desperate Offendresse against nature."

Helena sighs:

> That Wishing well had not a body in't,
> Which might be felt; that we, the poorer borne,
> Whose baser starres do shut us up in wishes,
> Might with effects of them follow our friends,
> And show what we alone must thinke, which never
> Returnes us thanks.[2]   [I, I]

She is irresistible with the force of Spring, the ferment, the mounting sap:

> Our remedies oft in ourselves do lie
> Which we ascribe to heaven: the fated skye
> Gives us free scope: onely doth backward pull
> Our slow designes when we our selves are dull.
> What power is it which mounts my love so hye;
> That makes me see, and cannot feede mine eye?
> The mightiest space in fortune Nature brings
> To joyne like likes, and kisse like native things.   [I, I]

[2] "And show by realities what we now must only think." — JOHNSON.

A Poet's Notebook

I. On the Poet's Nature

"The sun shone on all statues, but only the statue of Memnon gave forth a sound." — SCHOPENHAUER: "On the Senses," *The World as Will and Idea*. Trans. R. B. Haldane and J. Kemp.

"We naturalize ourselves to the employment of eternity." — BENJAMIN WHICHCOTE: *Aphorisms*.

The great artist is made of "the wild nature of the world" to use Boehme's expression. He is a native of the wild truth. — E. S.

"His step is the migration of peoples, a migration greater than all ancient invasions." — ARTHUR RIMBAUD: "Genius," *Les Illuminations*. Trans. Helen Rootham.

. . . "countries, and things of which countries are made, elements, planet itself, laws of planets and of men, have passed through this man as bread into his body, and become no longer bread, but body." — EMERSON: "Plato or the Philosopher," *Representative Men*.

"What" it will be Question'd, "when the Sun rises, do you not see a round disk of fire somewhat like a guinea?" "Oh no, no, I see an Innumerable Company of the Heavenly Host crying 'Holy, Holy, Holy, is the Lord God Almighty.' I question not my Corporeal or Vegetative Eye any more than

I would Question a Window concerning a Sight. I look thro' it and not with it." — BLAKE: *Vision of the Last Judgment.*

"The poets of the Kosmos advance through all interpositions and coverings and turmoils and stratagems to first principles. . . ." — WALT WHITMAN: Preface, *Leaves of Grass.* 1855.

"In him, the freest abandonment is united with the precision of the geometer. His daring imagination gives him the more solid grasp of facts — as the birds of highest flight have the strongest alar bones." — EMERSON: *Plato.*

"You never saw the Spiritual Sun. I have. I saw him on Primrose Hill." — WILLIAM BLAKE, in conversation with Crabb Robinson, who was much embarrassed.

The Processes of Inspiration

It will not be believed by the "Apôtres du Petit Bonheur," but the experience of the poet during the first processes of the inception and creation of a poem (I say this in all humility) is akin to the experience of the saint. — E. S.

"Professor Tyndall, in a letter, recalls Tennyson saying of this condition" (the trance state from which springs creation. — E. S.) "By God Almighty! there is no delusion in the matter. It is no nebulous ecstasy, but a state of transcendent wonder, associated with absolute clearness." — *Memoirs of Alfred Tennyson*, Vol. II, quoted by WILLIAM JAMES: *Varieties of Religious Experience.*

[154]

On the Poet's Nature

"The Word has sprung in me more than once: if It has entered frequently, I have not always been conscious of Its arrival. But I have felt It in me and I remember Its presence. Sometimes I have felt even the forerunning of Its entry.

"Whence did It enter my soul? Whither did It return on leaving me? What is the place of Its entry? . . . It does not enter through the eyes, for It is not a colour; nor through the ears, for it is not a sound." (*Note:* Here the experience of the saint and the poet differs. The Word, for a poet, *does* come as a sound. But one from far away. — E. S.)

"Nor by the nostrils, for it does not unite itself to the air. . . . By what way, then, did it enter? Perhaps it did not enter, for it does not come from without, like an external thing." (Here, again, the experience is different. The material world has delivered up its essence to the visiting Angel of the poet. — E. S.) "Nor does it come from within, since Goodness, I know, is not in me."

"I mounted to the highest part of my Self, and higher still reigned the Word. Strange exploration, I descended to the depth of myself, and I perceived It in still lower depths. It was more close to me than my Self." — ST. BERNARD: *Cantico*, Sermon 74.

"I am conscious of something within me that plays before my Soul and is as a light dancing in front of it; were this brought to steadiness and perfection in me it would surely be eternal life." — ST. AUGUSTINE.

". . . because it is generated in the centre or circle of life, as a bright shining light, like unto the heavenly birth or rising up of the Holy Ghost, with a fiery driving or impulse of the Spirit, therefore I cannot resist or withstand it, though the

[155]

world always made a mock of me for it." — JACOB BOEHME: *The Aurora.*

"When the flash is caught in the fountain of the heart, then the Holy Ghost riseth up in the seven qualifying or fountain spirits into the brain, like the daybreak, dawning of the day, or morning redness." — JACOB BOEHME: *The Aurora.*

"I am so placed and submerged in His immense love, that I seem as though in the sea entirely under water, and could on no side touch, see, or feel anything but water." — A saying of ST. CATHERINE OF GENOA.

"When we pray, we should open our heart to God, like a fish when it sees the wave coming." — JEAN BAPTISTE VIANNEY, the Curé d'Ars.

See William Blake on Prayer and Praise, page 207. — E. S.

"The first time we see light, in Condillac's phrase, we *are* it rather than *see* it. But all our later optical knowledge is about what the experience gives." — WILLIAM JAMES: *Principles of Psychology.*

"This worthless present was design'd you, long before it was a play, when it was a confus'd mass of Thoughts, tumbling over one another in the Dark: when the Fancy was yet in its first work, moving the Sleeping Images of Things towards the Light, there to be distinguish'd, and then either chosen or rejected by the Judgment." — JOHN DRYDEN: Dedication to the Earl of Orrery, of *The Rival Ladies.*

On the Poet's Nature

"I dropped it (my idea) for the time into the deep well of unconscious cerebration: not without the hope, doubtless, that it might eventually emerge from that reservoir, as one had already known the buried treasure to come to light, with a firm iridescent surface and a notable increase of weight." — HENRY JAMES: *Works,* New York Edition, II, VII.

Later Processes

"All we can hope from these inspirations which are the fruit of unconscious work, is to obtain points of departure for our calculations. As for the calculations themselves, they must be made in the second period of conscious work which follows the inspiration. . . . They demand discipline, attention, will, and consequently, consciousness. In the sublimal ego, on the contrary, there reigns what I would call liberty, if one could give this name to the mere absence of discipline and to disorder born of Chance. Only, this very disorder permits of unexpected couplings. . . . Their mutual collisions may produce new combinations. — HENRI POINCARE.

II. On the Nature of Poetry

1. On Poetry of the Greatest Kind

"The Son of God is sowed in every furrow." — JOHN DONNE: *Sermon* (An adaptation of a phrase from Irenaeus).

And in every line. — E. S.

The Fountain-Head.

"O eternal Truth! and true Charity! and dear Eternity!" — ST. AUGUSTINE: *Confessions.*

". . . the theme of the Gospel . . . proclaims Eternity as an event." — Barth: *The Epistle to the Romans.*

Is not this true of the greatest poetry? — E. S.

"The head sublime, the heart Pathos, the genitals Beauty, the hands and feet Proportion." — BLAKE: *The Marriage of Heaven and Hell.*

"In the words of one of the Saints, 'Blood of the Holy Ghost and its glow are in one sense eternal, and in another temporal.'" — MEISTER ECKHART: *Sermons and Collections XXXIX.*

The spirit of a poem is nothing unless its body has that glow. — E. S.

May not the following four aphorisms on Music be applied equally to Poetry of the greatest kind? — E. S.

[158]

On the Nature of Poetry

"Music, as Schopenhauer has made clear to us, is not a representation of the world, but an immediate voice of the world." — ARTHUR SYMONS: *Studies in Seven Arts.*

"Schopenhauer . . . recognises in Music itself an Idea of the world, wherein the world immediately exhibits its essential nature." — WAGNER: *Beethoven.* Trans. E. Dannreuther.

In Schopenhauer's own words "Music never expresses phenomena, but solely the inner being, the essence of phenomena." — "Metaphysics of Music," *The World as Will and Idea,* quoted as an epilogue in Wagner's *Beethoven.* Trans. E. Dannreuther.

"Music expresses the inner being, the essence of phenomena, the Will itself, and represents accordingly all that is physical in the world, the thing *per se*, which lies beyond all appearance." — *Ibid.*

"The poetic idea which disengages itself from the movement, in the lines, would seem postulate the existence of a vast being, immense, complicated, but of harmonious proportion — an animal full of genius, suffering and sighing all sighs and all human ambitions." — BAUDELAIRE: *Fusées.*

". . . Poetry, prophecy, and the high insight, are from a wisdom of which man is not master . . . the gods never philosophise." — EMERSON: "Plato, or the Philosopher," *Representative Men.*

"Music . . . would seem to reveal the most secret sense of scene, action, event, environment." — WAGNER: *Beethoven.* Trans. E. Dannreuther.
Is not this also true of Poetry? — E. S.

[159]

A Poet's Notebook

"As Christianity arose from under the civilisation of Rome, so from the Chaos of modern civilisation music burst forth. Both affirm 'Our kingdom is not of this world.' That is to say 'We come from within, you from without. We spring from the essential nature of things, you from its semblance.' " — WAGNER: *Beethoven*.

Poetry of the greatest kind springs from the essential nature of things, not from its semblance. But poetry has its phenomena in nature, its outward and revelatory being. Poetry is also the visible world, with its images of wonder. — E. S.

Cézanne declared, "I have not tried to produce Nature; I have represented it." — Quoted in MARTIN ARMSTRONG'S *The Major Pleasures of Life*.

This great painter must be held to be right, according to the necessities of the art of which he was a practitioner. But in Poetry the exact opposite is right. To represent Nature, in Poetry, would mean, not that Nature is heard or seen through a temperament, but that Nature was unassimilated by the poet, had not "passed into this man as bread into his body." (See page 153.) — E. S.

"The greatest poet has a strong solving sense to reconcile his poetry with the appearance of the world." — EMERSON: "Plato, or the Philosopher," *Representative Men*.

"Music blots out an entire civilisation as sunshine does lamplight." — WAGNER: *Beethoven*.

This is true of the greatest poetry in a certain kind. It is true of Shakespeare's Comedies. In another kind, poetry is a sun whose light does not blot out a civilization, but fuses it into a single being. This is true of certain of Shakespeare's characters. — E. S.

"The Greeks said that Alexander went as far as Chaos; Goethe went, only the other day, as far; and one step farther he hazarded, and brought himself straight back." — EMERSON: "Goethe," *Representative Men.*

"He [Goethe] had a power to unite the detached atoms again by their own law." — *Ibid.*

"He [Plato] from the sunlike centrality, and reach of his vision, had a faith without cloud." — EMERSON: "Plato," *Representative Men.*

"Can no father beget or mother conceive a man-child so entire and so elastic that whatever . . . syllable he speaks, it shall be melodious to all creatures, and none shall be an exception to the universal and affectionate 'yes' of the earth?" — WHITMAN: *Notebooks.*

"If I speak with the tongues of men and of angels, but have not love, I am become sounding brass, or a clanging cymbal. And if I have the gift of prophecy, and know all mysteries and all knowledge; and if I have all faith, so as to remove mountains, but have not love, I am nothing." — ST. PAUL: I *Corinthians,* XIII.

"We have done nothing . . . if we have not purified the will in the order of charity." — ST. JOHN OF THE CROSS: *Ascent of Mount Carmel.*

"Thought without affection makes a distinction between Love and Wisdom as it does between body and spirit." —

BLAKE (Annotations to Swedenborg's *Wisdom of Angels Concerning Divine Love and Divine Wisdom*): *Marginalia.*

"Now he has passed that way, see after him! there is not left any vestige of despair or misanthropy or cunning or exclusiveness, or the ignominy of a nativity or colour or delusion of hell or the necessity of hell; and no man thenceforward shall be degraded for ignorance or weakness or sin."
— WHITMAN: Preface to *Leaves of Grass.*
It may be held that the above should have been placed under the heading of "The Greatest Poet," but to my feeling, it belongs to where I have placed it. — E. S.

"See the mysteries which lie hid in that miracle of Our Lord" (the changing of Water into Wine). (The) "Scriptures were the water. He made the water wine when He opened unto them the meaning of these things, and expounded the Scriptures; for thus that came to have a taste which before had none, and that enebriated which did not enebriate before." — ST. AUGUSTINE, quoted in ST. THOMAS: *Catena Aurea.*
The poets, among the sons of God, must keep this miracle, humbly, before their minds. They must open the meaning of the visual world, which, for them, is among the Scriptures. — E. S.

"Now was I come up in spirit through the flaming sword into the Paradise of God. All things were new: and all the Creation gave another smell unto me than before." — GEORGE FOX: *Journal.*

"Poetry is the identity of all other knowledges, the blossom and fragrance of all human knowledge, human thoughts, human passions, emotions, language." — COLERIDGE: *Biographia Literaria.*

"All truths lie waiting in all things. . . . For their birth you need not the obstetric forceps of the surgeon. They unfold themselves more fragrant than . . . roses from living buds, whenever you fetch the spring sunshine moistened with summer rain. But it must be in yourself. . . . It shall be love." — WHITMAN: *Notebooks.*

"Poetry is the Honey of all Flowers, the Quintessence of all Sciences, the Marrow of Art and the very Phrase of Angels." — THOMAS NASHE.

"Bless Jesus Christ with the Rose and his people, which is a nation of living sweetness." — CHRISTOPHER SMART: *Rejoice with the Lamb.*

"Bless God with every feather from the Wren in the sedge to the Cherubs and their mates." — *Ibid.*

"I would believe only in a God that knew how to dance." — NIETZSCHE: *Thus Spake Zarathustra.*

"Rowland, Rowland, get up and see the sun dance." — A country woman of Hockley, early one Easter morning, to her husband. Told in MRS. WRIGHT's *Rustic Speech and Folklore.*
This is like reading *As You Like It* for the first time. — E. S.

"All the pain of existence is shattered against the immense delight of playing . . . with the power of shaping the incomprehensible. . . . Brahma, the Creator of worlds, laughs as he perceives the illusion about himself; innocence regained plays lightly with the sting of expiated guilt, Conscience set free banters itself with the torments it has undergone." — WAGNER: *Beethoven*. Trans. E. Dannreuther.

"Perfection of a thing is threefold; first, according to the constitution of its own being; secondly, in respect of any accidents being added as necessary for its perfect operation; thirdly, perfection consists in the attaining to something else as the end. . . . This triple perfection belongs to no creature by its own essence; it belongs to God only, in Whom alone essence is existence." — AQUINAS: *Summa Theologica*.

The perfection of the spiritual life, as given here, is of the same order as the perfection of a poem. — E. S.

"Essence is the Father, Unity the Son, and Goodness the Holy Ghost." — ECKHART: Sermon XXXVI.

Essence, Unity, and Goodness (or Love) are the three attributes of the greatest poetry. — E. S.

2. On the Great Poems from the Depths

"What prodigies may we not conceive of . . . [from] those primitive longaeval and antediluvian man-tigers, who first taught science to the world." — MARTIN SCRIBLERUS: *On the Origin of Science*.

". . . Satan's Mathematic Holiness, Length, Bredth, and Highth." — BLAKE: *Milton*, Book the Second.

"As I was walking among the fires of Hell, delighted with the enjoyments of Genius, which to Angels look like torment and insanity, I collected some of their Proverbs, thinking that as the sayings used in a nation mark its character, so the Proverbs of Hell show the nature of infernal wisdom." — BLAKE: *Marriage of Heaven and Hell.*

". . . the notion that man has a body distinct from his soul is to be expunged; this I shall do by printing in the infernal method, by corrosives, which in Hell are salutary and medicinal, melting apparent surfaces away, and displaying the infinite which was hid." — *Ibid.*

"I constantly thought of the saying that when Delacroix paints, it is exactly like a lion devouring a piece of flesh." — VAN GOGH: *Letters of a Post-Impressionist.* Trans. Anthony M. Ludovici.

Baudelaire, speaking of Delacroix, quotes an acquaintance as saying that his is "Cannibal painting." — BAUDELAIRE: *L'Art Romantique.*

Millet said, "In art, it is necessary to put our very skin." — Quoted in VAN GOGH's *Letters to an Artist.*

(*Note:* Which are the great poems from the depths? . . . Such works, say, as *King Lear, Timon of Athens,* Villon's *Le Grand Testament,* and our traditional *Tom O'Bedlam's Song.* — These I have named are only a few. "*The Tyger*" has moved through the depths, but he has also walked in heaven. — E. S.)

3. On Lyrical Poems and Other Poems of a Small,
But Perfect Kind

"Can the reptile joys of a bee rival the lion's colossal pleasures?" — HENRY FUSELI: *Remarks on the Writings and Character of J. J. Rousseau.*
They can. — E. S.

. . . "The lark is a mighty angel." — BLAKE: *Milton*, Book the Second.

"The verse which out of many vocables remakes an entire word, new, unknown to the language, and as if magical, attains this isolation of speech." — MALLARMÉ: Excerpt from a Lecture. Trans. Arthur Symons, in *The Symbolist Movement in French Literature.*

"I say: 'A flower!' and out of the oblivion to which my voice consigns every contour, so far as anything save the known calyx, musically arises, ideal, and exquisite, the one flower absent from all bouquets." — *Ibid.*

"To create a little flower is the labour of ages." — BLAKE: *The Marriage of Heaven and Hell.*
Little, but perfect. The verses of Austin Dobson, and kindred horrors are not perfect. They are merely slippery. Certain short poems of Blake, and such a poem as "He came al so stil where his mother was," are among the most wonderful examples of the little, yet perfect, kind. — E. S.

"A flower told me her name." — RIMBAUD: *Les Illuminations.* Trans. Helen Rootham.
The poems of Herrick might be an example of this small,

yet perfect kind. They have not the childlike humble ecstasy of the short Blake poems, or of "He came al so stil" — they are not the flower itself, like those mysterious growths, — but the flower certainly told its secret name to Herrick. — E. S.

"The greatest poet hardly knows pettiness or triviality. If he breathes into anything that was before thought small, it dilates with the grandeur and life of the universe." — WHITMAN: Preface to *Leaves of Grass*.

"Snow quickly becomes marble in the predestinate hands." — JEAN COCTEAU: "Carte Blanche," *Le Rappel à l'Ordre*.

"The artist who has the sentiment of reality must never fear to be lyrical. The objective world retains its power in his work, no matter to what metamorphoses lyricism may have subjected it." — JEAN COCTEAU: "Le Coq et l'Arlequin," *Le Rappel à l'Ordre*.

Of Light Ayres

"The Apothecaries have books of Gold whose leaves, being opened, are so light that they are subject to be shaken with the least breath; yet rightly handled, they serve both for ornament and use." — THOMAS CAMPION: Preface to the Fourth Book of *Ayres*.

"We must not omit to enquire how Breezes and Butterflies move their four wings." — SIR THOMAS BROWNE.

"The bird rises to a great height without beating its wings, by means of the wind." — DA VINCI: *Notebooks*. Trans. Edward MacCurdy.

"The bird weighs less which spreads itself out more, and conversely that weighs more which draws itself together more tightly; and the butterflies make experiments of this in their descents." — *Ibid.*

We must experiment like bird and butterfly. — E. S.

"They" (in this case the makers of light ayres) are "warming themselves at fantastick fires, and dancing in the light of glow-worms." — JEREMY TAYLOR.

"Poetry should be always 'running upon pleasant feet, sometimes swift, sometimes slow.' " — J. PUTTENHAM: *Art of English Poesy*, 1589.

"To know how cherries and strawberries taste, said he, ask children and birds." — GOETHE, listening to "the songs and yodelling of the cheerful Tyrolese." *Conversations of Goethe with Eckermann.* Trans. J. Oxenford.

The above seems to be applicable to some of the lovely folk songs that are the natural growth of our soil: "The Turtle-Dove," "Under the Leves Grene" (an early poem, anonymous, but not actually a folk song), "Oh dear, what can the matter be" and hundreds of others. Also to many of the sweet and exquisite nursery rhymes. In these respects I, for one, am both child and bird. — E. S.

The Metaphysical Bustard

"Instead of a covey of poetic partridges, with whirring wings of music, up came a metaphysical bustard, winging its slow, heavy, laborious, earth-skimming flight over dreary and level wastes." — COLERIDGE: complaining, quite unfairly, of certain of his own poetry. *Letters*, Vol. I.

On the Nature of Poetry

4. On Modern Poetry

"There are two kinds of beauty; they are, general beauty which attracts people as sun attracts the planet — (this is found chiefly in ancient Art) and the other, individual beauty which results from the observer himself becoming a sun, attracting beauty — this is the beauty of modern Art." — TOLSTOI: quoting from Arthur Müller, *What Is Art?* Trans. by Aylmer Maude.

"The direct trial of him who would be the greatest poet is to-day. If he does not flood himself with the immediate age as with vast oceanic tides — if he be not himself the age transfigur'd, and if to him is not opened the eternity which gives similitude to all periods and locations and processes and animate and inanimate forms, and which is the bond of time . . . [the eternity which] commits itself to the representation of this wave of an hour, and this one of the sixty beautiful children of the wave — let him merge in the general run and wait his development. . . ." — WHITMAN: Preface to *Leaves of Grass.*

This is right for the transcendentally great poet who wrote it, but it is not right for every poet, even every great poet. It is certainly never right for the small poet, under any circumstances. On this subject, van Gogh (*Letters of a Post-Impressionist*, trans. Anthony M. Ludovici) said we must "avoid squandering our modest powers in metaphysical brooding which cannot press chaos into a tumbler; for that is precisely why it is chaos, because it cannot enter into a tumbler of our calibre." This should be remembered. — E. S.

We must learn "to cram today with Eternity and not the next day." — KIERKEGAARD: *Christian Discourses.*

". . . poetry sheds no tears 'such as Angels weep,' but natural and human tears; she can boast of no celestial ichor that distinguishes her vital juices from those of prose; the same human blood circulates through the veins of them both." — WORDSWORTH: Preface to *Lyrical Ballads* (1800–1805).

This belief has produced, often, wonderful results in the case of the great poet who declared it. But it is profoundly dangerous. Poetry should "utter somewhat above a mortal mouth," to quote a phrase from Ben Jonson's *Discoveries*. — E. S.

"Art is Science become flesh." — COCTEAU: "Le Secret Professionnel," *Le Rappel à l'Ordre*.

"Pure draughtsmen are philosophers and the abstractors of the quintessence." — BAUDELAIRE: *Curiosités Esthétiques*.

Many modern poets may be considered as draughtsmen — in their precision, avoidance of superfluity, vagueness, or romanticism. — E. S.

"Ô Soleil, c'est le temps de la Raison ardente."

I read somewhere, and now cannot trace, this line by Guillaume Appollinaire. I think that poetry, at this time, lives in the weather of the "Raison ardente." — E. S.

"Genius can no more analyse itself than can electricity. Either one possesses it, or one does not possess it. . . . Stravinsky canalises a brute force and so uses it that it serves equally the apparatus from the workshop, and the pocket lamp." — COCTEAU: "Le Coq at l'Arlequin," Appendice 1924, *Le Rappel à l'Ordre*.

"As you see, we are not far from the religious spirit. . . . The primordial importance that is granted to lyricism by minds like ours, the most capable, one would have thought, of despising it, obliges us to recognise in it a divine essence.

"This can change the slightest object into an idol, and make it live, for us, in conditions of an astounding silence." — COC-TEAU: "Le Secret Professionnel," *Le Rappel à l'Ordre.*

"The spirit of poetry: the religious spirit outside all precise religion, is doubtless what Paul Claudel depicted perfectly when he told us that Rimbaud was a mystic in the wild state." — *Ibid.*

Among the characteristics of modern poetry at its best, as of modern painting at its best, is the extraordinary and almost terrifying *identity* of that idol, the subject, — an identity which is due, in part, to simplicity, to the stripping away of all superfluities (see the section on Simplicity, page 198), and the extraordinary, almost terrifying silence by which the idol is surrounded. — E. S.

To speak of certain modern painters, for in these qualities the poets resemble the painters, in a recent essay on Tchelit-chew, in the quarterly *View* (May 1942), Mr. Lincoln Kir-stein wrote, "In his [Tchelitchew's] later paintings, as in Seurat, objects indicated exist isolated in their own air. . . . Each has its own essential temporal and spatial independence."

In the same number of this quarterly, Nicholas Calas, writing of Yves Tanguy, said, "The appalling silence of Tanguy's pictures creates a longing for sound. . . . The changes of temperature are rhythmical." He adds, "The solitude of Tanguy is oceanic."

In poetry, the subject, itself a life of sound, is surrounded by this silence. — In certain poems, it might be said that the changes of rhythm, of speed, are like changes in temperature.

"The depths are fathomless, and therefore calm. The innocence and nakedness are resumed." — WHITMAN: Preface to *Leaves of Grass.*

"More enigmas are contained in the shadow of a man walking in the light of the sun, than in all religions, past, present, or future." — CHIRICO, writing in the quarterly *Minotaure.*

This is an exaggeration. To have said "as many" would have been truer. But it is from enigmas such as these that the modern poet waits to hear a voice, the voice that spoke in the groves of Dodona, the voice of the Sphinx. — E. S.

"Here you will see no trace of any monument or superstition. Morality and language are reduced to their simplest expression. . . . New Erinnyes haunt the cottage which is my country and the home of my desires — Death without tears our active handmaid, hopeless Love, and a pretty little crime whining in the street." — RIMBAUD: "A Town," *Illuminations.* Trans. Helen Rootham.

"Great is the faith of the flush of knowledge, and of the investigation of the depths of qualities and things. Cleaving and circling here swells the soul of the poet." — WHITMAN: Preface to *Leaves of Grass.*

"The culte of a ruin hides . . . the sound of the shock of intelligence against beauty." — COCTEAU: "Picasso," *Le Rappel à l'Ordre.*

5. On Works of a Certain Kind

(*Note:* There is more music than poetry of this nature. For instance, certain works of Stravinsky's are of this order. In poetry, my verses for William Walton's and my joint work *Façade* are examples of this kind. — E. S.)

Warning: The "raw elegance of the lion is dangerous." — COCTEAU: writing of Braque, "Le Coq et l'Arlequin," *Le Rappel à l'Ordre.*

Villiers de l'Isle Adam wrote of his own work, *Triboulat Bonhommet,* that it was "an enormous and sombre clowning, the colour of the century."

All nations, and particularly the English, are slow to understand works of this nature. At first, these works are derided, and their authors insulted; then, twenty years after their first appearance, the point of such works is seen.

It is certain that an empty work which appears to be serious because it is dull will be acclaimed as a masterpiece, while a work of the above order will be at first disdained. — E. S.

Cocteau, writing in "Le Coq et l'Arlequin" (*Le Rappel à l'Ordre*) of a great work of this nature, the ballet *Parade,* of which he, Picasso, and Satie were the authors, said, "For the majority of artists a work cannot be beautiful without a plot, involving mysticism, love, or boredom. Brevity, gaiety, sadness without romance are suspect. The hypocritical elegance of the Chinaman, the melancholy of the Little Girl's steamboats, the touching silliness of the Acrobats, all that which has remained a dead letter to the public, would have pleased them, if the Acrobat had been in love with the Little Girl, and had been killed by the jealous Chinaman, who had then been killed, in his turn, by the wife of the Acrobat — or any of the other thirty-six dramatic combinations."

". . . we become drunk with a strong honey, and that honey must sometimes be gathered from the paw of a very

[173]

young bear." — COCTEAU: writing about Poulenc, "Le Coq et l'Arlequin," *Le Rappel à l'Ordre*.

Works of this order have, from time to time, this wild and heady sweetness, attached to menace. — E. S.

"It is the poetry of childhood overtaken by a technician." — COCTEAU: writing of Satie's music for *Parade*. *Ibid*.

Works of this order, in poetry, are frequently technical experiments of an extreme difficulty. — E. S.

"Purely arithmetical relations," wrote Schopenhauer — "Metaphysics of Music," *The World as Will and Idea* — "lie at the foundation of both rhythm and melody; in the one case, the relative duration of the notes, in the other case, the relative rapidity of their vibrations. . . . The rhythmical element is the essential; for it can produce a kind of melody of itself alone . . . and without the other. . . ."

This is the case with a work such as *Façade*, where in many cases (though not, for instance, in such poems as "By the Lake," "Daphne," "Four in the Morning," or "Rose and Alice") the rhythmical element has produced the melody. — E. S.

(See "On Technical Experiments," page 189.)

The mention of technical experiments brings us to the question of distortion.

Guillaume Apollinaire (*Méditations Esthétiques*) wrote: "The Fourth Dimension, such as it is, offers itself to the intellect from the plastic point of view, is the immensity of space, eternalising itself in all directions at a determined moment. It is space itself, the dimension of the infinite; it is this which endows objects with plasticity. It gives them, in a word, the proportions they deserve, whereas in Greek Art, for example, a rhythm that is to a certain degree mechanical ceaselessly destroys the proportions.

"Greek Art had a purely human conception of beauty. It took Man as the measure of perfection. The Art of the new painters takes the infinite universe as the ideal, and it is to that ideal that we owe a new measure of perfection which allows the artist to give to the object proportions conformable to the degree of plasticity which he wishes to produce in it. Nietzsche divined the possibilities of such an Art.

" 'O Dionysus divine, why dost thou pull mine ears?' Ariadne asks her philosophical lover in one of the celebrated dialogues on the Isle of Naxos. 'I find there is something agreeable, something pleasant about thine ears. . . . Why are they not still longer?' . . .

"Nietzsche, when he recounts this anecdote, brings to trial, through the lips of Dionysus, Greek Art." — APOLLINAIRE: *Les Peintres Cubistes.*

"Words and thoughts, never before brought together since Babel, clash into a protesting combination, and in the very aspect of the page there is something startling." — ARTHUR SYMONS: writing on Villiers de l'Isle Adam, in *Baudelaire: a Study.*

I would have substituted "civilization" for "combination." — E. S.

"Charm needs a profound tact. One must cling to the edge of vacancy. Nearly all graceful artists fall over the edge. Rossini, Tchaikowski, Weber, Gounod, Chabrier . . . lean over, but do not fall. They have a deep root, and this allows them to lean very far." — COCTEAU: "Le Coq et l'Arlequin," *Le Rappel à l'Ordre.*

"Everything which grows with irresistible force is accused of arrivism." — COCTEAU: "Le Secret Professionnel," *Le Rappel à l'Ordre.*

"You will say to me 'No solitude lasts long. You will soon see the school of solitude, or the school of the tightrope.' It is possible; but as it is dangerous, it does not attract everybody.

"As for the rest, one of the secrets of the *tour de force* lies in deceiving disciples, if they appear.

"How shall they be deceived?

"Ah, gentlemen, turn over our worlds, our pockets. . . . One risks nothing in divulging the professional secret. The means of using it are lacking." — COCTEAU: "D'un Ordre considéré comme une Anarchie," *Le Rappel à l'Ordre.*

Alas, Monsieur Cocteau was over-optimistic. *Nothing* will prevent amateurs from imitating, and spoiling the works they imitate. I defy anyone to escape from them. Simplicity itself — the simplicity of the great master, that most uncopyable of all forces, is imitated. — E. S.

III. On Technical Matters

1. On Texture

"It is," wrote Richard Wagner in his book on Beethoven, "a matter of experience that, by the side of the world which presents itself as visible in waking as well as in dreaming, we are conscious of yet another world which manifests itself by sound . . . a true world of sound by the side of a world of light, of which it may be said that it bears the same relation to the latter as dreaming to waking."

It is with this world of sound that many of the notes in this book deal.

Histories of English prosody have occupied themselves mainly with the effect on rhythm of variety and changes of accent, and the effect of alliteration; but, as far as I know, although Mr. Robert Graves has written a highly interesting chapter on Texture itself ("Techniques of Modern Poetry") — as I said in my book on Alexander Pope, the effect of texture upon rhythm and upon speed has not been considered. The truth is, that the texture of a poem has been regarded as merely a matter of fatness or leanness — has been acknowledged only as producing richness, or sweetness, or harshness in the poem; but the fact that texture is largely responsible for rhythm, and for variations in the speed of the poem, has not been acknowledged. The particular part played by the varying uses of consonants, vowels, labials, and sibilants, has been insufficiently considered. — E. S.

[177]

A Poet's Notebook

With regard to the relationship of consonants and vowels, it might, perhaps, be said that the vowels are the spirit, the consonants and labials the physical identity, with all the variations of harshness, hairiness, coldness, roughness, smoothness, etc.[1] (E. S.), "the garment of the spirit, 'thus distinguished, marked off and announced . . . to the outer world, [as] the animal by the skin, the tree by its bark.' " — WAGNER: "Opera and Drama," Part II, *Prose Works.* Trans. W. A. Ellis.

"We have called" (Wagner explains in "The Theatre," *Prose Works*, Part III, trans. W. A. Ellis) "the consonants, the garments of the vowel, or, more precisely, the physiognomic exterior. . . . Just as it hedges the vowel from without, so does it also bound the vowel within . . . i.e. it determines the specific nature of the latter's manifestation, through the roughness or smoothness of the inward contact therewith . . . or, to elaborate the matter further, these enclosing consonants are playing the part of the fleshly covering of the human body, organically ingrown with the interior; we shall thus gain a faithful image of the essence both of consonant and vowel, as well as of the organic relations to one another. Take the vowel for the whole inner organism of man's living body, which prescribes from out itself the shaping of its outward show, as offered to the eye of the beholder." [2]

Cézanne declared that "when colour has its richness, form has its plenitude." [3] — This is applicable to the effect that vowels have upon consonants. — E. S.

[1] Dante wrote of consonants being "shaggy" and "buttered," *pesca et hirsuto*, "combed and hairy."
[2] In certain early, or fairly early poetry, and in certain fairly late poetry in which there is an alliterative scheme — such as Dunbar's "Blind Harry" — consonants have another rôle. See the note on Dunbar.
[3] Cézanne, quoted in *Major Pleasures of Life*, Martin Armstrong.

[178]

"It has been experimentally demonstrated that light exerts pressure on any body on which it falls. This pressure is due to the momentum of the moving light energy. It has also been proved . . . that light has weight. — W. M. N. SULLIVAN: *The Bases of Modern Science.*

Vowels play the part of light or of darkness, consonants that of matter. Sometimes consonants (that have "the most universal qualities of matter . . . such as gravity, cohesion, rigidity, fluidity, sensitiveness to light") seem soaked with light or with darkness. — E. S.

"Bodies serve light, which would not shine unless it could break against them; similarly it may be said that without rhythm music would not be perceptible." — WAGNER: *Beethoven.* Trans. E. Dannreuther.

This is the service rendered by the consonants to the spiritual force of the vowels.

Consonants have each, when in contact with the vowel, their own specific gravity, mobility, or want of elasticity, their power of refracting light, their behavior as magnetic or diagmagnetic.

Consonants shape; they do not affect time as do vowels: roughly speaking the realm of consonants is in Space: the realm of vowels in Time — although vowels, too, have their place, position, depth, and height, they do not give body.

Sibilants slow the line. — E. S.

2. On Technical Perfection

". . . the feature in Beethoven's musical productions which is so particularly momentous for the history of art is this: that here, every technical detail, by means of which for clearness' sake the artist places himself in a conventional relation to the external world, is raised to the highest significance of a spontaneous effusion." — WAGNER: *Beethoven.* Trans. E. Dannreuther.

This should be true of all technique. — E. S.

"Mechanical excellence is the only vehicle of genius." — BLAKE: *Marginalia*, Reynold's Discourses.

"Without innate Neatness of Execution, the Sublime cannot exist." — *Ibid.*

"The fruition of beauty is no chance of hit or miss — it is as inevitable as life — it is exact and plumb as gravitation. From the eyesight proceeds another eyesight, and from the hearing proceeds another hearing . . . eternally curious of the harmony of things with man." — WHITMAN: Preface to *Leaves of Grass.*

"His [Plato's] strength is like the momentum of a falling planet; and his discretion, the return of its due and perfect curve — so excellent is his Greek love of boundary, and his skill in definition." — EMERSON: "Plato, or the Philosopher," *Representative Men.*

"The great and golden rule of Art as well as of Life, is this: That the more distinct, (and) sharp . . . the bounding line, the more perfect the work of art, and the less keen and sharp, the greater is the evidence of weak imitation, plagiarism, and bungling. . . . What is it that distinguishes honesty from knavery, but the hard . . . line of rectitude and certainty, in the actions and intentions? Leave out this line, and you leave out life itself; all is chaos again, and the line of the Almighty must be drawn out upon it, before man or beast can exist." — BLAKE: *Descriptive Catalogue.*

This refers to drawing, but is equally applicable to poetry. It should be learned by heart by the woolly imitators of that great poet, Wordsworth. — E. S.

"Energy is the only life, and is from the Body; and Reason is the bound or outward circumference of Energy." — BLAKE: *Marriage of Heaven and Hell.*

All technical achievement is, as it were, the Etheric Body of the poet. — E. S.

3. On the Essence of Sound

"The *Species of Visibles* seeme to be *Emissions of Beames* from the *Object* seen; almost like Odours; save that they are more Incorporeall." — FRANCIS BACON: *Naturall History.*

So should be the sound of Poetry. — E. S.

SOCRATES: "Is there not an essence of colour and sound as of anything else which may be said to be an essence. . . . And if anyone could imitate the essence of each thing in letters and syllables, would he not express the nature of each thing?"

. . . . . .

SOCRATES: "That objects should be imitated in letters and syllables and so find expression may appear ridiculous, Hermogenes, but it cannot be avoided."

— PLATO: *Cratylus*

"Imitate": should not the word be "reproduce"? If we *imitate* an essence, it is false. — E. S.

"The angels, from the sound of the voice, know a man's love; from the articulation of the sound, his wisdom; and from the sense of his words, his science." — SWEDENBORG, quoted by EMERSON: "Swedenborg the Mystic," *Representative Men.*

"Sounds as well as thoughts have relation both between each other and towards that which they represent, and a perception of the order of those relations has always been found connected with a perception of the order of the relations of thoughts. Hence the language of poets has ever affected a certain uniform and harmonious recurrence of sound, without which it were not poetry, and which is scarcely less indispensable to the communication of its influence, than the words themselves, without reference to that peculiar order. Hence the vanity of translation; it were as wise to cast a violet into a crucible that you might discover the formal principle of its colour and odour, as seek to transfuse from one language into another the creations of a poet. The plant must spring again from its seed, or it will bear no flower — and this is the burthen of the curse of Babel." — SHELLEY: *A Defence of Poetry.*

This is true of translations in nearly all cases. But there are wonderful exceptions. The translations by Arthur Waley from the Japanese and Chinese are works of a transcendental beauty — the pure essence of beauty itself, as indefinable as the scent of a flower. I know nothing more lovely than these truly miraculous works. — E. S.

"Like the metamorphosis of things into higher forms, is their change into melodies. Over every thing stands its daemon or soul, and as the form of the thing is reflected by the eye, so the soul of the thing is reflected by a melody. The sea, the mountain-ridge, Niagara, and every flower-bed, pre-exist, or super-exist, in pre-cantations, which sail like odours in the air, and when any man goes by with an ear sufficiently fine, he overhears them, and endeavours to write down the notes, without diluting or depraving them, and herein is the legitimation of criticism in the mind's faith, that the poems are a corrupt version of some text in nature, with which they ought to be made to tally." — EMERSON: "The Poet," *Essays.*

"Melody," said Beethoven, "is the sensual life of poetry. Do not the spiritual contents of a poem become sensual feeling through melody?" — Quoted by G. H. LEWES: *Inner Life of Art.*

4. On Rhythm

Rhythm has been defined as "melody stripped of its pitch." — This should be remembered. — E. S.

Wagner wrote: "Rhythm is the mind of dance and the skeleton of tone." "Tone is the heart of man through which dance and poetry are brought to mutual understanding." "This organic being is clothed upon with the flesh of the world." — Quoted by ARTHUR SYMONS: *Studies in Seven Arts.*
For the word "Tone" substitute "texture," which is to poetry what tone is to music, — and for Wagner's use of the word "poetry" substitute "the spirit." — The flesh of the world is made, for poetry, of the varying and shaping consonants. Vowels are the heart of tone. — E. S. (See Notes on Texture, pages 178, 179.)

"Rhythm is in time what symmetry is in space." — SCHOPENHAUER: *The World as Will and Idea.* Trans. T. B. Haldane and J. Kemp.

"Time is primarily the form of inner sense." — SCHOPEN-HAUER: "Of Knowledge à Priori," *The World as Will and Idea.*

Rhythm, then, is the form of inner sense when it has attained full consciousness and has become executive. Rhythm is the executive Sense or Soul. — E. S.

". . . the Musician, moulding and shaping, stretches his hand, as it were, towards the waking world of phenomena, by the *rhythmical* succession of *time* in his productions, much as the allegorical stream connects with the habitual ideas of the individual, so that the waking consciousness, which is turned towards the external world, is able firmly to retain it." — WAGNER: *Beethoven.* Trans. E. Dannreuther.

Rhythm, therefore, is one of the principal translators between dream and reality. — E.S.

"Thus," Wagner continues, "by means of the rhythmical arrangement of tones, the musician touches upon the perceptible plastic world."

This is also true of the poet.

Rhythm might be described as, in the world of sound, what light is in the visible world. It shapes, and it gives new meaning. — E. S.

"Beethoven contemplates life, and appears to contemplate how he is to play a dance for life itself." — WAGNER: *Beethoven.*

5. On the Modern Use of Rhythm

"It is a weakness not to comprehend the beauty of a machine. The fault lies in depicting machines instead of taking from them a lesson in rhythm, in stripping away the superfluous." — COCTEAU: "Carte Blanche," *Le Rappel à l'Ordre.*

"To describe a dreadnought is no more new than to describe a galley. What is new is that one should feel in the poem the rhythm of a dreadnought, as Racine evokes the pomp of a galley. Onomatopea relegates us to the rank of a parrot — (even that which Marinetti calls 'abstract onomatopea'). A spectacle, a sound, which enters through the eye and the ear, should be subjected, before it reissues by the hand, to profound metamorphoses." — *Ibid.*

6. On Form

"In each era of poetry, outward structure must inevitably undergo a change. In the Augustan age, the outward structure of poetry was the result of logic alone, while variations of speed, the feeling of heat and of cold, the variations of the different depths and heights, were produced by means of texture and were the result of sensibility and of instinct in this matter. Poetry was therefore, in that age, as far as outward structure was concerned, the sister of architecture. With the Romantics and their more poignant vowel-sense, resulting in a different kind of melodic line, poetry became the sister of music. Now she appears like the sister of horticulture — each poem growing according to the laws of its own nature, but in a line which is more often the irregular though entirely natural shape of a tree, — bearing leaves, bearing fruit, — than a sharp melodic line, springing like a fountain." — E. S.: *Aspects of Modern Poetry.*

"The true . . . mistake lies in confounding mechanical regularity with organic form. The form is mechanic, when on any given material we impress a predetermined form, not necessarily arising out of the properties of the material; as when to a mass of wet clay we give whatever shape we wish it to retain when hardened. The organic form, on the other hand, is innate; it shapes, as it develops, itself from within, and the fullness of its development is one and the same with . . . its outward form." — COLERIDGE: *Lectures* (1818).

> For of the soul the body form doth take;
> For soul is form, and doth the body make.
>   — SPENSER: "Hymn in Honour of Beauty"

"To speak . . . with the perfect rectitude and insouciance of the movements of animals, and the unimpeachableness of the sentiment of trees in the woods and grass by the roadside, is the flawless triumph of art. If you have look'd on him who has achieved it, you have look'd on one of the greatest masters of all nations and times. You shall not contemplate the flight of the grey gull across the bay, or the mettlesome action of the blood-horse, or the tall leaning of sunflowers on their stalk, or the appearance of the sun journeying through heaven, or the appearance of the moon afterward, with any more satisfaction than you shall contemplate him." — WHITMAN: Preface to *Leaves of Grass*.

"No work of true genius dares want its appropriate form, neither indeed is there any danger of this. As it must not, so genius cannot, be lawless; for it is ever this that constitutes its genius — the power of acting creatively under laws of its own origination." — COLERIDGE: *Lectures* (1818).

7. On Harmony and Proportion

"The world is made by symmetry and proportion, and is in that respect compared to music, and music to poetry . . . what music can there be where there is no proportion observed?" — T. CAMPION: *Observations on the Art of English Poesie.*

"Harmony itself is a thing of thought." — WAGNER: *Prose Works,* Chapter IV, Part III.

In other words, there must be no division between the thought and the clothing flesh, the harmony. — E. S.

"Harmony and Proportion are Qualities and not Things. The Harmony and Proportion of a Horse are not the same with those of a Bull. Every Thing has its own Harmony and Proportion, Two Inferior Qualities in it. For its Reality is its Imaginative Form." — BLAKE: annotations to Berkeley's *Siris.*

Consider this saying of Blake's, young men. All spiritual Imagination is not fitted for the Harmony and Proportion of a Sonnet.

The swiftness of the Horse is not to be found in the Harmony and Proportion of a Sonnet. — E. S.

8. On Style

"His [Wordsworth's] remark was by far the weightiest thing we ever heard on the subject of style, and it was this: that it is in the highest degree unphilosophic to call language the *dress* of thoughts. . . . He would call it the '*incarnation* of thoughts.' Never in one word was so profound a truth conveyed. . . . And the truth is apparent on consideration: for if language were merely a dress, then you could separate the two; you could lay the thoughts on the left hand, the language on the right. But, generally speaking, you can no more deal thus with poetic thoughts than you can with soul and body. The union is too subtle, the intertexture too ineffable." — DE QUINCEY: *Style.*

". . . Descartes has only ideas, and no visible style. His thought has a skin which clings to the flesh — not a flowered dress. This is equally true of Pascal. Their style is naked, sometimes sweating with fever, yellow from fasting, or suddenly red from the blood that has fled from the heart, leaving it turned to ice. It is naked as a soul." — DE GOURMONT: *Le Problème du Style.*

"The living language of dream, the dead language of awakening. We need an interpreter, a translator." — COCTEAU: *Opium.* Trans. Ernest Boyd.

9. On Technical Experiments

". . . every great poet must inevitably innovate upon the example of his predecessors in the exact structure of his peculiar versification." — SHELLEY: *A Defence of Poetry.*

Many and varied are the experimental inquiries made by modern poets into the effect on rhythm, and on speed, of the use of rhymes, assonances, and dissonances, placed outwardly, at different places in the line, in most elaborate patterns: and the effect on speed of equivalent syllables, that system which produces almost more variation than any other device.

On Technical Matters

The rhythm and speed of a skillful unrhymed poem differ from the rhythm and speed of a rhymed poem containing the same number of feet, — and both the rhymed and the unrhymed poem differ slightly in rhythm and speed from a poem ending with assonances or dissonances, but containing the same number of feet. Again, assonances and dissonances put at different places within the lines and intermingled with equally skillfully placed internal rhymes, have an immense effect upon rhythm and speed; and their effect on rhyme, and sometimes, but not always, upon speed, is different from that of lines containing elaborately schemed internal rhymes without assonances or dissonances. — E. S.

* * *

How slight, how subtle, are the changes in speed or of depth in English poetry, due to the fact that the English, in their cunning over the matter of poetry, have adopted the system of equivalence. For is it really to be supposed that two words of one syllable each, equal in speed one word of two syllables? The two-syllabled words, if unweighted by heavy consonants, move far more quickly. The system, therefore, of equivalent syllables gives variation. — E. S.: *Alexander Pope.*

Sometimes, in the actual texture, subtle variations of thickness and thinness (and consequently of darkness or faint shadow) are brought about in assonances and rhymes by the changing of a consonant or labial, from word to word.

This change from thickness to thinness can actually affect, very faintly and subtly, rhythm and speed.

I have made innumerable experiments of each of the above kinds. Indeed, my verses *Façade* and certain other poems are, in a very great many cases, experiments of these orders. — E. S.

It must not be thought, however, that all matters of form derived from texture are superimposed, — are planned or deliberated by the poet: they are the result of instinct, and arise from the necessities of the material. — E. S.

Schopenhauer, in *The World as Will and Idea*, wrote: "[Nature] accomplishes that which appears so designed and planned, without reflection and without conception of an end. . . . The six equal radii of a snowflake, separating at equal angles, are measured beforehand by no knowledge; but it is the simple tendency of the original Will, which exhibits itself to knowledge when knowledge appears."

The poet accomplishes his design instinctively, but at the same time with knowledge. In him, knowledge has become instinct, and during the conception of the poem, knowledge works in him as if it were nature alone.

When the work is almost completed, when the inspiration has pronounced its will, then, and only then, does the knowledge become conscious knowledge once again.

The difference between the poet and the person who is not a poet, although he may (and no doubt does) write reams of verse, lies partly in the fact that the poet has this instinctive knowledge. — E. S.

10. On Free Verse

Orlando Gibbons, the composer, in a dedicatory address to Sir Christopher Hatton the younger, wrote, "It is Proportion that beautifies everything."

This should be remembered. — E. S.

Rhythm has been defined as "Melody stripped of its pitch."

"The Impressionist school substitutes sunshine for light, and sonority for rhythm." — COCTEAU: "Le Coq et l'Arlequin," *Le Rappel à l'Ordre*.

[190]

On Technical Matters

Free Verse does not substitute sunshine for light, but it does, to a certain degree, substitute sonority for rhythm. — E. S.

Wagner wrote of Palestrina (*Beethoven*), "Here rhythm is only perceptible through changes in the harmonic succession of chords, while apart from these it does not exist at all as a symmetrical division of time. Here the successions in time (*Zeitfolge*) are so immediately connected with the essential nature of harmony, which is itself connected with time and space, that the laws of time cannot aid us to understand such music. The sole succession of time in music of this description is hardly otherwise apparent than in exceedingly delicate changes of the same fundamental colour, which changes retain their connection through the most varied transitions, without our being able to trace any direct drawing of lines."

Is not this applicable to some of the verse of our time, — verse in which the shaping is not architectural, but is the result of the inward movement brought about by the texture, and particularly by the vowels . . . i.e. the "exceedingly delicate changes of some fundamental colour"? — E. S.

Swinburne, writing of Rossetti (*Essays and Studies*), said that his line was "as sinuous as water or as light, flexible and penetrative, delicate and rapid; it works on its way without halt, or jolt or collapse."

Should this not be true of the line in Free Verse? — E. S.

Free Verse should have "an astonishing sense of linear rhythm, a rhythm which is . . . extremely elastic, that is to say it is capable of extraordinary variations from the norm without loss of continuity. . . . Imagine the rhythm rendered the least bit tight and mechanical in its regularity, and

[191]

the whole system . . . would break down." — ROGER FRY:
Matisse.

Young men, beware. Whitman described himself as "apparently lawless; but on closer examination a certain regularity appears, like the recurrence of lesser and larger waves on the sea-shore, rolling without intermission, and fitfully rising and falling." — WHITMAN: *Notebooks.*

I would like a strong and lovely movement — a movement belonging to the morning, the rush onward of

Horses, young horses, and the waves of the sea.

I do not know who wrote that wonderful phrase, nor where I found it. — E. S.

11. On Rhyme

"The profit of Rhyme is that it drops seeds of a sweeter and more luxuriant rhyme, and of uniformity that it conveys itself into its own roots in the ground out of sight. The rhyme and uniformity of perfect poems show the free growth of metrical laws, and bud from them as unerringly and loosely as lilacs or roses on a bush, and take shapes as compact as the shapes of chestnuts and oranges, and melons and pears, and shed the perfume impalpable to form." — WHITMAN: Preface to *Leaves of Grass.*

". . . the accident of a rhyme calls forth a system from the shadow." — H. POINCARÉ, quoted by COCTEAU: "Le Secret Professionnel," *Le Rappel à l'Ordre.*
And a whole planetary system. — E. S.

12. On the Sonnet

"The irregular in the regular, the lack of correspondence in symmetry — what could be more illogical or more thwarting? Every infraction of the rule disturbs us like a false or doubtful note in music. The Sonnet is a sort of poetic fugue of which the theme should pass and repass until it is resolved according to its determined form. We must, therefore, submit ourselves absolutely to the laws of the Sonnet, or else, if we find those laws superannuated, pedantic, and restricting, abandon the writing of Sonnets." — THÉOPHILE GAUTIER: "Charles Baudelaire" — attached as a Preface to Baudelaire's *Les Fleurs du Mal*.

"False or doubtful note?" Gautier was not decrying strangeness, or the use of the unexpected sound by a musician. He was speaking of the false note played by the amateur in music. — E. S.

IV. Some Necessities of Poetry

"The hero is he who is immovably centred" (Emerson, quoted by Baudelaire, in *The Work and Life of Eugène Delacroix*). "This," says Baudelaire, "can equally be applied to the domain of poetry and art. The literary hero — that is to say the true writer, is he who is immovably centred. . . . It is not surprising, then, that Delacroix has a very pronounced sympathy for those writers who are concise and concentrated, those whose prose, laden with but few ornaments, has the air of imitating the rapid movements of thought, and whose phrase resembles a gesture."

"That which marks most visibly the style of Delacroix, is the conciseness, and a species of intensity without ostentation, the result of the habitual concentration of all his spiritual forces upon a given point." — BAUDELAIRE: *Ibid.*

"It is . . . a metre-making argument that makes a poem, — a thought so passionate and alive that, like the spirit of a plant or an animal, it has an architecture of its own, and adorns nature with a new thing." — EMERSON: "The Poet," *Essays.*

Blake said: "A Spirit and a Vision are not, as the modern philosophy supposes, a cloudy vapour or a nothing: they are organised and minutely articulated beyond all that the mortal and perishing nature can produce. He who does not imagine in stronger and better lineaments, and in stronger and better light than his perishing and mortal eye can see, does not imagine at all." — BLAKE: *Descriptive Catalogue.*

"Perhaps the efforts of the true poets, founders, religions, literatures, in all ages, have been, and always will be, essentially the same — to bring people back from their persistent strayings and sickly abstractions, to the costless, average, divine, original concrete." — WALT WHITMAN.

"J'ai breuvé mon sang," wrote Rimbaud. And Nietzsche: "Of all writings I love only those which the writer writeth with his blood. Write in blood, and thou shalt learn that blood is spirit."

Poetry must be "full of strong sensual germs." — WALT WHITMAN.

. . . "The problem of essence must take precedence of all others. . . . Moses, Jesus, work directly in this problem." — EMERSON.

"Activity flows from essence. . . . Heat comes from fire: No fire, no heat." — MEISTER ECKHART: Sermon XXXVII. Trans. C. de B. Evans. (See page 181.)

"The infusion of the Holy Ghost into the Apostles at Pentecost was with fire . . . for then does God truly shine to us." — JOHN DONNE: Sermon CLIV.

SOCRATES: There is fire within us, and in the universe.
PROTARCHUS: True.
SOCRATES: And is not our fire small and weak and mean?

But the fire in the universe is wonderful in quantity and in beauty, and in power that fire has.

PROTARCHUS: Most true.

SOCRATES: And is the fire in the universe nourished and generated and ruled by the fire in you and me, or is the fire in you and me, and in other animals, dependent on the universal fire?

PROTARCHUS: That is a question which does not deserve an answer. — PLATO: *Philebus Dialogue.*

V. On Morality in Poetry

". . . We shall find a mere philosophy of morals without explanation of nature, such as Socrates wished to introduce . . . analogous to melody without harmony, which Rousseau desired exclusively; and contrariwise, mere Physics and Metaphysics without Ethics would be equivalent to harmony without melody." — SCHOPENHAUER: "On the Metaphysics of Music," quoted in Wagner's *Beethoven*. Trans. E. Dannreuther.

Never was a more valuable statement made. In addition to this harmony and melody, we need, as Emerson said ("Uses of Great Men," *Representative Men*), "fire enough to fuse the mountain of ore." — E. S.

VI. On Simplicity

"As a man raises himself towards Heaven, so his view of the spiritual world becomes simplified and his words fewer." — DIONYSIUS THE AREOPAGITE: *Mystical Theology*.

The best poetry of our time, although it is held to be of an extreme complication, has actually attained to a new kind of simplicity and compression. That so much of a varying character should be compressed into a line is startling, because it involves the fusion of exceedingly complicated cross-currents and cross-lights into an element.

It is only by attaining to this fusion, that poetry becomes "the voice of the world." — E. S.

To attain to this simplicity, involves the problem of *becoming* our subject. — E. S. "Everything that is not believed remains decorative." — COCTEAU: *Opium*. Trans. Ernest Boyd. "It is a question of the painter who likes to paint trees becoming a tree." — EMERSON, quoted by COCTEAU: in *Opium*. Trans. Ernest Boyd.

"The Beautiful is invariably of a double composition, in spite of the fact that the impression it makes is single; for the difficulty of discerning the varying elements of beauty in the unity of the impression, in no way invalidates the need for variety in the composition. The Beautiful is composed of an eternal, invariable element, of a quantity difficult to deter-

[198]

mine, and of a relative, circumstantial element, which may be the epoch, the mode, ethics, or passion (either alternatively, or together). Without this second element . . . the first element would be indigestible, unappreciable, not adapted or appropriate to human nature." — BAUDELAIRE: *L'Art Romantique.*

"What is style? For many people, a very complicated way of saying very simple things. According to us, a very simple way of saying very complicated things." — COCTEAU: "Le Secret Professionnel," *Le Rappel à l'Ordre.*

"Satie invents a new simplicity. The transparent air undresses the lines. Pain does not grimace." — COCTEAU: "Carte Blanche," *Le Rappel à l'Ordre.*

"A true poet does not trouble about the poetical. In the same way as a horticulturist does not scent his roses. He makes them follow a system that perfects their cheeks and their breath." — COCTEAU: "Le Secret Professionnel," *Le Rappel à l'Ordre.*

"Simplicity changes sides. That which is simple, is the mass, the unformed. That which is composed, is the element.
"The elementary form reveals itself as polymorphous and iridescent.
"Often unity scintillates." — GASTON BACHELARD: "Irrationalism," appeared in the review *Minotaure.*

"One need only look closely at a drawing by Ingres, to see that it sparkles with little touches, chips from the spiritual mine. Yet they speak of Ingres as if they were seeing a pure

line." — COCTEAU: "Le Coq et l'Arlequin," *Le Rappel à l'Ordre.*
Simplicity is not paucity. — E. S.

"The Greek temple is beautiful because taste has banished from it the superfluous. The sky-scraper is beautiful because utility has banished from it the superfluous. These beauties are antipodal, but the antipodes resemble each other." — COCTEAU: "Carte Blanche," *Le Rappel à l'Ordre.*

"Machinery and American sky-scrapers resemble Greek Art, in the sense that utility bestows on them a dryness and a grandeur deprived of the superfluous. But that is not art. The rôle of art is to seize the sense of the epoch and extract from the contemplation of this practical aridity an antidote to the beauty of the useless, which encourages superfluity." — *Ibid.*

A valuable example of modern simplicity and compression occurs in the scene in Cocteau's *Orphée,* in which Orpheus and Eurydice have returned from Hades. This scene, however, is in prose, not verse:

EURYDICE: If you knew how unimportant are these "histoires" — [scenes about? stories about? — the word can mean either. — E. S.] the moon and the sun.
ORPHEUS: Madame is above such things.
EURYDICE: If I could only speak . . .

VII. On the Senses

"The Four Senses are the Four Faces of Man & the Four Rivers of the Water of Life." — BLAKE: annotations to Berkeley's *Siris*.

The poet's mind has become a central sense, interpreting and controlling the other five senses; for we have rediscovered the truth uttered by Blake, that "Man has no Body distinct from his soul, for that called Body is a portion of Soul discern'd by the five Senses, the chief inlets of Soul in this age." — BLAKE: *Marriage of Heaven and Hell*.

"By the very right of your senses you enjoy the world. Is not the beauty of the Hemisphere present to your eye? Doth not the glory of the Sun pay tribute to your sight? Is not the vision of the world an amiable thing? Do not the stars shed influences to perfect the Air? . . . Prize these first, and you shall enjoy the residues: Glory, Dominion, Power, Wisdom, Honour, Angels, Souls, Kingdoms. . . ." — TRAHERNE: *Centuries of Meditation*.

". . . it is asserted, that God invented and bestowed sight on us for this purpose, that, on surveying the circles of intelligence in the heavens, we might properly employ those of our own minds, which, though disturbed when compared with the others that are uniform, are still allied to their circulations; and that, having thus learned, and being naturally possessed of a correct reasoning faculty, — we might, by imitating the uniform revolutions of divinity, set right our own wanderings and blunders." — PLATO: *Timaeus*.

"By experiments of Sense we become acquainted with the lower faculties of the Soul, and from them, whether by a gradual evolution or ascent, we arrive at the highest." — BERKELEY: *Siris;* quoted by BLAKE: *Marginalia*.

"The inmost kernel of all genuine and actual knowledge is a perception; and every new truth is the profit or gain yielded by a perception. . . . Merely abstract thoughts, which have no kernel of perception, are the cloud-structures, without reality.

"Wisdom and genius, those two summits of the Parnassus of human knowledge, have their foundation not in the abstract and discursive, but in the perceptive faculty; Wisdom proper is something intuitive, not something abstract. It does not consist in principles and thoughts which one can carry about ready in his mind." — SCHOPENHAUER: *The World as Will and Idea*. Trans. R. B. Haldane and J. Kemp.

"Helvétius forced on Rimbaud the conception of the mind as the product of the senses, which, to one of such sensual activity as Rimbaud, gave great comfort. Even Memory, Helvétius demonstrated, is simply a continuation of sensation, weakened but conserved, so that the mind, whether in itself it be material or not, is completely the product of the nervous sensibility.

"One of the examples chosen by Helvétius to illustrate his theory is the low mentality of animals such as the horse. The extremities of these creatures, their hoofs, are covered with insensitive horn, and if we consider how much knowledge we owe to the delicacy of our hands, the reasoning of Helvétius appears most plausible. This, I imagine, was the starting point of Helvétius' reasoning: 'Let us refine our fingers, that is *all* our points of contact with the external world, and our minds will become proportionally superior to those of ordinary men, as theirs are now to horses.' " — EDGELL RICKWARD: *Rimbaud: The Boy and the Poet.*

"The poet makes himself a seer by a long, immense, and reasoned unruliness of all his senses." — RIMBAUD: Letter to Delahaye, 1872.

This is only true of a certain kind of poetry. But it is true that where the language of one sense is insufficient, we use that appertaining to another. — E. S.

VIII. On Over-Civilization

"We have just passed through a long period of error in art, caused by the knowledge of physical and mechanical chemistry, and by the study of nature. Artists having lost their savagery, and no longer able to rely upon instinct, one might better say imagination, have strayed off on so many different paths to find the productive elements they no longer have the strength to create; and now they cannot work except in disorderly crowds, feeling frightened, almost lost, if left to themselves." — GAUGUIN: *Letters*. Trans. Ruth Pielkova.

"I have found that in the composition of the human body as compared with the bodies of animals, the organs of sense are duller and coarser. Thus it is composed of less ingenuous instruments, and of spaces less capacious for receiving the faculties of sense. I have seen in the Lion Tribe that the sense of smell is connected with part of the substance of the brain which comes down from the nostrils." — LEONARDO DA VINCI: *Notebooks*.

"The eyes in the Lion Tribe have a larger part of the head for their sockets, and the optic nerves communicate at once with the brain; but the contrary is to be seen in Man, for the sockets of the eyes are but a small part of the head, and the optic nerves are very fine and long." — *Ibid*.

We must have the eyes, the nose, of the Lion, the Lion's acuity of sense, and with these, the Sun of Man's reason.

On Over-Civilization

Remember the "animal full of genius," of whom Baudelaire wrote. (See page 159.) — E. S.

". . . of this great personage Pan we have a very particular description in the ancient writers, who unanimously agree to represent him . . . hairy all over, half a man and half a beast. . . .

"Since the chief thing to which he applied himself was the civilising of mankind . . . it should seem that the first principle of science must be received from that nation to which the gods were by Homer said to resort twelve days every year for the conversation of its wise and just inhabitants." — MARTIN SCRIBLERUS: *On the Origin of Sciences.*

". . . In all the western parts of the world there was a great and memorable era in which they [the beast-philosophers] began to be silent. . . . Men's heads became too much puzzled to receive the simpler wisdom of these ancient Sylvans." — *Ibid.*

IX. On the Need for the Refreshing of the Language

"Their [the poets'] language is vitally metaphorical; that is, it marks the before unapprehended relations of things and perpetuates their apprehension, until the words which represent them become, through time, signs for portions or classes of thoughts instead of pictures of integral thoughts; and then if no new poets should arise to create afresh the associations which have been thus disorganised, language will be dead to all the nobler purposes of human intercourse. These similitudes or relations are finely said by Lord Bacon to be 'the same footsteps of nature impressed upon the various subjects of the world' (*De Augment. Scient.* Cap. I. Lib. III) — and he considers the faculty which perceives them as the storehouse of axioms common to all knowledge." — SHELLEY: *A Defence of Poetry.*

"We need a language fann'd by the breath of Nature, which leaps overhead, cares mostly for impetus and effects, and for what it plants and invigorates to grow." — WALT WHITMAN: *Democratic Vistas.*

X. On the Poet's Labor

Prayer is the Study of Art,
Praise is the Practice of Art.

— BLAKE: sentences engraved above the plate of the Laocoön
Group.

XI. On Imagery in Poetry

"The rise, the setting of imagery, should, like the sun, come natural to him [the reader], shine over him, and set soberly, although in magnificence, leaving him in the luxury of twilight." — KEATS: *Letters.*

". . . those ornaments can be allowed that conform to the perfect facts of the open air, and that flow out of the nature of the work, and come irrepressibly from it, and are necessary to the completion of the work." — WHITMAN: Preface to *Leaves of Grass.*

(After a comparison of poetry to a ship, and poets to a mariner) ". . . some, to goe the lighter away, will take in their fraught of spangled feathers, golden Peebles, Straw, Reedes, Bulrushes or anything, and then they heave out their sayles as proudly as if they were balisted with Bulbeefe." — THOMAS NASHE: Preface to the first quarto edition (1591) of Sidney's *Astrophel and Stella.*

XII. *On the Poet, the Natural World, and Inspiration*

"The Heat, Light, and Atmospheres of the Natural World only open Seeds . . . but this not by Powers derived from their own Sun . . . but by Powers from the spiritual Sun . . . for the image of Creation is Spiritual; nevertheless, that it may appear, and furnish Use in the natural world . . . it must be clothed in Matter." — SWEDENBORG: *Wisdom of Angels Concerning Divine Love and Divine Wisdom:* quoted in Blake's *Marginalia.*

"Often before dawn," said Goethe, "I am awake, and lie down by the open window to enjoy the splendour of the three planets at present visible together, and to refresh myself with the increasing brilliance of the morning-red. I then pass almost the whole day in the open air, and hold spiritual communion with the tendrils of the vine, which say good things to me, and of which I could tell you wonders." — *Conversations of Goethe with Eckermann.*

"When I see where the east is greater than the west . . . or a father is more needful than a mother to produce me — then I guess I shall see how spirit is greater than matter." — WHITMAN: *Notebooks.*

"The soul or spirit transcends itself into all matter, — into rocks, and can live the life of a rock — into the sea, and can

[209]

feel itself the sea . . . into the earth — into the motions of the suns and stars.

"Never speak of the soul as anything but intrinsically great. The effusion or corporation of the soul is always under the beautiful laws of physiology." — *Ibid.*

"The sap in the tree denoteth pure Deity." — JAKOB BOEHME: *The Aurora.*

XIII. *On the Power of Words*

"I am not yet so lost in lexicography, as to forget that words are the daughters of earth, and that things are the sons of heaven." — DR. JOHNSON: Preface to *Dictionary of the English Language.*

William Rossetti, in his Foreword to Whitman's *Leaves of Grass,* says: "Whitman's language has a certain ultimate quality."

It is this "ultimate quality" in language, — and "speech above a mortal mouth," to quote from Ben Jonson's *Discoveries* — that is needed in the poetry of to-day. — E. S.

". . . The grammar, the arid grammar itself, becomes something like an evoked sorcery, the words are alive again in flesh and in blood, the substantive, in its substantial majesty, the adjective, a transparent vestment that clothes and colours it . . . and the verb, angel of movement." — BAUDELAIRE: *Les Paradis Artificiels.* Trans. and quoted by Arthur Symons.

Furious old lady, complaining of my own poems: "Words, Words, nothing but Words."

Not *only* words, my dear lady. Yet see what only words will do for us. Compare these lines,

> And we'll gang nae mair a-rovin,
>   A rovin in the nicht,

from "The Jolly Beggar," by James V of Scotland, and the final lines of Byron's "So we'll go no more a-roving," a poem that begins with lines which are almost those of King James, but ends with

> Yet we'll go no more a-roving
> By the light of the moon.

— E. S.

The Poet and His Audience

"Devant plusiers hommes, je causai tout haut avec un moment de leurs autres vies." — ARTHUR RIMBAUD: *Une Saison en Enfer.*

On Stupidity

"No individual must think himself more brilliant than his fellows. We must have no intellectuals. Each mind is of equal importance." — BERNHARD RUST, Reichsminister of Culture and Education: *Education and Instruction*, quoted in *Our Time*, January 1946.

STRANGER: I do seem to see one very large and bad sort of ignorance which . . . may be weighed in the scale against all other sorts of ignorance put together.
THEATETUS: What is it?
STRANGER: When a person supposes that he knows, and does not know: this appears to be the great source of all the errors of the intellect.
THEATETUS: True.

[212]

On the Power of Words

A certain Dr. F. R. Leavis touches nothing that he does
not adorn. He is delightful, for instance, on the subject of
Milton, whom he decided to "show up" in his magazine
Scrutiny.

Dr. Leavis has "scrutinized" Milton, and has decided that
there is very little there. The sound of a great deal of Milton,
too, affects Dr. Leavis much as the sound of a motor-bicycle
affects my less sensitive nervous system. "We find ourselves
. . . flinching from the foreseen thud that comes so inevitably, and at last, irresistibly; for reading *Paradise Lost*
is a matter of resisting, of standing up against the verse-
movement, of subduing it into something tolerably like sensitiveness, and in the end our resistance is worn down, we
surrender at last to the inexplicable monotony of the ritual."

We are warned, however (for he is scrupulously fair), that
"a writer of Mr. Allen Tate's repute as critic, poet, and intellectual leader" can see something in the poor old gentleman. But then, having from a sense of justice handed Milton
this necessary testimonial we are told that "He exhibits a
feeling for words rather than a capacity for feeling through
words. . . . The extreme and consistent remoteness of Milton's medium from any English that was ever spoken is an
immediately relevant consideration. It became, of course, habitual to him; but habituation could not sensitize a medium
so cut off from speech — speech that belongs to the emotional
and sensory texture of actual living and is in resonance with
the nervous system; it could only confirm an impoverishment
of sensibility."

[213]

"These lines," according to Dr. Leavis, are an "offence."

Thus was the place,
A happy rural seat of various view;
Groves whose rich trees wept odorous Gummes and Balme,
Others whose fruit burnisht with Golden Rinde
Hung amiable, Hesperian fables true,
If true, here onely of delicious taste.

These thunderbolts are followed by a lot of the usual wincing and whimpering about "sensitiveness," and by an analysis of the following passage:

The hasty multitude
Ad*mi*ring enter'd, and the *work* some praise
And *some* the Architect, his *hand* was known
Where Scepter'd *An*gels held their *re*sidence
And *sat* as Princes.

I hasten to add that the stressing is Dr. Leavis's, not mine. The unfortunate thing about his analysis is that it transpires that Dr. Leavis does not hear where the stresses fall. And (which is equally delightful) he does not realize that the passage in question is, *comparatively* speaking, light in texture, and he has therefore chosen it as an example of "thudding." Yet "praise" and "Princes" are the only words beginning with heavy consonants. If there is any "thudding" at all, it is to be found only in the *p* and in the thickness of the *m* in "multitude," and "admiring." As for his interpretation of the stressing, it is sad to see Milton's great lines bobbing up and down in the sandy desert of Dr. Leavis's mind with the grace of a fleet of weary camels. — E. S.

But then, according to the late L. Trotsky: "It is well to have the problems of life ground by the grinders of proletarian thought. The grinders are strong, and will master anything they are given to grind." — L. TROTSKY: *Problems of Life*. Trans. by Z. Venerova.

Misunderstandings

After admiring "the pure realism" of Blake's illustration for "The Tyger," Dante Gabriel Rossetti continued: "Certainly an unaccountable perversity in colour may now and then be apparent, as where . . . the tiger is painted in fantastic streaks of red, green, blue, and yellow, while a tree stem at his side tantalisingly supplies the tint which one might think his due, and is perfect tiger-colour."

Rossetti did not realize that Blake was expressing the oneness of the wild nature of the world. — E. S.

There was, in my youth, a great deal of opposition to the revivification of rhythmic patterns. But we must remember that, in past ages, even the greatest of all rhythmic patterns, those not made by the hand of Man, have been misapprehended. The otherwise great mind of Bishop Burnet, who died in 1715, was so seriously disturbed by the unsymmetrical arrangement of the stars that he rebuked the Creator for His lack of technique. "What a beautiful hemisphere they would have made," he exclaimed, "if they had been placed in rank and order; if they had all been disposed of in regular figures . . . all finished and made up into one fair piece, or great composition, according to the rules of art and symmetry."

We must not complain, therefore, if the patterns in the humble works of Man are not perceived immediately by the unobservant. — E. S.

The Amateur

"Sir George Beaumont found great advantage in learning to draw from Nature through gauze spectacles." — COLERIDGE: *Anima Poetae.*

The amateur invariably softens and blurs. — E. S.

XIV. *On Ben Jonson*

"If," says Professor Saintsbury (*History of Prosody*), "we were playing the old children's game of 'Animal, Vegetable or Mineral' in respect of Jonson's prosody, I should say about his lyrics 'Animal,' and of all but the very highest animation; of his couplets 'Vegetable,' and first-rate Vegetable; but of his blank verse, 'Mineral': weighty, sometimes brilliant, but not alive."

I do not think that all the lyrics of Jonson come under the heading of "Animal"; some, for instance, grow like a flower, from the soil, but with the clear beauty of a flower. "The Sad Shepherd" has a fresh and invigorating, shaggy, forestial roughness, — "hairy" language, as Dante would have said. But Professor Saintsbury's qualifications are useful. — E. S.

XV. On the Augustans

". . . the dry light which did scorch and offend most men's natures." — BACON: *Essays*, quoted by Emerson.

"Architecture . . . [brings to] greater distinctness some of those ideas which are the lowest grade of the objectivity of the Will; such as gravity, cohesion, rigidity, hardness, those universal qualities of stone, those first, simplest, most inarticulate manifestments of Will: the bass notes of Nature." — SCHOPENHAUER: "Architecture." *The World as Will and Idea.*

In this, Augustan poetry, as I have remarked elsewhere, bears a strong resemblance to Architecture; not only because of its rigid outward structure (which contains, however, within the lines, from pole to pole, great variation) — but because the consonantal system, the mass of the planet (see Note on Dunbar), is the base of those inward variations. — E. S.

XVI. On Alexander Pope

1. On His Personal Character

"Of his personal character" (Swinburne, *A Century of English Poetry*) "it is nothing to say that he had the courage of a lion: for a beast's or an athlete's courage must have something of physical force to back it: something of a body to base itself upon: and the spirit which was in Pope, we might say, was almost as good as bodiless. And what a spirit it was! How fiery bright and dauntless!

"We are invited, and not always unreasonably, to condone or palliate much that was unworthy of manhood in Byron, on just and compassionate consideration of the bitter burden attached to his bodily and daily life; but what was his trial and what was his courage to Pope's? how less than little the one, how less than nothing the other! For Byron we should have charity and sympathy: but it rouses the blood, it kindles the heart, to remember what an indomitable force of heroic spirit, and sleepless always as fire, was enclosed in the pitiful body of the misshapen weakling whose whole life was spent in fighting the good fight of sense against folly, of light against darkness, of human speech against brute silence, of truth and reason and manhood against all the banded bestialities. . . ."

2. On the Perfection of Pope

"Whatever Pope has left us is 'as round and smooth as Giotto's O,' whatever Dryden has left us is liable to come short of this especial and surely precious praise. The strength of Dryden never wholly fails him, but the skill of Pope never fails him at all." — SWINBURNE: *Ibid.*

3. On the Work of Pope

Wagner, on the subject of Mozart (*Prose Works*), wrote "with him grey was always grey and red red; only that this grey and this red were equally bathed with the freshening dew of his music, were resolved into all the nuances of the primordial colour, and thus appeared as many-tinted grey, as many-tinted red."

4. On the Technical Side of Pope's Work

Actually melody was absent from the poems of Pope, in spite of their technical splendour and unsurpassed flawlessness, — and this lack is due to their unvaried outward structure. For to produce melody, in spite of the variations caused by texture, those variations are not alone sufficient. We must also have variations in the outward structure; and it was to this that we were restored by Shelley, Blake, and Coleridge.

It must be remembered, however, that melody is not the only technical or oral joy to be gained from poetry. — E. S.

5. On the Heroic Couplet

"The heroic couplet, which is kept strictly within the limits of its outward structure, is yet as variable within those limits as waves, as the air with its light variations of wind, indeed, as variable as the earth itself with its mountains and plains. The reason why, to an insensitive ear, the heroic couplet seems monotonous, is because structure alone, and not texture also, has been regarded as the maker of rhythm." – E. S.: *Alexander Pope.*

6. On Pope's Sense of Texture

"He stated repeatedly that everything he knew about versification he learned from Dryden, and that even at the age of twelve he could distinguish the difference between softness and sweetness in the texture of the several poets; for his feeling for this most important matter of texture was so phenomenally sensitive that had the verses been transformed into flowers, he could have told lily from rose, buttercup from cowslip, in no matter how starless and moonless the night, merely by touching one petal. In these matters, he found Dryden to be softer, Waller sweeter; and that the same difference, the same subtle distinction, separated Ovid from Vergil." – E. S.: *Alexander Pope.*

I presume he was referring to such poems of Dryden's as "Annus Mirabilis" and "Ode to Mrs. Anne Killigrew." He could not, of course, have referred to the satires.

XVII. On Blake

Schopenhauer, in *The World as Will and Idea*, spoke of "the naïveté with which every plant expresses and lays open its whole character in its mere form, reveals its whole being and will. This is why the physiognomy of plants is so interesting. . . . The plant reveals its whole being at the first glance, and with complete innocence. . . . This innocence in the plant results from its complete want of knowledge. . . . Every plant speaks to us, first of all, of its home, of the climate, and the nature of the ground in which it has grown. . . . Besides this, however, every plant expresses the special will of its species, and says something that cannot be uttered in any other tongue."

Blake had the innocence of the flower, but his innocence did not come from ignorance, but from wisdom. The extreme poles, want of knowledge, and wisdom, are alike. — E. S.

"It is the supreme quality of this wisdom that it has never let go of intuition. It is as if intuition itself ripened." — ARTHUR SYMONS: *William Blake*.

"At the birth of Blake — to paraphrase a sentence in Rimbaud's 'Fairy' (*Les Illuminations:* Trans. Helen Rootham), "were present the saps of beauty in the untrodden shadows and the still radiancy of the astral silence." — For his childhood, "the thickets and the deep shadows trembled, the hearts of the poor and the legends of heaven were stirred."

[222]

On Blake

Blake, in a letter to Hayley (27 January 1804), wrote of verses that "still sound upon my ear like the distant approach of things mighty and magnificent, like the sound of harps which I hear before the Sun's rising."

Wonderful — and strange. He was speaking of verses by a poet of little, or no worth. But might he not have been speaking of some of his own verses? Not all: not the *Songs of Innocence*, in which, as Gilchrist wrote in his *Life of William Blake*, we hear "an angelic voice singing to an oaten pipe." — E. S.

Blake, in his own words, "entered into Noah's rainbow, and made a friend and companion of one of those images of wonder. . . ."

"Nothing can withstand the fury of my Course among the Sons of God & in the Abysses of the Accuser." — BLAKE: Letter to Thomas Butts, Jan. 19, 1802.

"The root of all is God. But it is not the way to receive fruits to dig to the root, but to reach to the boughs. I reach for my creation to the Father, for my redemption to the Son, and for my sanctification to the Holy Ghost: and so I make the knowledge of God, a tree of life unto me, and not otherwise." — DONNE: Sermon CIX, preached at Court, April 1629.

Such also was the wisdom of Blake. — E. S.

Blake might have said, with Smart (*Rejoice with the Lamb*), "In my nature I quested for Beauty — but God, God hath sent me to the sea for pearls."

To the salt, the bitter waters of affliction. — E. S.

"In heaven the angels are advancing continually to the springtime of their youth, so that the oldest angel appears the youngest." — SWEDENBORG, quoted by EMERSON: "Swedenborg, or the Mystic," *Representative Men.*

This might have been said of Blake in his old age. — E. S.

XVIII. On Baudelaire

"Happy, happy they that in Hell feel not the world's despite."
— The last words written by Dowland for *Lachrimae, or Seven Teares, figured in Seven Passionate Pavanes.*

"Could we not believe ourselves in Palmyra unruined. . . ."
— THÉOPHILE GAUTIER: "Charles Baudelaire" (attached as a Preface to *Les Fleurs du Mal*).
"Intact" was the word in French — it seems unsuitable in English. — E. S.

"A profound light that the ear fathoms without fatigue
. . ." (a work of art) "vegetable and architectural as a banana-tree of Rio." — COCTEAU, writing of a work by Milhaud: "Carte Blanche," *Le Rappel à l'Ordre.*
This saying of Monsieur Cocteau's might equally apply to certain words of Baudelaire's, although Milhaud's music would seem to bear no relation to Baudelaire's strange spirit. — E. S.

". . . I was once told by a near relative of mine, that having in her childhood fallen into a river, and being on the very verge of death . . . she saw in a moment her whole life, clothed in its forgotten incidents, arrayed before her . . . not successively, but simultaneously; and she had a faculty developed as suddenly for comprehending the whole and every part." — DE QUINCEY: *Confessions of an English Opium-Eater.*

It is this simultaneity, a kind of water-clearness (into which he fell as into a river) on the verge of death, to which Baudelaire has attained. — E. S.

"This poet . . . loved what one wrongly calls the style of decadence, which is no other thing than the arrival of art at this extreme point of maturity that determined in their oblique suns the civilisations that aged; a style ingenious, complicated, learned, full of shades and of rarities, turning for ever backward the limits of the language, using technical vocabularies, taking colour from all the palettes, notes from all the keyboards. . . . In regard to his verse there is the language already veined in the greenness of decomposition, the tainted language of the later Roman Empire, and the complicated refinements of the Byzantine School, the last form of Greek Art fallen in delinquencies.' " — THÉOPHILE GAUTIER: *Charles Baudelaire*. Quoted and translated by Arthur Symons in *Baudelaire, a Study*.

"Polysyllabic and ample-sounding words are pleasing to Baudelaire, and with three or four of these words, he often makes verses which seem immense and in which these vibrating sounds prolong the measure." — THÉOPHILE GAUTIER: *Charles Baudelaire*. Trans. E. S.

His "great Alexandrines . . . come, in a time of calm, to die on the shore with the tranquil and profound undulation of the wave arriving from the open sea." — *Ibid*.

XIX. *On Verlaine*

"Sometimes in a kind of melting jargon of the countryside, he spoke of death which brings repentance, of the unhappy, of painful labours, of partings that rend the heart. In the hovels where we used to get drunk he wept while he contemplated those who surrounded us, Poverty's cattle. He raised up drunkards in the foul streets. He had the compassion of a wicked mother for little children." — ARTHUR RIMBAUD: *A Season in Hell*. Trans. Helen Rootham.

"I felt an extreme pleasure this morning, on seeing again a little picture of mine. There was nothing in it, but it was charming and seemed as if it had been painted by a bird." — Letter from COROT, quoted in *Opium*, by Jean Cocteau. Trans. Ernest Boyd.

The following would be true of Verlaine, were he spiritually evil, instead of pure:
"Only a bird could trust itself to paint the Profanation of the Host. Only a bird could be pure enough, selfish enough, cruel enough." — JEAN COCTEAU: *Opium*. Trans. Ernest Boyd.

On Certain Poems of Verlaine

"I know several sculptures of Giacometti which are so solid, so light, that they look like snow on which a bird has left its footmarks." — *Ibid*.

[227]

". . . aspects of people and things in which a butterfly seems to have left a little of its coloured dust as it alights and pauses." — ARTHUR SYMONS on Whistler: *Studies in Seven Arts.*

". . . They have their brief coloured life like butterflies, and with the same momentary perfection." — ARTHUR SYMONS on Whistler and Verlaine: *Ibid.*

"A white which is like the soul of a colour caught and fixed there by some incalculable but precisely coloured magic. It ends, of course, by being the ghost of a colour . . . but all things end, when their particular life is over, by becoming the ghost of themselves." — ARTHUR SYMONS on Whistler: *Ibid.*

Dr. D. S. MacColl, in his *19th Century Painting*, said of Manet that his mind is "that joyful, heedless mind of summer, beneath or above thought, the intense sensation of life, with its lights and colours, coming and going in the head."

"Words serve him with so absolute a negation that he can write *Romances sans Paroles* — songs almost without words, in which scarcely a sense of the interference of human speech remains." — ARTHUR SYMONS: *The Symbolist Movement in French Literature.*

"He created in verse a new voice for nature, full of the humble ecstasy with which he saw, listened and accepted . . . and with the same attentive simplicity with which he found words for the sensations of hearing and the sensations of sight, he found words for the sensations of the soul, for the fine shades of feeling. . . . Here . . . are words which startle one by their delicate resemblance to thoughts, by their winged flight from so far, by their alighting so close." — *Ibid.*

XX. *On Chaucer*

Blake said of Chaucer (*Descriptive Catalogue*): "as Newton numbered the stars, and as Linnaeus numbered the plants, so Chaucer numbered the classes of men."

*   *   *

Swinburne wrote of Ariosto that he "threw across the windy sea of glittering legend and fluctuant romance the broad summer lightnings of his large and jocund genius."

This might, in one sense, have been said equally of Chaucer, were it not that his movements are neither sharp, like those of lightning, nor fluctuant, like those of a sea.

Those fresh and shining poems *The Canterbury Tales* have a curiously strong and resilient line, an urgent life. Their strength is of nature, and the will which is in them, and which forms their purpose and guides their direction, is instinctive. Close to the earth as are these poems, often the strength and movement of the lines, for all the warmth and humanity in them, are like the strength and movement of a slow plant life.

Sometimes the line is divided by a pause that is both long and deep, but the two halves divided by the pause have a movement and impetus of a peculiar strength, and this is not the rushing, tumultuous swelling movement of the march of waves (for it is often slow, and it has more direction than that of waves); it has, rather, the inevitability and urgency of sap rising in a plant. At moments the growth is horizontal, its urgency keeps close to the earth, as with a melon (because the vowels are equal in length, in height, or in depth), — but more often, owing to a rising system of sharp vowels, it springs into the air, like sap rising in a tree.

A beautiful example of the first kind is the following song of Troilus, — "If no love is, O God, what fele I so?" — where some, but not all, the lines are divided — in this case after the fourth syllable — by a stretching pause. The line then continues in its resistless way, in its plant-life (though, like the plant, it has its variations of leaves and flowers), — the other lines being undivided. — The levels of the earth are different, however, in the lines, and are sometimes uneven. Sometimes the vowels rise, and fall again; yet the lines stretch onwards, they do not soar.

> If no love is, O God, what fele I so?
> And if love is, what thing and which is he?
> If love be good, from whennes cometh my wo?
> If it be wikke, a wonder thynketh me,
> When every torment and adversite
> That cometh of him, may to me savory thinke;
> For ay thurst I, the more that ich it drinke.
>
> And if that at myn owen lust I brenne,
> Fro whennes cometh my wailing and my pleynte?
> If harm agree me, where-to pleyne I thenne?
> I noot, ne why unwery that I feynte.
> O quike deth, O swete harm so queynte,
> How may of the in me swich quantite,
> But if that I consente that it be?
>
> And if that I consente, I wrongfully
> Compleyne, y-wis; thus possed to and fro,
> Al stereless with-inne a boot am I
> Aymdde the see, by-tuixen wyndes two,
> That in contrarie stonden evere-mo.
> Alas! what is this wonder maladye?
> For hete of cold, for cold of hete, I dye.

On Chaucer

The assonances, dissonances, and alliterations have much effect here, — "whennes," "wikke," "wonder," — "thynketh" echoing "wikke"; — the change, in the second verse, from "myn" to "pleyne," and the dulling from "pleyne" to "thenne"; the echo of "wailing" and "pleynte" — the first being long yet broken, the second dying away at once.

An example of the second kind (the line whose impetus, owing to its vowel system, rises with a strong sharp strength) is the following magnificent line:

> The mighty tresses in hir sonnish heres.

— I know, and have been reminded of the fact by correspondents, that the *o* in "sonnish" was usually pronounced as the letter *u* is now pronounced in German. But variations were in use in the time of Chaucer, and I think that here is a case. If, then, "sonnish" was pronounced as we now pronounce the word "sun," each accented vowel-sound rises, sharply, after the other, springing upward. In this line, incidentally, there is no pause. Air, however, plays around the line, owing to the long vowels; it has not, therefore, as have many pauseless lines, a huddled quality.

Much of the variation in sound of this wonderful poetry is due (as I have said already) to the fact that some lines are divided sharply in two by a deep pause, whilst at other times there is no pause at all, or else several small pauses. An example is that miracle, the first rondel of "Merciles Beaute" — to me the only perfect rondel in the English language:

> Your eyen two wol slee me sodenly,
> I may the beaute of hem not sustene,
> So woundeth hit through-out my herte kene.
>
> And but your word wol helen hastily
> My hertes wounde, whyl that hit is grene,

Your eyen two wol slee me sodenly,
I may the beaute of hem not sustene.

Upon my trouthe I sey yow feithfully,
That ye ben of my lyf and deeth the quene;
For with my deeth the trouthe shal be sene.
Your eyen two wol slee me sodenly,
I may the beaute of hem not sustene,
So woundeth hit through-out my herte kene.

The English rondel is usually a giggling, trivial horror; but this poem has a most clear, noble, and grave beauty.

Turning from this, let us consider the variations, the peculiar softness and sweetness given by the pauses changing from line to line in number, in length, in depth, — sometimes rising, sometimes stretching faintly outward, sometimes dropping, — and, too, by the faint dissonances of "softe" and "cougheth," and the deeper dissonances of "semysoun" and "honeycomb" in these lines:

And softe he cougheth, with a semysoun:
What do ye, honey-comb, sweete Alisoun,
My faire byyd, my sweete cynamome.

Here the actual texture is affected by the pauses. Part of the beauty is due, also, to the marvelously managed, sweet *s* and *c* sounds, and to the fact that the second syllable of "cynamome," coming after the high-voweled first syllable, has a soft dropping movement.

Was that sweetness and softness the original inspiration, though not the subject, of this wonderful passage in James Joyce's *Ulysses:* "And in New Place a slack dishonoured body that once was comely, as sweet, as fresh, as cinnamon, now her leaves falling, all bare, frighted of the narrow grave and unforgiven"?

Chaucer has been accused, by persons incapable of hearing

subtleties of difference, of a lack of variety. But how great are the differences in these two fragments from "Troilus and Criseyede":

> O sterre, of which I lost have al the light,
> With herte soor wel oughte I to biwaille,
> That evere derk in torment, nyght by nyght,
> Toward my deth with wind in steere I saille;
> For which the tenthe nyght, if that I faille,
> The gydyng of thi bemes bright an houre
> My ship and me Caribdis wol devoure.
>
> This song whan he thus songen hadde, soone
> He fel ayeyn into his sikkes olde.

In this wonderful fragment the vowels that are at once dark and shining, like water seen by clear moonlight (and this is not a matter of association only) — of "sterre," "herte," "derk" — these assonances alternating with the faint cloudiness of the vowels in "deth," "tenthe," — these changing again to the long bright clear vowels of "light," "nyght," "bright" (and these latter are the high points of the scheme), — the handling of these assonances, and the alliterations, give a flawless beauty to the movement.

The consonants are never thick or heavy.

In the "ardent harmony, the heat of spiritual life guiding the movement" of the second fragment quoted below, there is more body. This supreme magnificence is indeed a song of the morning.

PLESAUNCE OF LOVE

> O blissful light, of whiche the bemes clere
> Adorneth all the thridde hevene faire!
> O sonnes lief, O Joves doughter dere,
> Plesaunce of love, O goodly debonaire,
> In gentil hertes ay redy to repaire!

O verray cause of hele and of gladnesse,
I-heried be thy myght and thy goodnesse!

In hevene and helle, in erthe and salte see
Is felt thi myght, if that I wel descerne;
As man, brid, best, fissh, herbe, and grene tree
Thee fele in tymes with vapour eterne.
God loveth, and to love wol nought werne;
And in this world no lyves creature
With-outen love is worth, or may endure.

Ye Joves first to thilke effectes glade,
Thorugh which that thynges liven alle and be,
Comeveden, and amorous him made
On mortal thing, and as yow list, ay ye
Yeve hym in love or adversitee;
And in a thousand formes doun hym sente
For love in erthe, and whom yow liste, he hente.

Ye fierse Mars apeysen of his ire,
And as yow list, ye maken hertes digne;
Algates, hem that ye wol sette a-fyre,
They dreden shame, and vices they resygne;
Ye do hem corteys be, fresshe and benigne,
And hye and lowe, after a wight entendeth,
The joies that he hath, youre myght him sendeth.

Ye holden regne and hous in unitee;
Ye sothfast cause of frendship ben also;
Ye knowe al thilke covered qualitee
Of things which that folk on wondren so,
Whan they can not construe how it may jo,
She loveth him, or whi he loveth here,
As whi this fissh, and nought that cometh to were.
Ye folk a lawe han set in universe;
And this knowe I by hem that lovers be,

On Chaucer

That who-so stryveth with yow hath the werse:
Now, lady bright, for thi benignite,
At reverence of hem that serven the,
Whos clerk I am, so techeth me devyse
Som joye of that is felt in this servyse.

Ye in my naked herte sentement
Inhielde, and do me shewe of thy swetnesse. —
Caliope, thi vois be now present,
For now is nede; sestow not my destresse,
How I mot telle anon-right the gladnesse
Of Troilus, to Venus heryinge?
To which gladnes, who nede hath, God him bringe!

GLOSSARY. — *Hele:* health. *Werne:* refuse. *Thilke:* that same. *Comeveden:* didst instigate. *Yeve:* give. *Hente:* seized. *Algates:* in every way. *Jo:* how it may come about. *Were:* weir. *Inhielde:* pair in.

Chaucer, when he wrote of love, had that "sublimity in tenderness" that Swinburne, with truth, said was the reason of Wordsworth's genius at its highest. Chaucer has also the sublimity in sweetness which Wordsworth had not, and which is one of the rarest of qualities, — yet, although Chaucer had all the lightness and brightness of a fiery spirit as Swinburne said of Nash, he has not, like Wordsworth, seen the Burning Bush.

He is a poet of light. It is interesting to compare the peculiar shining quality of Chaucer with the lucency of Marlowe. The former glitters, like dew upon a forest under the sun. The latter has a still, bright lucency like that upon still water, or a "faint eternal eventide of gems."

Chaucer knew nothing of the black powers that rule the world, or the dark places of the heart. It was to the sweet things of the earth, and "the blisful light," to an earthy God of growing things, that this gentle giant knelt, "with dredful hart and glad devocioun."

[235]

XXI. On Certain Poems by Dunbar, Skelton, Gower, and a Poem by an Anonymous Poet

"Poets," Swinburne said in his *Miscellanies*, may be divided into two exhaustive but not exclusive classes, — "the gods of harmony and creation, the giants of energy and invention."

If this be so, Dunbar, Dryden, and Whitman are the ungod-like giants of our poetry.

The sounds arising from these Titans vary from the hot, earthy sound, the rumbling noise of volcanoes about to burst into flames, of Dryden, to the sonorous and oceanic harmony of certain of Whitman's greatest poems, — or the sound of the huge thundering footsteps of that Blind Harry, William Dunbar.

Sometimes Dunbar is a blinded, blundering, earthy giant, sometimes he has the vastness and strength of a genial, bluster-ing, boisterous north wind, — a geniality that can blacken and turn dangerous. Yet even when he is most windlike, his spirit has at the same time a queerly animal quality, — almost a smell; his genius has a terrible animal force, stinking and rank like that of Swift; but it is for the most part a genial and friendly rankness, unlike that of Swift. This rank darkness and animal stink is present, or can be present, in nearly all genius, but in most, "the angel that stands near the naked man" has inter-fused it with sweetness and light.

[236]

Dryden, to return to him for a moment, is a Cyclops, a giant with one red eye; he is formed of thick earth and of raging fire, but light, apart from the light that comes from that fire, that huge forge of earthy things, is not for him.

But here comes the sound of the tempestuous voice, the huge thundering footsteps of Blind Harry:

> Harry, Harry, hobillschowe!
> Se quha is cummyn nowe,
> Bot I wait nevir howe
>   With the quhorle wynd?
> A soldane owt of Seriand land,
> A gyand strang for to stand,
> That with the strength of my hand
>   Beres may bynd.
>
> Yet I trowe that I vary,
> I am the nakit Blynd Hary,
> That lang has bene in the Fary
>   Farleis to fynd;
>
> And yit gif this be nocht I,
> I wait I am the spreit of Gy;
> Or elkis go by the sky
>   Licht as the lynd.

*   *   *

> Quha is cummyn heir, bot I,
> A bauld bustuous bellamy,
> At your Corss to mak a cry,
>   With a hie sowne.
> Quhilk generit am of gyandes kynd,
> Fra strang Hercules be strynd;
> Of all the occident of Ynd,
>   My eldaris bair the crowne.

[237]

My fore grantschir, hecht Fyn MacKnowle,
That dang the devill and gart him yowle,
The skyis rangd quhen he wald scowle,
    And trublit all the air;
He got my grantschir Gog Magog;
Ay quhen he dansit, the warld wald schog,
Five thousand ellis yeid in his frog
    Of heiland pladdis, and mair.

Yet he was bot of tendir youth;
Bot eftir he grewe mekle at fouth
Ellevyne myle wyde was his mouth,
    His teith was ten myle squwair.
He wald upon his tais stand,
And tak the sternis downe with his hand,
And set them in a gold garland
    Above his wyfis hair.

He had a wyf was lang of clift;
Hir hed wan hier than the lift;
The hevyne rerdit quhen scho wold rift;
    The lass was no thing sklendir:
Scho spittit Lock Lomond with her lippis,
Thunner and fyre-flaucht flewe fra her hippis;
Quhen scho was crabit, the son tholit clippis;
    The fende durst nocht offend hir.

For cald scho tuke the fever tertane;
For all the claith of Fraunce and Brettane,
Wald nocht be till her leg a gartane,
    Thocht scho was ying and tender;

*   *   *

My father, mekle Gow Mackmorne,
Out of that wyfis wame was schorne,
For litilness scho was forlorne,
    Sic a kempe to beir:

[238]

Or he of eld was yeris thre'
He wald step our the Ocean fe',
The Mone sprang never above his kne;
   The hevyn had of him feir.

One thousand yere is past fra mynd
Sen I was generit of his kynd,
Full far among the deserts of Ynde,
   Amang lyoun and beir:
Baith the King Arthur and Gawaine
And mony bauld berne in Brettane,
Ar deid, and in the weris slane,
   Sen I couth weild a speir.

*   *   *

GLOSSARY. — *Farleis:* wonders (?). *Bustuous:* boisterous. *Bellamy:* boon companion. *Strynd:* race, offspring, kindred. *Dang:* knocked out, struck. *Yowle:* scream, howl. *Schog:* shake. *Yeid:* went. *Frog:* coat. *Fouth:* abundance. *Tais:* toes. *Lift:* firmament. *Rift:* belch. *Fyre-flaucht:* lightning, wildfire. *Crabit:* peevish, crabbed. *Berne:* man. *Weris:* wars.

As we have already seen in the Note on Texture (page 178), consonants are organically ingrown with the vowels: consonants "determine the specific nature of the latter's manifestment."

"In the deepest tones of harmony," wrote Schopenhauer, quoted by Wagner in his book on Beethoven, "in the fundamental bass-notes, I recognise the lowest degree of the objectivation of the Will, inorganic nature, the mass of the planet. All the higher tones . . . are to be regarded . . . as the accessory vibrations of the deep fundamental tone, at the sound of which they are always to be heard softly vibrating. . . . This is analogous to the view which requires that all bodies and organisations of nature shall be taken as arising in course of gradual evolution from the mass of the planet: this development is their support as well as their source. . . . Thus the ground bass is to us in harmony, as inorganic nature is to the world, the rudest mass upon which everything rests, and from which everything rises and is developed."

If we apply, as we may do, the above to poetry, we may substitute consonants for the bass-notes, vowels for the higher tones.

Now, it would be impossible to say that the higher tones, the vowels, of the terrific Blind Harry, "can be heard softly vibrating." But certainly the huge consonantal system is "the rude mass of the planet," only endowed with a gigantic Will.

*   *   *

Dunbar's other poems are roared out by a genial, blustering boisterous north wind, caring nothing for smoothness, — invigorating, not appeasing. Sometimes the roughness dies down, and the sound is like that of a stilled cold wind blowing in the branches of a tree heavy with leaves, creaking discordantly in the tree's veins.

Both the girl in Dunbar's "Ane Brash of Wowing" and the girl of Skelton's "Lullay, lullay" are strayed from Fairyland — but how different is the untamed rough vigor of the first from that strange lullaby, blown by a stilled wind out of a cold fairyland beyond our sight, — the fairyland out of which, one day, will drift "La Belle Dame sans Merci."

Dunbar's is a fairyland inhabited by the kind of fairies that colts and calves might see, — and from that land, the cuckoo, the wood grouse, have flown, bringing back a "rubye appil" from the same tree from which Eve had plucked an apple for Adam.

Everything is vaster than real life. The woman in "Ane Brash of Wowing" and the strange lout she is wooing, are giants. He is the naked Blind Harry as he was in youth.

Sometimes the consonants used are slightly rough or hairy, the words have a kind of coltish roughness and uncouthness of surface and movement, and the vowel-sounds change from a cold tunelessness, sharp as the sound of a wind creaking in a tree, to a piercing, harsh, high, inhuman curlew cry, as in

> . . . My clype, my unspaynit jyane

and

> Fow leis me that graceles gane,

which is very strange, contrasted with the wooden clapping sound brought about by the dulled yet hard consonants of "clype" and "gane," and the later "claver" and "curldodie," — and the dulled, closing-in vowels of the following passage:

> Quod he, my claver, and my curldodie,
> My hony soppis, my sweit possodie,
>
> .   .   .   .   .   .
>
> Ye brek my hairt, my bony ane!

ANE BRASH OF WOWING

In secreit place this hyndir nycht
I hard ane beyrne say till ane bricht,
My hunny, my hairt, my houp, my heill,
I haif bene lang your lufar leill,
    And can of yow gett comfort nane;
How lang will ye with denger deill?
    Ye brek my hairt, my bony ane.

*   *   *

"Te he" quod scho, and gaif ane gowf,
Be still my tuchan and my calfe,
My new-spain'd howphyn fra the sowk;
And all the blithnes of my bowk;
My sweit swankyng, saif yow allane
Na leid I luiffit all this owk;
    Fow leis me that graceles gane.

[241]

A Poet's Notebook

Quod he, my claver, and my curldodie,
My hony soppis, my sweit possodie,
By nocht oure bosteous to your billie,
Be warme hartit and nocht illwillie:

. . . . .

    Ye brek my hairt, my bony ane.

Quod scho, my clype, my unspaynit jyane,
With muderis milk yit in your michane,
My belly huddroun, my sweit hurle bawsy,
My huney gukkis, my slawsy gawsy,
    Your musing wald perss ane hairt of stane;
So tak gud confort, my gritheidit slawsy;
    Fow leis me that graceles gane.

Quoth he, my kid, my capirculyoun,
My tender gyrle, my wally gowdy,
My tirly mirly, my crowdy mowdy;

    *   *   *

    Ye brek my hairt, my bony ane.

Quoth scho, Now tak me by the hand,
Wylcum, my golk of maryland,
My chirry and my maikles myneyeoun,
My sowker sweit as ony unyeoun,
    My strummil stirk, yit new to spane,
I am applyid to your opinyoun;
    Fow leis me that graceles gane.

He gaif til hir ane appill ruby;
Grammercy! quod scho, my sweit cowhuby.

    *   *   *

    Fow leis me that graceles gane.

GLOSSARY. — *Hyndir:* last. *Beyrne:* youth. *Ane bricht:* a fair one. *Hunny:* honey. *Houp:* hope. *Heill:* welfare. *Lufar:* lover. *Denger:* disdain. *Howphyn:* dolt. *Bowk:* body. *Curldodie:* ribwort plantain. *Clype:* colt. *Gukkis:* fool. *Golk:* cuckoo. *Maryland:* fairyland. *Chirry:* cherry. *Sowker:* sugar. *Strummil:* stumbling. *Stirk:* Ox. *Spane:* wean. *Cowhuby:* cowherd, or booby. *Gane:* face.

John Skelton's "Lullay, lullay" is one of the most drowsy-sounding poems in our language:

> With Lullay, lullay, like a chylde,
> Thou slepyst to long, thou are begylde.

> My darlyng dere, my daysy floure,
>   Let me, quod he, ly in your lap.
> Ly styll, quod she, my paramoure,
>   Ly styll hardely, and take a nap,
>   Hys bed was hevy, such was his hap,
> All drowsy dremyng, dround in slepe,
> That of his loue he toke no kepe,
>   With hey, lullay.

> With ba, ba, ba, and bas, bas, bas,
>   She cheryshed hym both cheke and chyn,
> That he wyst never wher he was;
>   He had forgotten all dedely syn.
>   He wantyd wyt her love to win.
> He trusted her payment, and lost all hys pray:
> She left hym slepyng, and stole away,
>   With hey, lullay.

> The rivers rowth, the waters wan;
>   She sparyd not to wete her fete;
> She wadyd over, she found a man
>   That halysed her hartely and kyst her swete:
>   Thus after her cold she caught a hete.
> My lefe, she sayd, rowtyth in hys bed;
> I wys he hath an hevy hed
>   With hey, lullay.

> What dremyst thou, drunckard, drowsy pate!
>   Thy lust and lykyng is from thee gone;
> Thou blynkerd blowboll, thow wakyst to late,
>   Behold, thou lyeste, luggard, alone.

[243]

Well may thou sygh, well may thou grone,
To dele with her so cowardly;
I wys, powle hachet, she bleryd thyne eye.
With hey, lullay.

The sleepy movement owes much to the drone-sound of the alliteration. I know no poem to equal it for drowsiness, excepting the lines about the House of Sleep in John Gower's "Ceix and Alcyone" (and of this I will speak later) and the even earlier (fourteenth century) anonymous "Maid of the Mor," [1] which might have been the song of a wandering bee on some sleepy afternoon. It has, indeed, the circling, wandering, returning movements of the bee:

Maiden in the mor lay,
   In the mor lay,
Seuenyst fulle, seuenist fulle,
Maiden in the mor lay,
   In the mor lay
Seuenistes fulle ant a day.

Welle was hire mete;
   Wat was hire mete?
   The primerole ant the, —
The primerole ant the, —
Welle was hire mete;
Wat was hire mete?
   The primerole ant the violet.

Welle (was the hire dryng);
   Wat was hire dryng?
The chelde water of (the) welle-spring.

[1] *Fourteenth Century Verse and Prose*, edited by Kenneth Sisam, Clarendon Press.

Welle was hire bour;
Wat was hire bour?
The rede rose ant te lilie flour.

GLOSSARY. — *Mor:* moor. *Seuenyst:* seven nights. *Hire:* her. *Mete:* meat. *Primerole:* primrose. *Dryng:* drink. *Chelde:* child.

This really is a miracle of poetry, with the change in the vowel sounds of the alliteration, — the darkening from "maiden" to "mor" and the lightening again to the non-alliterative but assonantal "lay," — the change in the second verse from "welle" to "wat" (this latter having less an effect of darkening than of wandering).

The sound produces a strange effect of moving further away at the end of each line, — not dying away exactly, — and then of returning with the beginning of the next line. Perhaps this is because the accent falls on the first syllable in many of the lines.

The slight change in speed (I use this word for want of a better one, since it is a sleepy poem, and yet slowness is not the word either) is due to the pause between the echoes of

Maiden in the mor lay,
In the mor lay

(where the accent, in the two lines, is changed), crossed by the line

Seuenyst fulle, seuenist fulle

— which is faintly quicker, because of the three-syllabled "seuenyst."

* * *

Dionysius the Areopagite, speaking on the Divine Names, said: "All things in motion desire to make known their own proper movement, and this is an aspiration after the Divine Peace of the whole, which, unfalling, preserves all things

[245]

from falling, and, unmoved, guards the idiosyncrasy and life of all moving things, so that the things moved, being at peace among themselves, perform their own proper functions."

John Gower lived but in the light of a mortal day; but Poetry is only another of the Divine Names, and each poet, even if his day is but mortal, is part of the great light. Gower did, though neither a seraph nor an archangel nor a giant, make known the proper movement of his theme, — as in the sleepy sound of these lines from "Ceix and Alcyone":

> This Iris, fro the hihe stage
> Which undertake hath the message
> Hire reyny cope dede upon,
> The which was wonderlie begone
> With colours of diverse hewe,
> An hundred mo then men it knewe;
> The hevene lich into a bowe
> Sche bende, and as sche cam down lowe,
> The God of Slep when that sche fond;
> And that was in a strange lond,
> Which marcheth upon Chymerie:
> For ther, as seith the Poesie,
> The God of Slep hath mad his hous,
> Which of entaille is merveilous.
>   Under an hell there is a cave,
> Which of the sonne mai naught have,
> So that noman mai knowe ariht
> The point between the dai and nyht:
> Ther is no fyr, ther is no sparke,
> Ther is no dore, which mai charke,
> Whereof an ihye scholde unschette,
> So that inward ther is no lette.
> And for to speke of that withoute,
> Ther stan no gret tree nyh aboute
> Wher on ther myhte crowe or pie

Alihte, for to clepe or crie;
Ther is no cok to crowe day,
No beste non which noise may;
The hell bot al aboute round
Ther is gravende upon the ground
Popi, which beith the sed of slep,
With other herbes suche an hep.
A stille water for the nones
Rennende upon the smale stones,
Which hihte of Lethe's the rivere,
Under that hell is such manere
Ther is, which gifth gret appetit
To slepe. And thus full of delit
Slep hath his hous; and of his couch
Withinne his chambre if I schal touche,
Of hebenus that slepi tree
The bordes al aboute be.

GLOSSARY. — *Hihe:* high. *Hire:* her. *Reyny:* rainy. *Lich:* light. *Sche:* she. *Hell:* hall. *Charke:* shut loudly. *Ihye:* eye. *Unschette:* unshut. *Lette:* prevention. *Gravende:* growing. *Rennende:* running. *Hihte:* called, named. *Hebenus:* ebony.

The sleepy sound owes much to the rarity of pauses.

In other poems of Gower's, the shining, glistening quality that was part of the physical and spiritual nature of Chaucer's poetry was present, too, in his contemporary, Gower, though Gower's day was not universal, like Chaucer's, nor was he living in the midst of that day; it was, with him, a lovely memory of youth, — the memory of one hot morning when, like the Orfeo of a still earlier poet,

He might se him bisides
Oft in hot undertides,
The king o' fairy, with his rout
Com to hunt him al about
With dim cri and bloweing
And houndes also with him berking.

[247]

For Gower it was *one* day, never to be lived again, not all days:

> The Flees he tok and goth to Bote,
> The Sonne schyneth bryhte and hote,
> The Flees of Gold schon forth withal,
> The water glistreth overal.
>   Medea wepte and sigheth ofte —
> And stod upon a Tour aloft:
> And prively withinne hirselfe,
> Ther here it nouther ten, ne twelve,
>   Sche preide, and seide "O God him spede,
>   The kniht which hath my maidenheide."
>   And ay sche loketh toward thyle,
>   But whan sche sih withinne a while
>   The Flees glistrende ayein the Sonne,
>   Sche saide "Ha lord, now al is wonne,"
>   Hir kniht the field hath overcome;
>   Hir lord, that he ne were alonde,
>   Bot I dar take this on honde,
>   If that sche hadde wynges two,
>   Sche wolde have flowe with him tho
>   Strawht ther he was in the Bot.

GLOSSARY. — *Ther here it nouther ten, ne twelve:* in other words, she did not heed the passing of time. *Thyle:* the isle. *Alonde:* on the land.

We were to see that sun of youth again, shining like the Golden Fleece, four hundred years later, in certain poems of William Morris.

But to return to John Skelton. Certain of his poems to young girls have the notes we hear in the woods in spring, wild bird-songs, a murmuration of starlings, a watch of nightingales, and a charm of goldfinches. Sometimes they grow sharp as a spring flower, and from the same ground from which sprang this refrain of an Elizabethan song by an anonymous author, rediscovered by Mr. Norman Ault:

> With lily, germander and sops-in-wine,
> With sweet-briar
> And bonfire
> And strawberry wire
> And columbine.

. . . . . .

Never, for a moment, is there heard the voice of a man.

In the lovely "To Maystres Isabell Pennell," after the first three lines, each line is the shape of a honeycomb.

"In the construction," says Mr. Tickner Edwardes in his book on the honey-bee (Methuen), "of the six-sided cell, with its base composed of three rhombs or diamonds, the bee has adapted a form which our greatest arithmeticians admit to be the best possible for her requirements, and she endeavours to keep to this form whenever practicable."

Here, then, is the six-sided cell, with its base composed of six rhombs or diamonds:

> My mayden Isabell,
> Reflaring rosabell,
> The flagrant camamell;
>
> The ruddy rosary,
> The soverayne rosemary,
> The praty strawbery;

. . . . . .

and the "endless welth" of which we hear at the end of the poem, is that which the dusky workers in fields and gardens bring home to their hives when they

> . . . having laboured hard from light to light
> With golden thighes come singing home at night;

and like John Day's bee,

> The windowes of my hive, with blossoms dight,
> Are porters to let in our comfort, light.

"To Maystres Isabell Pennell," as Mr. de la Mare has said in *Come Hither*, "is the loveliest and gayest song of praise and sweetness to 'a young thing' I have ever seen."

> By saynt Mary, my lady,
>   Your mammy and your dady
> Brought forth a godely babi!
>
>   My mayden Isabell,
> Reflaring rosabell,
> The flagrant camamell;
>
>   The ruddy rosary,
> The soverayne rosemary,
> The praty strawbery;
>
>   The columbyne, the nepte,
> The ieloffer well set,
> The propre vyolet;
>
>   Enuwyd your colowre
> Is lyke the dasy flowre
> After the Aprill showre;
>
>   Sterre of the morrow gray,
> The blossom on the spray,
> The fresshest flowre of May;
>
>   Maydenly demure,
> Of womanhode the lure;
> Wherfore I make you sure,

It were an hevenly helth,
It were an endeles welth,
A lyfe for God hymselfe,

To here this nightingale,
Amonge the byrdes smale,
Warbelynge in the vale,

Dug, dug,
Iug, iug,
Good yere and good luk,
With chuk, chuk, chuk, chuk!

In the twist of this poem we have the spring bird's song, and the closely juxtaposed assonances "May" and "Maydenly demure" are round like buds.

"Ieloffer," says Mr. de la Mare in a note upon this poem in *Come Hither,* "gelofer, gelofre, gillofre, gelevor, gillyvor, gillofer, jerefloure, gerraflour — all these are ways of spelling 'gillyflower,' 'gelofre' coming nearest to its original French: 'giroflée,' meaning spiced like the clove.[2] There were of old, I find, three kinds of gillyflowers: the clove, the stock, and the wall. It was the first of these kinds that was meant in the earlier writers by the small clove carnation (or Coronation, because it was made into chaplets or garlands). Its Greek name was dianthus (the flower divine): and its twin sister is the Pink, so called because its edges are pinked, that is, jagged, notched, scalloped. Country names for it are Sweet John, Pagiants, Blunket, and Sops-in-Wine, for it spices what it floats in, and used to be candied for a sweetmeat. Blossoming in July, the gillyflower suggests July-flower, and if Julia is one's sweetheart, it may also be a Julie-flower. So one name may carry many echoes. It has been truly described as a

---

[2] "Gelevor" — a sweet red fire coming after the frost? — E. S.

[251]

gimp and gallant flower, and, says Parkington, who wrote *Paradisus Terrestris*, it was the chiefest of account in Tudor gardens. There was a garden in Westminster in his own time belonging to a Master Ralph Tuggie, famous all London over for the beauty and variety of its gillyflowers: e.g. 'Master Tuggie his Princesse,' 'Master Bradshaw his daintie Ladie,' 'The Red Hulo,' 'The Fair Maid of Kent,' 'Lustie Gallant,' 'The Speckled Tawny,' and 'Ruffling Robin.' "

To these enumerated by Mr. de la Mare, I might add these pinks or carnations that once grew in Master Tuggie's garden, and that I have gathered from my brother Sacheverell Sitwell's book, *Old-fashioned Flowers:* "Master Tuggie his Rose Gillyflower," the "Striped Tawny," the "Flaked," and the "Feathered Tawny," the "Chrystall" or "Chrystalline," the "Red Chrystall," the "Fragrant" and the "Striped Savadge," the "Rose Savadge," the "Greatest Granado," the "Cambersine," the "Bristol Blush," the "Red Dover," the "Queen's Dainty," the "Brazil," the "Turkey . . . ," together with Master Parkinson's "Feathered or Jagged Pinks," "Star Pinks," and "Great Thrifts" — which are called, also, "Sweet Johns" and "Sweet Williams."

The sweet perfume of those pinks remains to us after four centuries. It blows through a later garden:

.　　.　　.　　.　　.　　.

> To smell those odours that do rise
> From out the wealth and spiceries:
> So smels the flowre of blooming Clove,
> Or roses smother'd in the stove:
> So smels the Aire of spicèd wine;
> Or essences of Jessamine:
> So smels the breath about the hives,
> Where wel the work of hony thrives,
> And all the busy Factours come

Laden with wax and hony home;
So smell those neat and woven Bowers
All over-archt with Oringe flowers,
And almond blossoms, that so mix
To make rich those Aromatikes.
So smell those bracelets and those bands
Of Amber chaft between the hands,
When thus embalmed they transpire
A noble perfume from the fire.

. . . . . .

Though here, the perfume is more spiced, and the air in which it lives, less cool.

XXII. On Herrick

The spirit of Herrick might have been the "apparition" seen Anno 1670, near Cirencester, of whom John Aubrey tells us in his *Miscellanies:* "Being demanded whether a good spirit or a bad, returned no answer, but disappeared with a curious perfume and a most melodious Twang. Mr. W. Lilly believes it was a Fairie."

Or again, he could have appeared among those spirits that Mr. Thomas Allen, "in those darke (Elizabethan) times Astrologer, Mathematician, and Conjurer," met "coming up his stairs like bees" (John Aubrey, *Brief Lives*). At other times his spirit resembles those small birds which, according to Antonio Galvano of New Spain, "live of the dew, and the juyce of flowers and roses. Their feathers bee small and of divers colours. They be greatly esteemed to work gold with. They die or sleepe every yeare in the moneth of October, sitting upon a little bough in a warme and close place. They revive or wake againe in the moneth of April after the flowers be sprung."

*   *   *

The poems are as subtle, and as delicate, as the warm airs that awaken those little birds "whose feathers be greatly esteemed to work gold with," — they are faint as the breaths of air and perfume wafting through the branches of the flowering plum, or the stillness of a sweet night.

On Herrick

The night is still,
The darkness knows
How far away
A wavering rill
Of darkness goes;
Though no bough hums,
Between April and May
A streak of plum-blossom comes.

But that exquisite fragment is from a song by Gordon Bottomley, not by Herrick.

In the flawlessly beautiful "Lovers how they come and part," the only emphasis is in the shapes of the pear and plum, the only color that which steals into them:

A Gyges Ring they beare about them still,
To be, and not seen when and where they will.
They tread on clouds, and though they sometimes fall,
They fall like dew, but make no noise at all.
So silently they one to th' other come,
As colours steale into the Peare or Plum,
And Aire-like, leave no pression to be seen
Where e'er they met, or parting place has been.

To these shapes of the fruit the p's give body, — the first shape being longer and more delicate, tapering down from the roundness, through the long double vowels, to the fading r, — the second rounder, and with more body, because of the enclosing pl and m. ". . . So silently," with the alliterative s's, the rising vowels, gives another, but fainter, embodiment, "clouds" melts into "come," "come" fades into "colours." "Peare or Plum" has the faintest echo in the p and the pl of "parting place." There is the slightest possible lengthening of line, — a lengthening so faint as to be hardly perceptible, that comes from the wavering movement of the double-

[255]

voweled "Peare" and "Aire" (with that hardly perceptible flutter caused by the *r*) — and the echo of these in "Where e'er." "Beare" has not the same wavering movement, because the *b*, which begins the word, concentrates it.

In these lovely lines from "Corinna going a-Maying":

> Rise: and put on your Foliage, and be seene
> To come forth, like the Spring-time, fresh and greene;
>   And sweet as *Flora*. Take no care
>   For Jewels for your Gowne, or Haire:
>   Feare not; the leaves will strew
>   Gemms in abundance upon you,

the leaves strew their gems upon us, in the very sound of those incredibly faint, wavering, dropping movements of "care" and "Haire" (the latter being a little longer in fading than the former) — and in the immaterial fluttering sound of the internal *r*'s in "Spring," "greene," "strew."

These wavering airs, these faint rills of air that come and go, as with the subtle dropping sound of "dew" and the wavering sound of "air" in the poem "Upon Julia's Haire fill'd with Dew" — the faint sharpening sound of "dew" softening to the warmer sound of the *Ju* in "Julia" and the sound of "too," the points of light given by the long assonantal *e*'s of "Leaves," "Beames," "Streames," — the dewy *l*'s, — these subtleties are like the bloom upon the poem, the differences in the glitter of that dew on leaves and hair.

>   Dew sate on Julia's haire,
>   And spangled too
>   Like Leaves that laden are
>   With trembling Dew:
>   Or glitter'd to my sight,
>   As when the Beames
>   Have their reflected light
>   Daunc't by the Streames.

On Herrick

In "The Night-Piece to Julia" there is a firefly-like darting of the movement, due to the fact that the rhyme occurs internally, in the last word but one, in the first, second, and fifth lines of each verse (excepting in the third verse, where the opportunity does not arise, as the last word is a double-syllabled one):

Her Eyes the Glow-worme lend thee,
The Shooting Starres attend thee,
　　And the Elves also,
　　Whose little eyes glow,
Like the sparks of fire, befriend thee.

No Will-o'-th'-Wispe mis-light three;
Nor Snake, or Slow-worme bite thee:
　　But on, on thy way
　　Not making a stay,
Since Ghost ther's none to affright thee.

Let not the darke thee cumber;
What though the Moon do's slumber?
　　The Starres of the night
　　Will lend thee their light,
Like Tapers cleare without number.

Then Julia let me wooe thee,
Thus, thus to come unto me:
　　And when I shall meet
　　Thy silv'ry feet,
My soule Ile poure into thee.

Excepting in the third verse, where it does not occur, this internal rhyme gives emphasis, and we have the droning end, in the first two verses, caused by the fact that these lines end, invariably, with the same word, "thee."

Her Eyes the Glow-worme lend thee,
The Shooting Starres attend thee, [etc.]

[257]

The whole movement gives us the feeling of a lady in rustling silks flying down the midnight branch-shadowed paths, followed by the firefly-darting sound caused by the much shorter and quicker internal lines:

> And the Elves also,
> Whose little eyes glow.

The quickness is due to the running movement of "And the" in the first two lines, and "little" in the second — words much faster than those in the previous lines — words on which no pause is made. So that we understand from the sound that the lady is in a hurry, as she flies across the moonlit grass, for fear of the will-o'-the-wisp, the snake, and the slow-worm — and that all tiny and bright things are darting from the skies and from the dark woods to help her on her way with their sudden and lovely gleaming.

The poem "Upon Julia's Voice," with the subtlety of the longer rhyme to "voice" of "noise" and the dropping sound from "chamber" to "Amber," is largely dependent for beauty on the extremely sweet vowels, enclosed, sometimes, in a most intricate scheme of *s*'s; the only loud sound in the whole poem being produced by the *D* in "Damned." In fact, the whole of the verse is built upon a subtle foundation of *s*'s, — there are only three words beginning with hard consonants in the song, and of these, two are almost muted. I know of no poet — not even Milton or Pope — who could manage sibilants better than Herrick. As for the vowel-sounds in this poem, they are as smooth and as un-poignant as the lovely voice the poem is praising:

> So smooth, so sweet, so silv'ry is thy voice,
> As, could they hear, the Damn'd would make no noise,
> But listen to thee, (walking in thy chamber),
> Melting melodious words to Lutes of Amber.

On Herrick

In the first two lines of "The Weeping Cherry,"

> I saw a Cherry weep, and why?
> Why wept it? but for shame,

the alliteration, and the profound vowel-sound in "weep,"
prolong the length of the lines (but almost imperceptibly)
and make them heavier, as though the cherry, and the light
and lovely branch from which it sprang, were made heavier
by that rich weight of dew:

> I saw a Cherry weep, and why?
>   Why wept it? but for shame,
> Because my Julia's lip was by,
>   And did out-red the same.
> But pretty Fondling, let not fall
>   A tear at all for that:
> Which Rubies, Corralls, Scarlets, all
>   For tincture, wonder at.

And we, too, may wonder at the "Rubies, Corralls, Scar-
lets." But how are we to explain the faint, soft beauty of "The
Primrose," — a poem whose life is as faint as that of the flower,
whose perfume is as intangible:

> Aske me why I send you here
> This sweet Infanta of the yeere?
> Aske me why I send to you
> This Primrose, thus bepearl'd with dew?
> I will whisper to your eares
> The sweets of Love are mixt with teares.

> Aske me why this flower do's show
> So yellow-green, and sickly too?
> Aske me why the stalk so weak
> And bending (yet it doth not break?)
> I will answer, These discover
> What fainting hopes are in a Lover.

These songs and sounds, the faint warm rills of air, and drafts of cooler air, these whispers of air, ripples of air, steal on the ear; the primrose-pale, primrose-scented dews of the early morning poems, fleeting and immaterial, are gone in the moment of a dream. There is neither harshness nor pain, nor is there agony in death, — there is scarcely sorrow. . . . Only the dew fades on the primrose, the golden beauty of the daffodil.

> . . . We die,
> As your hours doe, and drie
> Away
> Like to the Summer's raine;
> Or as the pearles of Morning's dew,
> Ne'er to be founde againe.

And that fading is only the reason for a new invocation:

> So when or you or I are made
> A fable, song, or fleeting shade;
> All love, all liking, all delight
> Lies drown'd with us in endless night.
> Then while time serves, and we are but decaying;
> Come, my Corinna, come, lets goe-a-Maying.

All his funeral songs are only for the passing of a honey-bee, dead in the first delicate snows of winter; his bass-notes are like the deep droning sound that comes from a hive. To him, death, and life, and the business of life, were a sweet scent, intangible but rich, like the uncorrupted fame of which he wrote in his epigram "To His Honoured Kinsman, Sir William Soame"; — a fame that

> Casts forth a light like to a Virgin flame,
> And as it shines, it throws a scent about,
> As when a Rain-bow in perfume goes out.

XXIII. On Smart, with a Note on Gerard Manley Hopkins

To this earth-bound St. Francis, this earth-covered incomplete saint, comforting those who are not irradiated, with the words "The glory of God is always in the East, but cannot be seen for the Cloud of the Crucifixion," "all things have become light, never again to set, and the setting has believed in the rising. This is the new Creation." [1] All things were light come from above: "For water is not of solid constituents, but is dissolved from precious stones above"; — though the Crucifixion was his, amid the deathly cold of Bedlam, his madness was not a darkness but a light. His body knew the lack of bread, and had known the sin of drunkenness, but yet to the end of his life, his soul, his apprehension of the world, were those of Thomas Traherne's child:

"Certainly Adam in Paradise had not more sweet and curious apprehensions of the world than I, when I was a child.

. . . . . .

"All appeared new, and strange at first, inexpressibly rare and delightful and beautiful. . . . My knowledge was Divine, I knew by intuition those things which since my Apostasy, I collected, again by the highest reason. My very ignorance

[1] St. Clement: Address to the Greeks.

[261]

was advantageous. I seemed as one brought into the Estate of Innocence. All things were spotless and pure and glorious: yea, and infinitely mine, and joyful and precious. I knew not that there were any sins or complaints or laws. I dreamed not of poverties, contentions, or vices. All tears and quarrels were hidden from mine eyes. Everything was at rest, free and immortal. I knew nothing of sins and death or rents or exaction, either for tribute or bread. In the absence of these I was entertained like an Angel with the works of God in their splendour and glory, I saw all in the peace of Eden; Heaven and earth did sing my Creator's praises, and could not make more melody to Adam, than to me. All Time was Eternity, and a perpetual Sabbath. . . .

"The corn was orient and immortal wheat, which never should be reaped, nor was ever sown. I thought it had stood from everlasting to everlasting. The dust and stones were as precious as gold: the gates were at first the end of the world. The green trees when I saw them first through one of the gates transported and ravished me, their sweetness and unusual beauty made my heart leap, and almost mad with ecstasy, they were such strange and wonderful things. The men! O what venerable and reverend creatures did the aged seem! Immortal Cherubims! And young men glittering and sparkling Angels, and maids strange seraphic pieces of life and beauty! Boys and girls tumbling in the street, and playing, were moving jewels. I knew not that they were born or should die; But all things abided eternally as they were in their proper places. Eternity was manifest in the Light of the Day, and something infinite behind everything appeared: which talked with my expectation and moved my desire. The city seemed to stand in Eden, or to be built in Heaven. The streets were mine, the temple was mine, the gold and silver were mine, as much as their sparkling eyes, fair skins and ruddy faces. The skies were mine, and so were the sun and moon and stars, and all the world was mine; and I the only spectator and enjoyer of it. I knew no churlish proprieties, nor lands, nor divisions; but all proprieties and divisions were mine: all treasures and the possession of them."

In that great poem, "A Hymn to David," descending like an Angel to the madman of genius, the saint of love, in his earthly prison, all things of clay, all objects of our daily life, were changed into beings formed from the light that is in Heaven. The colors, the light, are deeper, are richer, like

> The topaz blazing like a lamp
> Among the mines beneath.

The saint in him pierced down to the essence of all things seen — and that essence was light, with all its variations of warmth, richness, piercingness, glow. It is impossible to know how he produces that quintessence of light. But if, for instance, we take Verse LXV:

> For Adoration, beyond match,
> The scholar bulfinch aims to catch
> The soft flute's ivory touch;
> And, careless on the hazle spray,
> The daring redbreast keeps at bay
> The damsel's greedy clutch,

we shall see how in the lovely softening from the *fl* of "flutes" to the *i* of "ivory," the change from the fullness of the one-syllabled word "flutes" to the long warm *i* of "ivory" with the quavering two syllables that follow, in that word, — the transposition of the *ulf* of "bulfinch" to the *flu* of "flutes," — the actual sound seems to echo the warmth, the very glow, of the scholar bulfinch's and the daring redbreast's sweet bosoms.

In Verse LII

> For Adoration seasons change,
> And order, truth, and beauty range,
> Adjust, attract, and fill:
> The grass the polyanthus cheques:
> And polish'd porphyry reflects
>   By the descending rill.
>
> Rich almonds colour to the prime
> For Adoration; tendrils climb;
>   And fruit-trees pledge their gems;
> And Ivis with her gorgeous vest
> Builds for her eggs her cunning nest,
>   And bell-flowers bow their stems.

the color is so rich as not to be of this world.

And yet, the flowers plucked by Smart are flowers of this earth, though they are known by the angels, "worshipping Christ with the People of the Rose, which is a nation of living sweetness."

Blake's lily of the vale was the white and ineffably sweet soul of the lily. Blake's marigold was a flower known to Persephone:

"Art thou a flower? Art thou a nymph? I see thee as a flower,
Now a nymph! I dare not pluck thee from thy dewy bed."

The Golden Nymph replied, "Pluck thou my flower, Oothoon the mild!
Another flower shall spring, because the soul of sweet delight
Can never pass away." She ceas'd, and clos'd her golden shrine.
Then Oothoon pluck'd the flower, saying: "I pluck thee from thy bed,
Sweet flower, and put thee here to glow between my breasts:
And thus I turn my face to where my whole soul seeks."

Over the waves she went in wing'd exulting swift delight.

*   *   *

On Smart

A beautiful though perhaps less great poet than Smart, Gerard Manley Hopkins (less great because he was not visited directly by angels of the heavenly fire and light), had, in an almost equal degree, this acute and strange visual sense, piercing, as I said above, to the essence of the thing seen. Hopkins, unlike Smart, heightened the truth, the essence, by endowing them with attributes which at first seem alien, with colors that are sharper, clearer, more piercing than those that are seen by the common eye.

This acute and piercing visual apprehension, this sharpening, and concentration into essence by the means of which I have spoken, may be found in these lovely lines from "The May Magnificat":

> Ask of her, the mighty mother:
> Her reply puts this other
> Question: What is Spring?
> Growth in everything —
>
> Flesh and fleece, fur and feather,
> Grass and greenworld all together.
> Star-eyed strawberry-breasted
> Throstle above her nested
>
> Cluster of bugle blue eggs thin
> Forms and warms the life within;
> And bird and blossom swell
> In sod or sheath or shell.
>
> . . . . . .
>
> When drop-of-blood-and-foam-dapple
> Blooms light the orchard-apple
> And thicket and thorp are merry
> With silver surfed cherry

And azuring-over greybell makes
Wood banks and brakes wash wet like lakes
And magic cuckoocall
Caps, clears, and clinches all.

This ecstasy all through mothering earth
Tells Mary her mirth till Christ's birth
To remember and exultation
In God who was her salvation.

In the sharply seen image of the star-eyed strawberry-breasted thrush, Hopkins says "strawberry-breasted" because of the freckles on her breast. In the enhanced and deepened color of the bugle-blue eggs, the sharp *u* of "bugle" melting into the softer *u* of "blue" gives the reflection of one in the other, the sisterhood of the deep blue heaven, the flower, and the egg, their colors changing and shifting in the clear light.

The same piercing truth-finding vision produced for us the fair hair of the country youth in this lovely fragment:

The furl of fresh-leaved dog-rose down
His cheeks the forth-and-flaunting sun
Had swarthed about with lion-brown
Before the Spring was done.

His locks like all a ravel-rope's-end
With hempen strands in spray —
Fallow, foam-fallow, hanks — fall'n off their ranks
Swung down at a disarray.

Or like a juicy and jostling shock
Of bluebells sheaved in May
Or wind-long fleeces on the flock
A day off shearing-day.

Then over his turnèd temples — here —
Was a rose, or, failing that,
Rough-Robin or five-lipped campion clear
For a beauty-bow to his hat,
And the sunlight sidled, like dewdrops, like dandled diamonds,
Through the sieve of the straw of his hat.

In this lovely fragment, the comparison of the youth's fair hair with a sheaf of bluebells gives, to me, the fairness of the hair, and shows the straightness of it, the way in which it flaps, — for, of all flowers, only a sheaf of bluebells has this particular limpness.

Here we have a youth, in the midst of his walk, suddenly leaping into the air and dancing for a step or two, because of the fun of being alive on this lovely morning of the late spring. The innocent and sweet movement of this very beautiful fragment is due, partly, to the skillful interposition of an extra syllable from time to time, and an occasional rare extra rhyme; and the clearness and poignant colors of the morning are conveyed by the sounds of "juicy," "bluebells," and "sheaved," with their varying degrees of deep and piercing color.

We find the same heightening and concentration again, in these beautiful lines about the skies on a May night:

For how to the heart's cheering
The down-dugged ground-hugged grey
Hovers off, the jay-blue heavens appearing
  Of pied and peeled May!
Blue-beating and hoary glow-height; or night, still higher,
With belled fire and the moth-soft Milky Way,
What by your measure is the heaven of desire,
The treasure never eyesight got, nor was ever guessed what for
  the hearing?

A lovely movement, a sense that all is well, that all Creation is part of a controlled and gigantic design, is given by the internal rhymes and assonances, — the movement being like that of a bird flying through the bright air, swooping downward to its nest, then up again through the holy and peaceful light.

XXIV. On Wordsworth

"Three kinds of men," said Eckhart in *Sermons and Collations*, "see God. The first see Him in faith; they know no more of Him than they can make out through a partition. The second behold God in the light of grace but only as the answer to their longings, as giving them sweetness, devotion, inwardness, and other such-like things which are issuing from His gift. The third kind see Him in the divine light."

Of these three kinds of men, George Herbert belongs to the second category, Smart and the yet more irradiated Blake to the third. Wordsworth belongs to neither kind, for although to Blake "even Wordsworth seemed a kind of atheist, who mistook the changing signs of vegetable nature for the unchanging realities of imagination" (Arthur Symons), he was wrong. Wordsworth did not see God through a partition — even one which is of living matter and not made by the hands of men from bricks and dead sticks: to him, "the lights of faith and of nature are subordinate John Baptists." He was, indeed, more of the nature of the disciples than, like Shelley, an order of being like the archangels.

The difference between Wordsworth, and Blake, Smart, and their brother in prose, Traherne, is the difference in nature between certain men of God — difference, not separation.

"It is written," said St. Bernard,[1] "the angel who spoke in me.

[1] On consideration.

"And yet there is a difference even here. The angel is in us suggesting what is good, not bestowing it: stimulating us to goodness, not creating goodness. God is so in us as to give the grace, and infuse it into us; or rather, so in us that He Himself is infused and partaken of, so that one need not fear to say that He is one with our substance. For you know 'He that is joined unto God is one spirit.' The Angel, therefore, is with the soul; God is in the soul. The Angel is in the soul as a comrade, God as life."

"I am a companion of angels," wrote Blake to his friend Hayley. But these were the companions of his earthly side. He had deeper, more terrible communions than these.

It is the comrade, the angel, that Wordsworth knew on the levels of his life. Though there were days, those moments which contain eternity, when he saw the Burning Bush.

On the levels of his life, he knew light, but it was the light of Reason rather than the innermost secret Flame. He brought to his poetry all the "household stuffe of Heaven on earth." And it is a poetry more of the reason than the intellect . . . a reason which is Life. It is that reason of which St. Augustine spoke when he said, "The earth was made; but, the earth itself which was made is not life. In the Wisdom of God, however, there is spiritually a certain Reason after which the earth was made. This is life."

Reason and Tranquillity were the companion Angels of Wordsworth, as he walked through an everyday world made splendid by the light of a genius which illuminated but did not transform. Common speech and common experience were here, but all made radiant and unforgettable by inspiration. There were days — the *Intimations of Immortality from Recollections of Early Childhood* was such an undying day — when the Pentecostal Flames came, for a moment, to our common speech. The ordinary objects of life became supernatural.

On Wordsworth

The common celandine was still the common celandine, but it was also a star. For Wordsworth had the warmth of the earth and of the human heart; and that genius which was rather of the heart than of the soul had taken all the chill from Reason, till Reason had the pulse of a human, yet a holy, heart.

For his poems are ineffably holy:

> The earth, and every common sight,
>   To me did seem
> Apparelled in celestial light.

In the note to that ode which was the mountain on which he and his angels spoke with God (*the Intimations of Immortality from Recollections of Early Childhood*), he says, speaking of his early years: "I was often unable to think of eternal things as having external existence, and I communed with all that I saw as something not apart from, but inherent in, my own immaterial nature. Many times while going to school have I grasped at a wall or tree to recall myself from this abyss of idealism to the reality."

The kernel of all his poems — even when we have to cut to that kernel through an unnecessary husk furred with earth, has a singular purity and fidelity. Matthew Arnold said of him, "It might seem that Nature not only gave him the matter for his poem, but wrote his poem for him." That fine critic Arthur Symons, quoting this, adds, "He has none of the poet's pride in his own invention, only a confidence in the voices that he has heard speaking when others were aware of nothing but silence. Thus it is that in the interpretation of natural things he can be absolutely pellucid, like pure light, which reveals to us every object in its own colours."

Indeed, the sublimity of his simplicity is such that it is not so much an interpretation as "an Idea of the World," as Wagner said of music, in his work on Beethoven, "wherein the world immediately exhibits its essential nature."

The light he knew was that which illuminates our common earth, but whose source, whose beginning, is beyond our knowledge, — the "celestial light."

"The Peace of the celestial city is the perfectly ordered and harmonious enjoyment of God and of one another in God. The peace of all things is the tranquillity of order." — ST. AUGUSTINE, *The City of God.*

To this peace, Wordsworth attained. — E. S.

Wordsworth, at his highest, has the tranquillity, the activity of the saints: the "tranquillity according to His essence, activity according to His Nature: perfect stillness, perfect fecundity" of which Rusbroeck wrote in *De Vera Contemplatione.*

"The nobler things are, the commoner they are. Love is noble, because it is universal." — TAULER: *Sermons.*

"God is so omnipresent, as that the Ubiquitary will needs have the body of God everywhere; so omnipresent, as that the Stancarest will needs have God not only to be in everything, but to be everything — that God is an angel in an angel, and a stone in a stone, and a straw in a straw." — JOHN DONNE: Sermon VII.

"Can you take too much joy in your Father's works? He is himself in everything. Some things are little on the outside, and rough and common, but I remember the time when the dust of the streets were as pleasing as gold to my infant eyes, and now they are more precious to the eye of reason." — THOMAS TRAHERNE: *Centuries of Meditation.*

"Suppose a river, or a drop of water, an apple, or a sand, an ear of corn, or an herb: God knoweth infinite excellencies in it more than we: He seeth how it relateth to angels and men; how it proceedeth from the most perfect Lover to the most perfect Beloved; how it conduceth in its place, by the best of means to the best of ends: and for this cause it cannot be beloved too much. God the author and God the end are to be beloved in it; angels and men are to be beloved in it; and it is highly to be esteemed for their sakes. O what a treasure is every sand when truly understood! Who can love anything that God made too much. What a world would that be, were everything loved as it ought to be." — *Ibid.*

Emerson said of Goethe: "There is a certain heat in the breast, which attends the perception of a primary truth, which is the shining of the spiritual sun down into the shaft of the mine."

This was the common experience, also, of Wordsworth. —E. S.

"He . . . has a certain gravitation towards truth." — *Ibid.*

"The peculiar note of Wordsworth's genius at its very highest, is that of sublimity in tenderness." — SWINBURNE: *Essays and Studies.*

"The Beatific Vision has come to him in tangible embodied form, through a kind of religion of the eye, which seems to attain its final rapture, unlike some forms of mysticism, with open eyes." — ARTHUR SYMONS: *The Romantic Movement in English Poetry*.

On Certain Flaws in This Great Poet

". . . It seems to me undeniable that Wordsworth, who could endow such daily matters, such modest emotion and experience, with a force of contagious and irresistible sympathy which makes their interest universal and eternal, showed no such certitude of hand when dealing with the proper and natural elements of tragedy." — SWINBURNE, writing on Wordsworth's "Tribute to the Memory of a Dog."

"We hate poetry that has a palpable design upon us, and if we do not agree, seems to put its head into its breeches pocket. . . . Old Matthew spoke to him some years ago on some nothing, and because he happens in an evening walk to imagine the figure of the old man, he must stamp it down in black and white, and it is henceforth sacred. I don't mean to deny Wordsworth's grandeur . . . but I mean to say we need not be teased with grandeur and merit when we can have them uncontaminated and unobtrusive." — KEATS: Letter to Reynolds, 3 Feb. 1818.

Lord Houghton, in his *Life of Keats*, remarks: "Keats was perhaps unconsciously swayed in his estimate of Wordsworth at this moment by an incident which had happened at Mr. Haydon's. The young poet had been induced to repeat to the elder the Hymn to Pan, out of 'Endymion.' . . . Wordsworth only said, 'It was a pretty piece of Paganism.'"

A monstrous remark. In any case, Keats's criticism had justice in it, and Wordsworth's had none. — E. S.

On Wordsworth

"... Part of [his] singular power over certain minds was doubtless owing to the might of will, the solid individual weight of mind, which moulded his work into the form he chose for it; part to the strong assumption and high self-reliance which grew in him so close to the self-confidence and presumption; part to the sublimity and supremacy of his genius in its own climate and proper atmosphere — one which forbids access to all others and escape to him, since only there can he breathe and range, and he alone can breathe and range there; part to the frequent vapour that wraps his head and the frequent dust that soils his feet, filling the softer sort with admiration of one so lofty and so familiar; and part, I fear, to the quality which no great poet shared or can share with him, his inveterate and invincible Philistinism, his full community of spirit, and faith, in certain things of import, with the vulgarest English mind — or that which, with the Philistine, does duty for a mind. To those who, like Shelley and Landor, could mark this indomitable chillness and thickness of sense which makes him mix with magnificent and flawless verse, the 'enormous folly' of those stupid staves, his pupils could always point out again the peculiar and unsurpassable grandeur of his higher mood; it was vain to reply that these could be seen and enjoyed without condonation or excuse of his violent and wearisome peculiarities. This is what makes his poetry such unwholesome and immoral reading for Philistines; they can turn upon their rebukers and say, 'Here is one of us who by your own admission is also one of the great poets.'" — SWINBURNE: *Essays and Studies.*

"What Wordsworth's poetic life lacked was energy, and he refused to recognize that no amount of energy will suffice for a continual production. ... When one has said that he wrote instinctively, without which there could be no poetry, one must add that he wrote always. Continual writing is really a bad form of dissipation; it drains away the very marrow of the brain." — ARTHUR SYMONS: *The Romantic Movement in English Poetry.*

On the Difference between Sorrow in the Poems of Wordsworth and Shelley

Of Wordsworth it might be said, "God places a watery cloud in the eye, that when the light of heaven shines upon it, it may produce a rain-bow to be a sacrament." — JEREMY TAYLOR, in a Sermon.

To Shelley might be applied the words of St. Ignatius: "My Eros is crucified."

*   *   *

Here, then, is the end of my two first Notebooks. But my habit of compiling Notebooks is by no means at an end. There are more books of this kind to come. I intend to examine Blake at great length, and the poetry of Pope at far greater length than in my biography of him. I intend to write on Dryden, and on Donne.

And, as I said in my Preface, there are many notes made by me — I should say gathered — from works on the subject of color, and of light, and of all the works of life.

How sad it is that there are only twenty-four hours in the day, and that some of those precious hours must be passed in sleep.

[276]